A Quiet Revolution

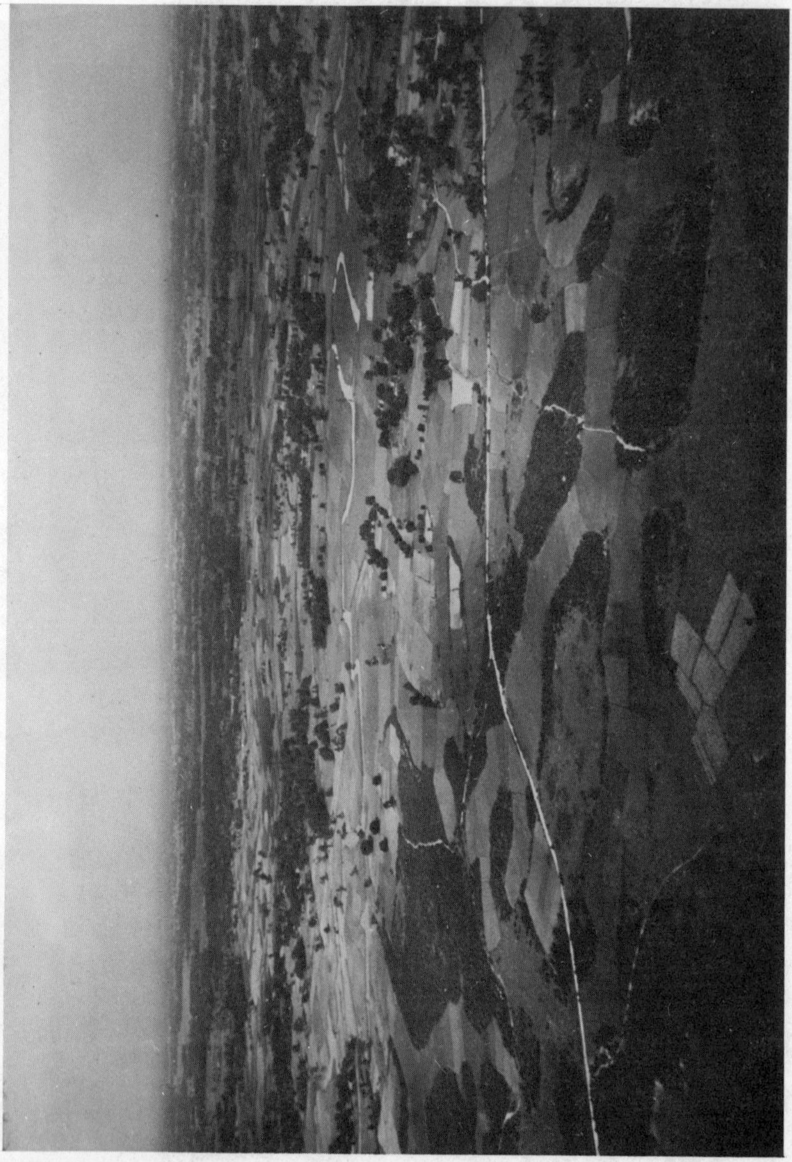

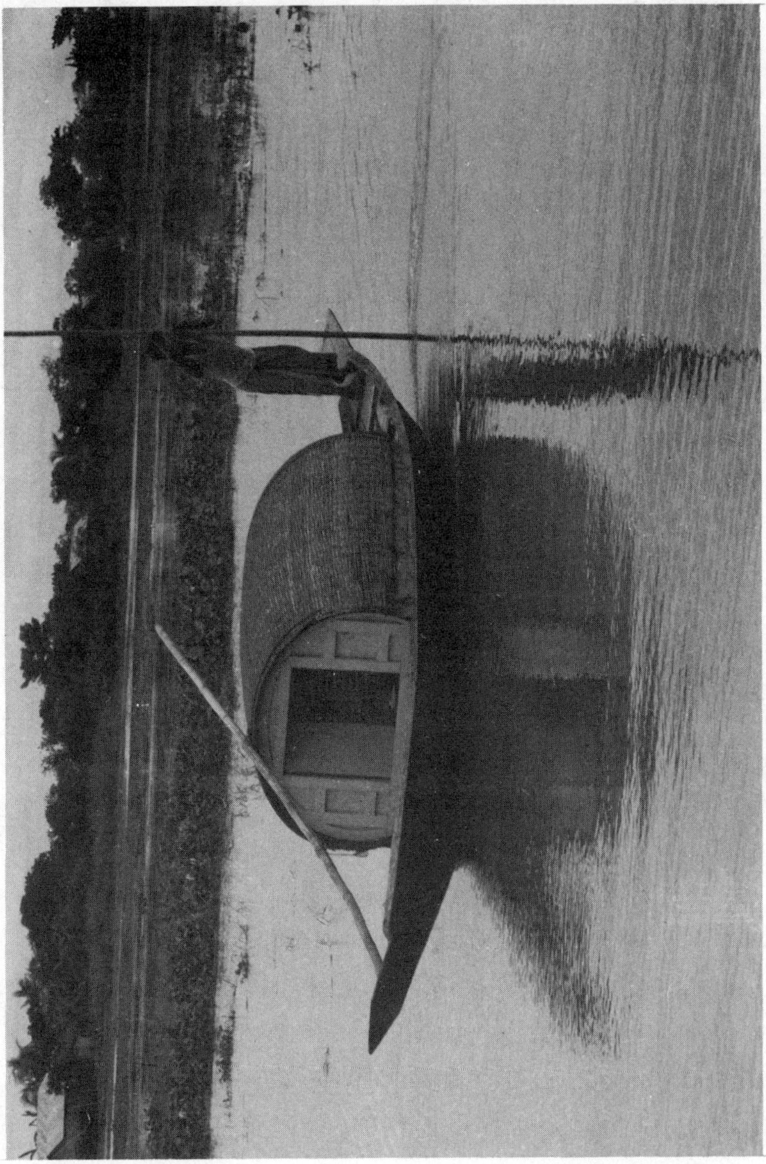

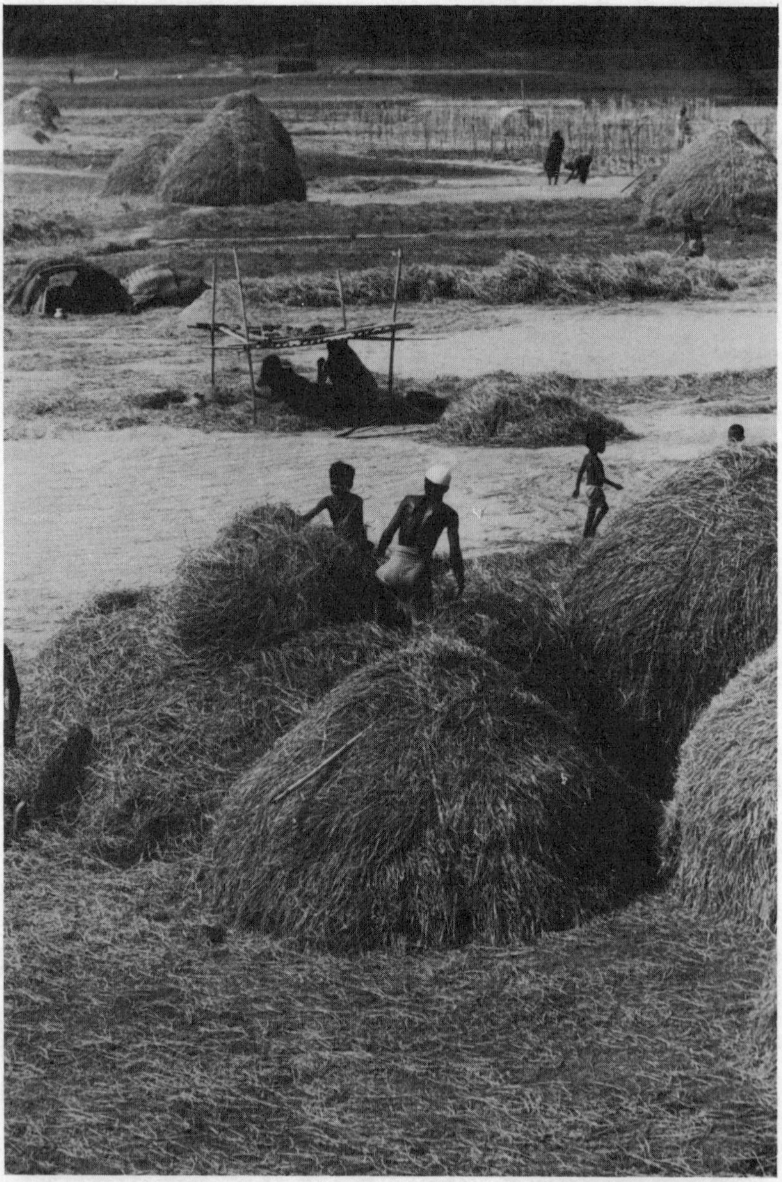

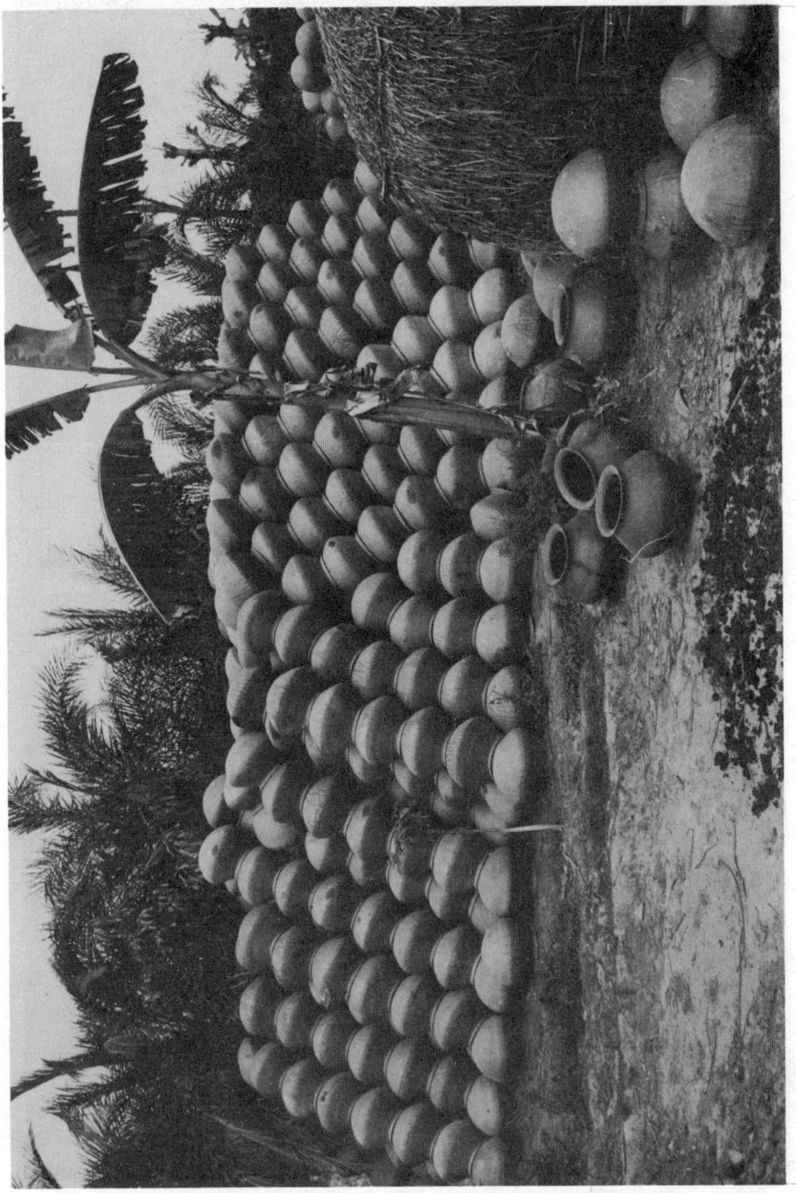

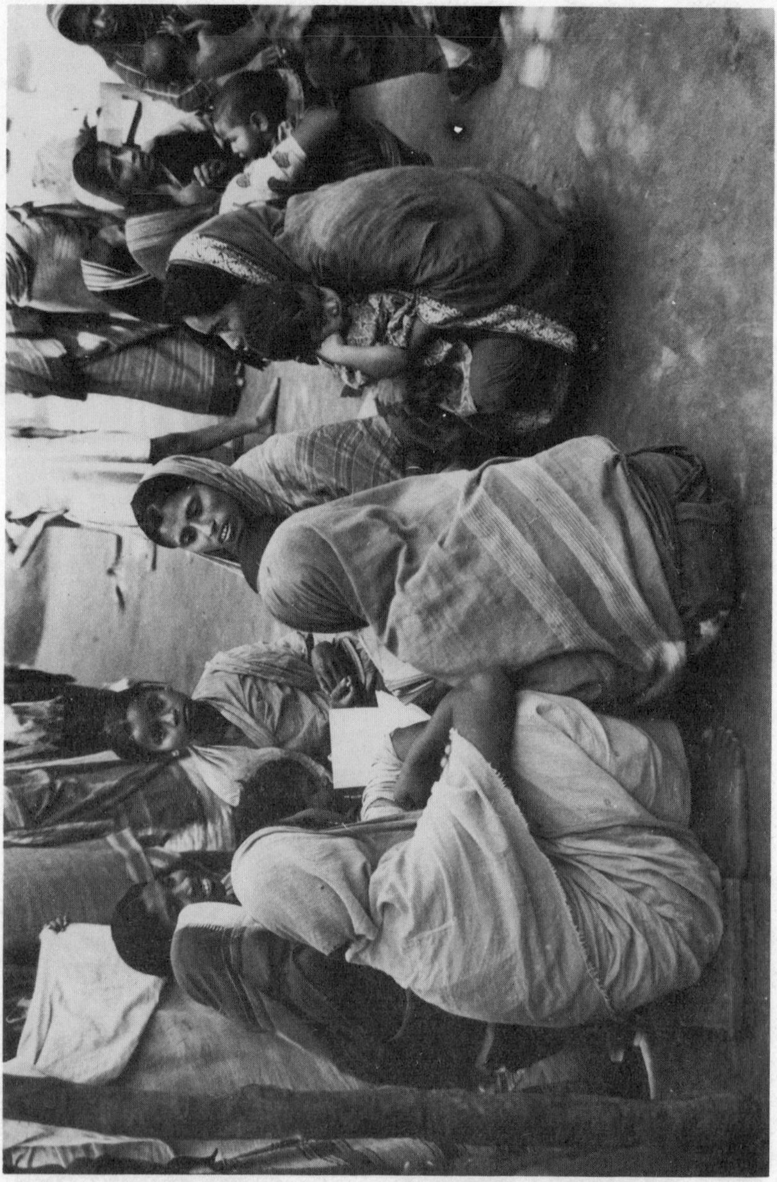

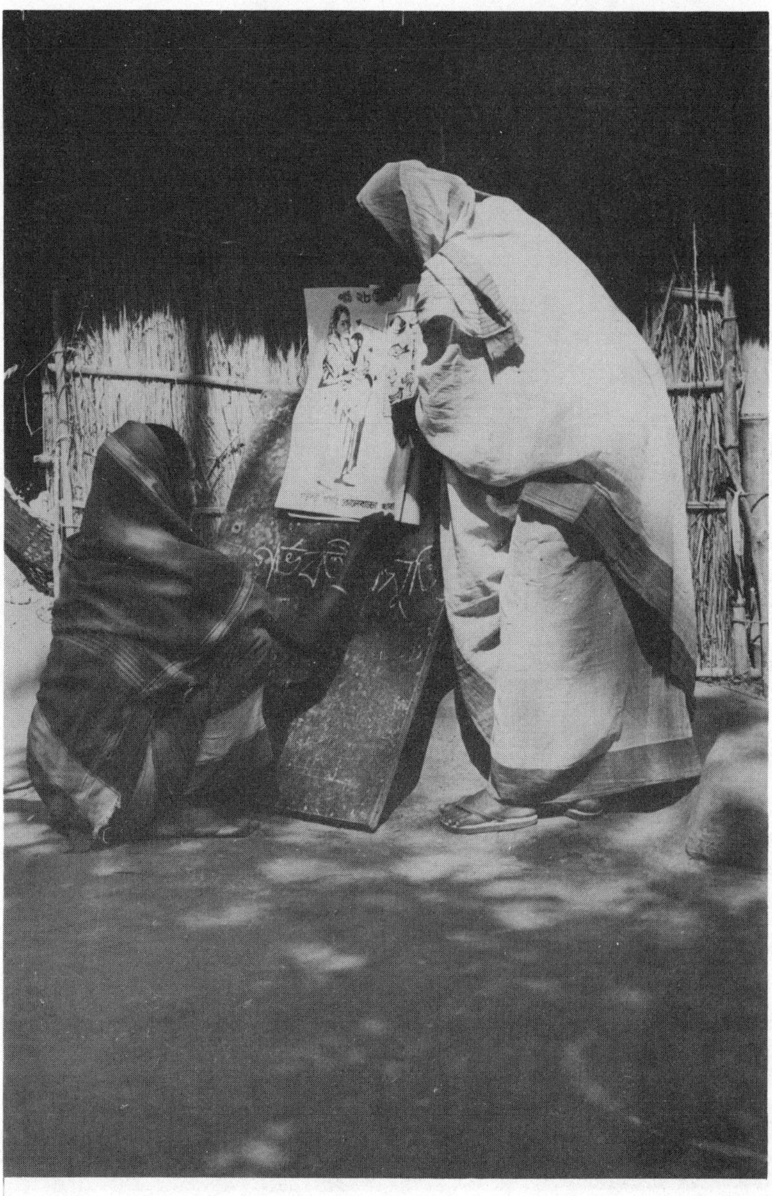

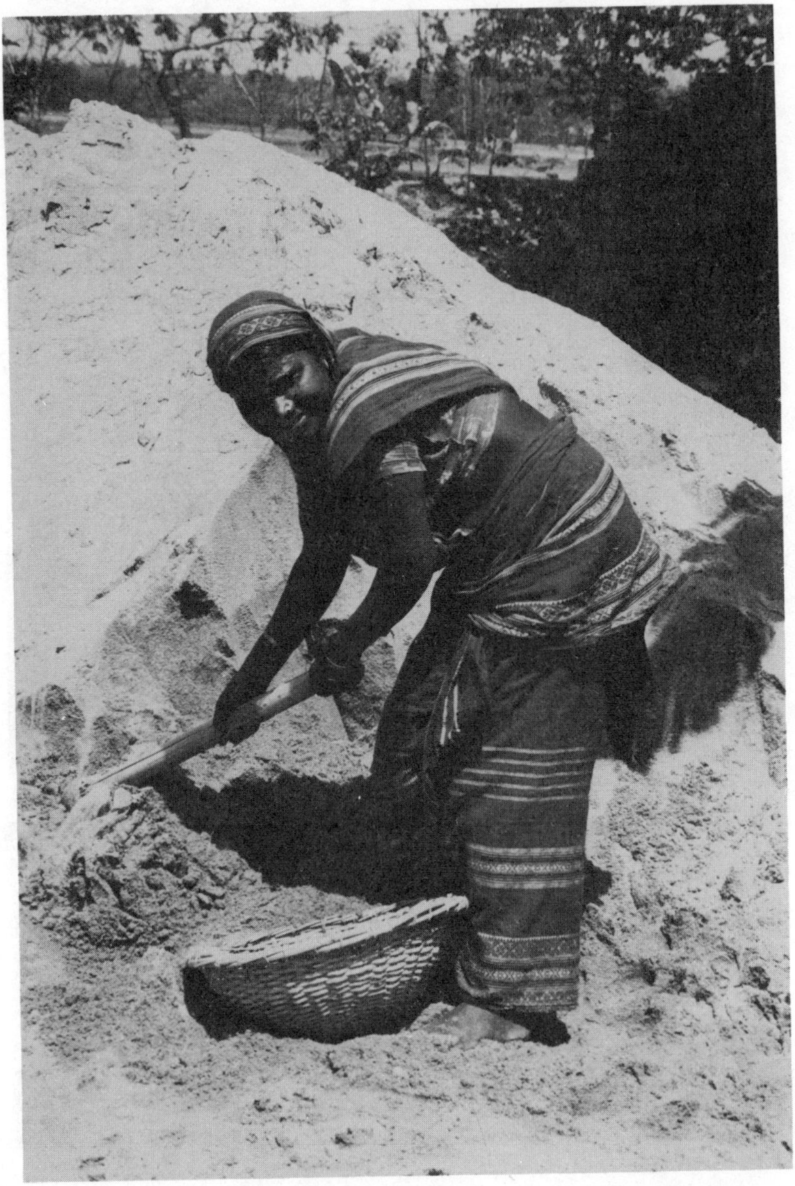

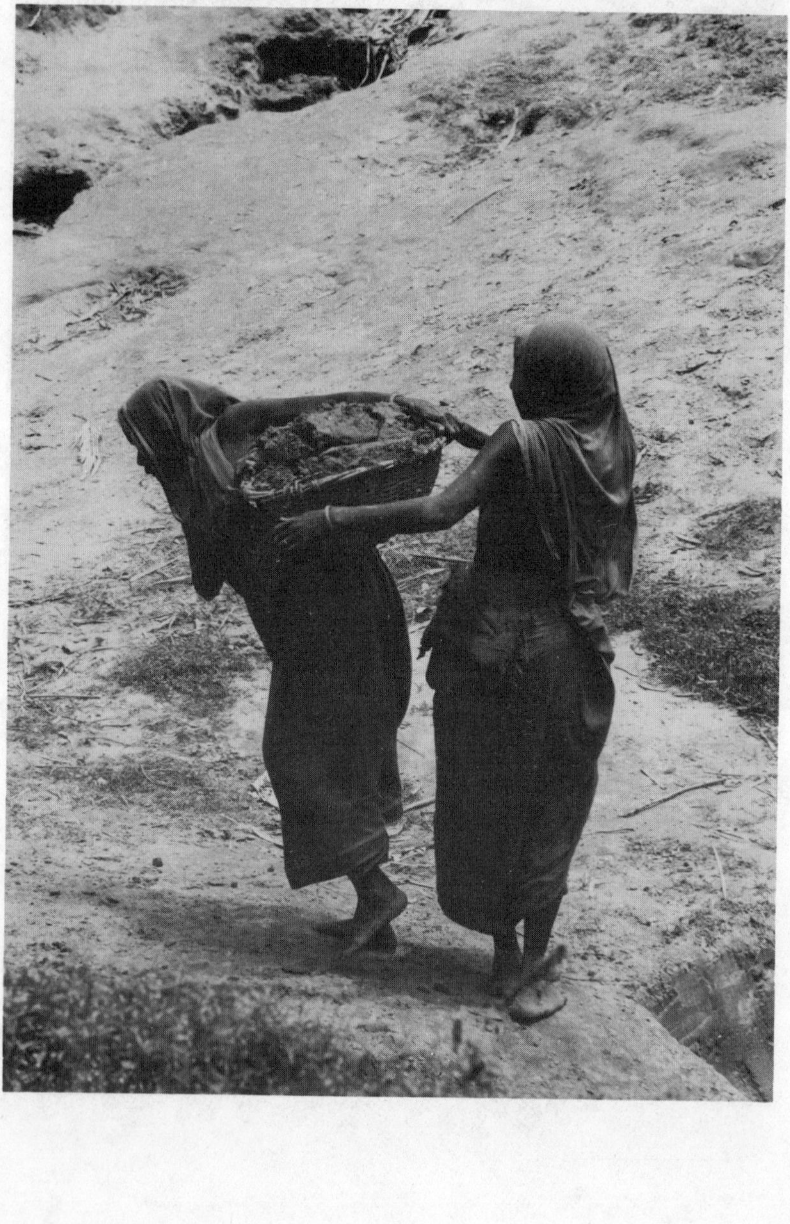

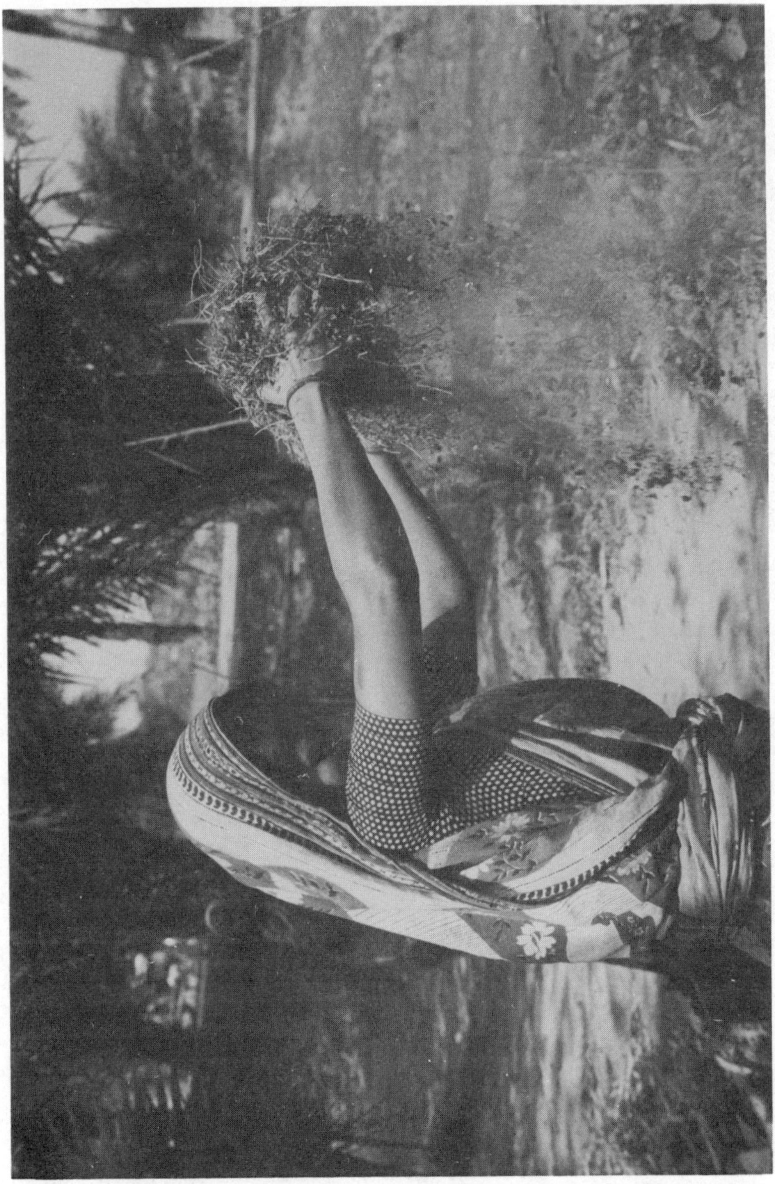

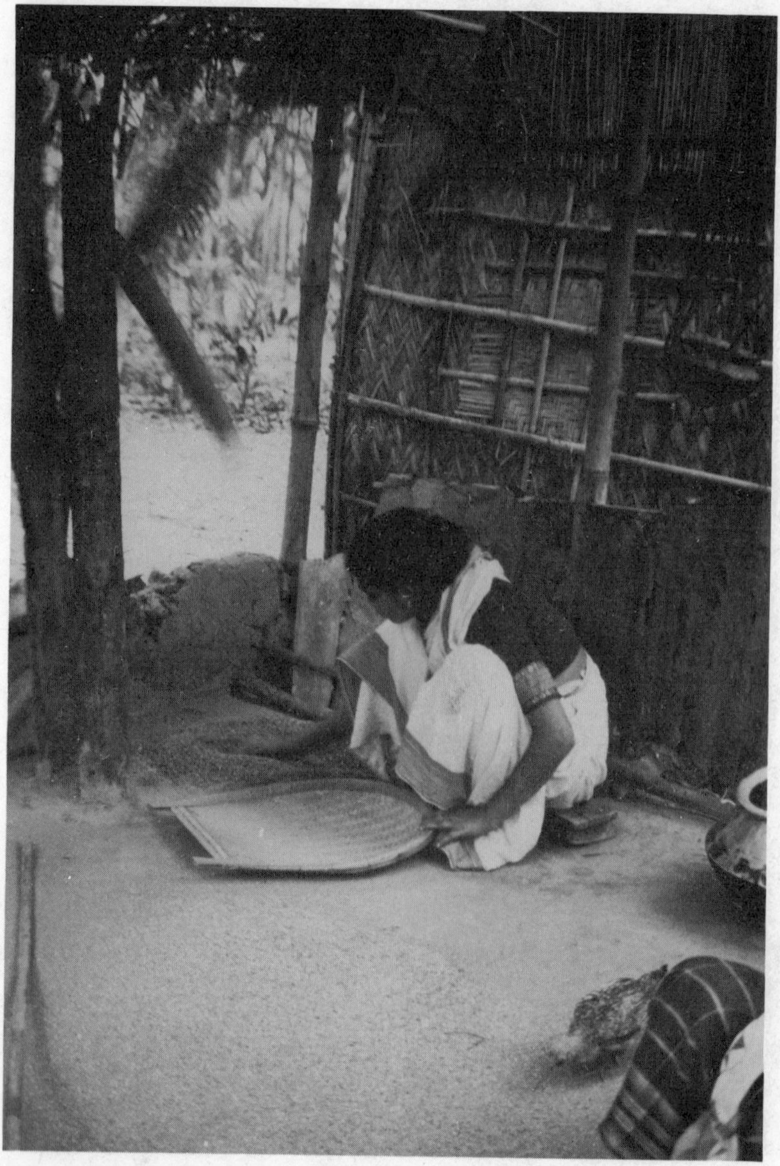

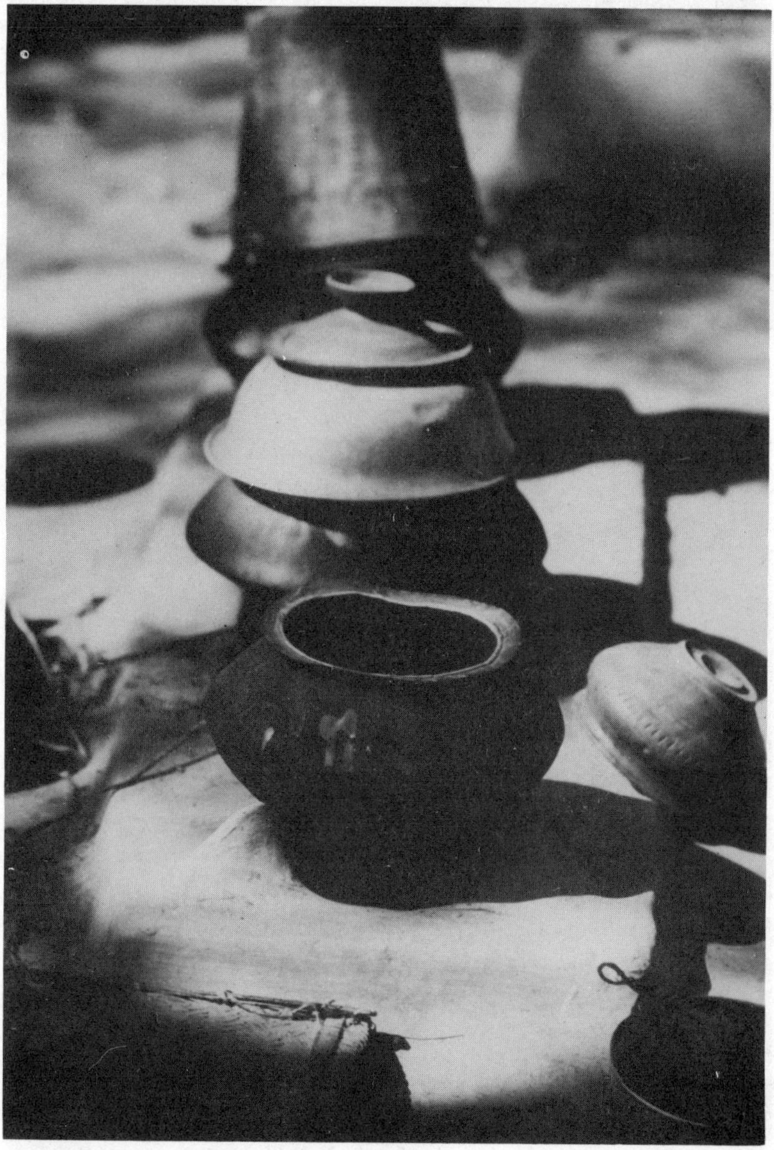

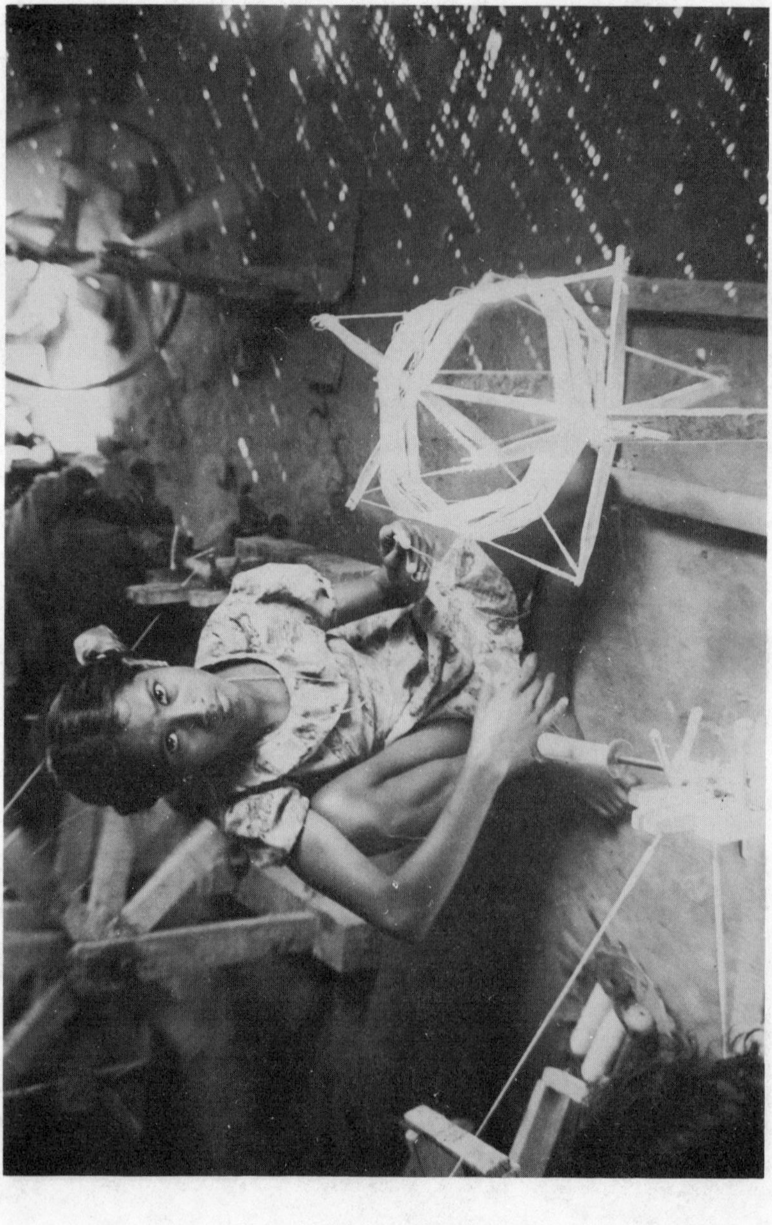

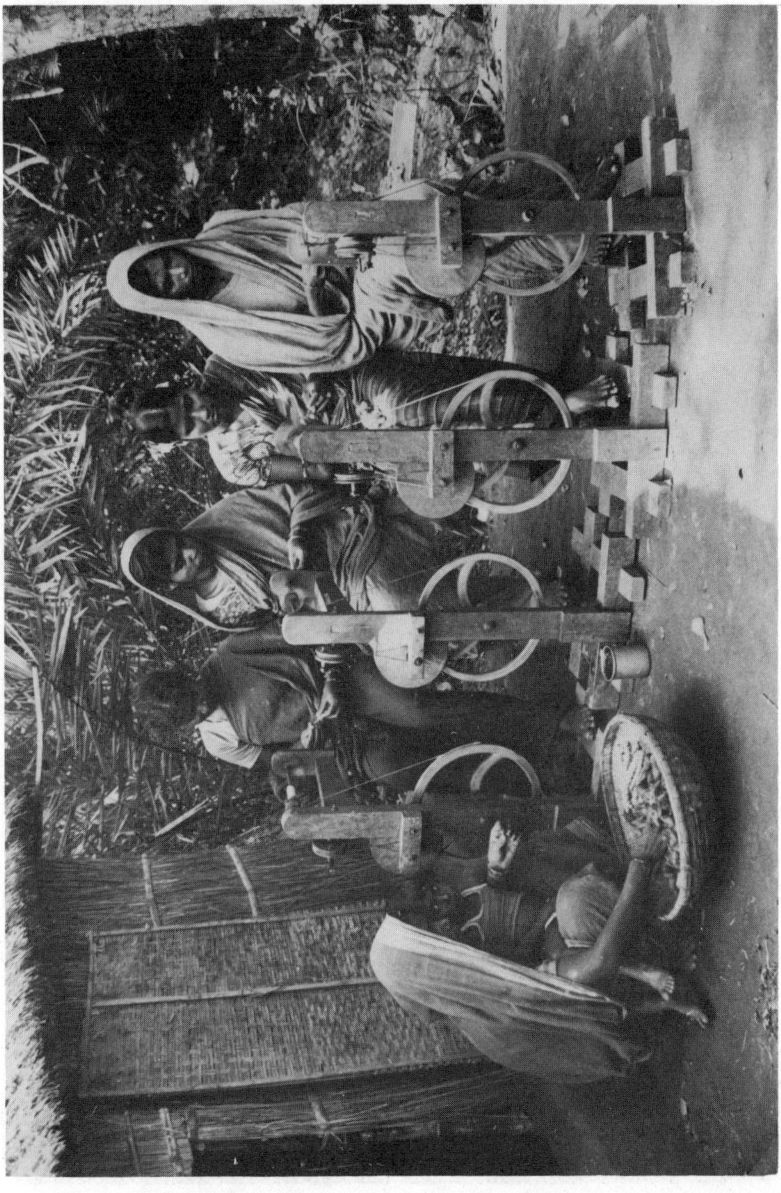

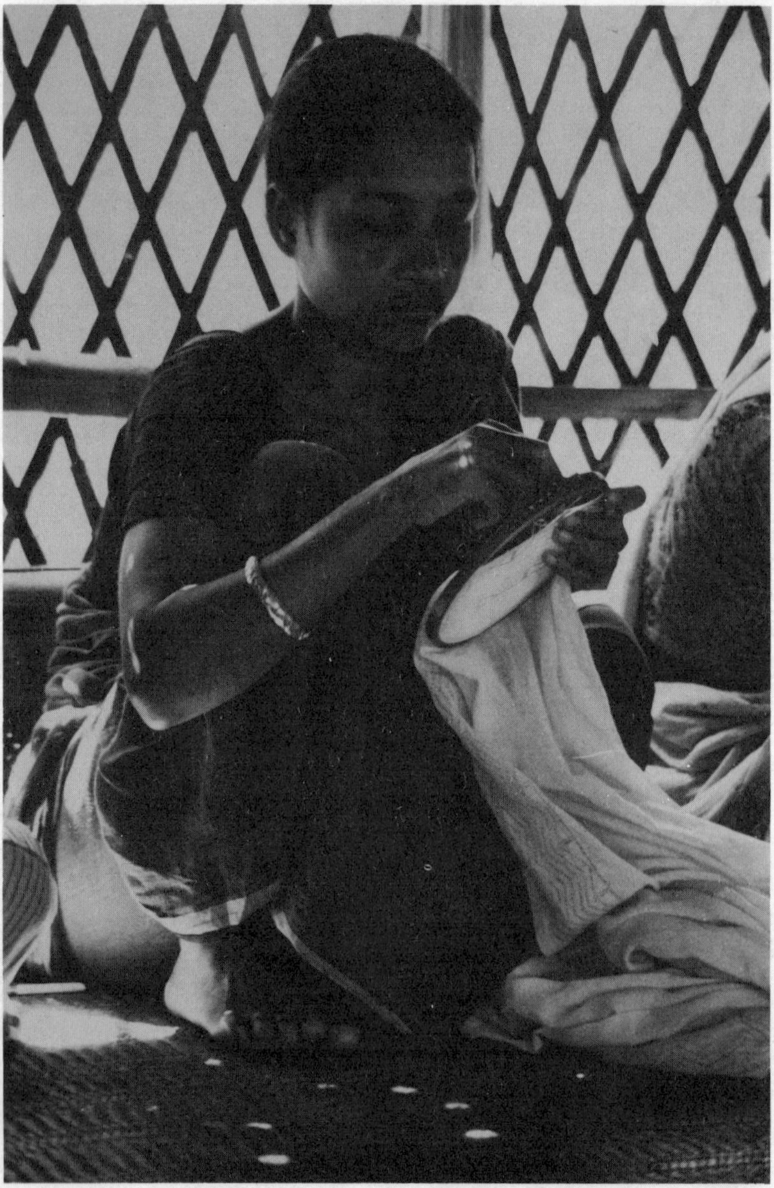

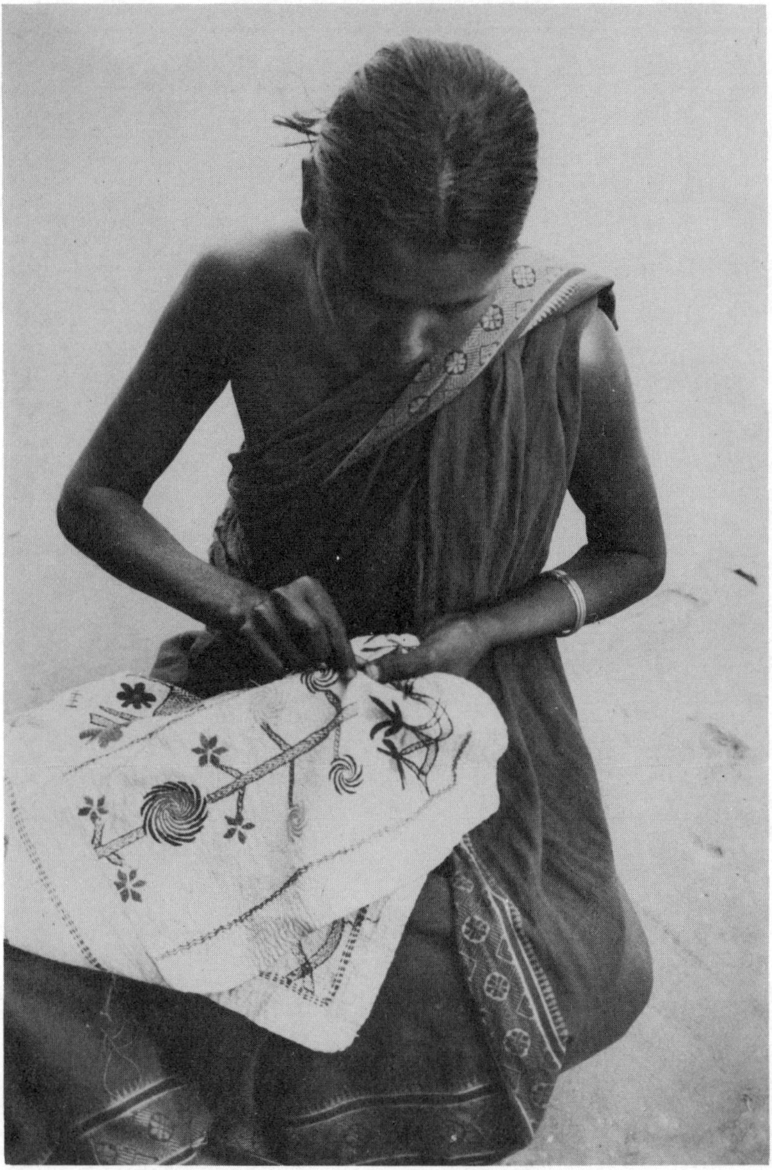

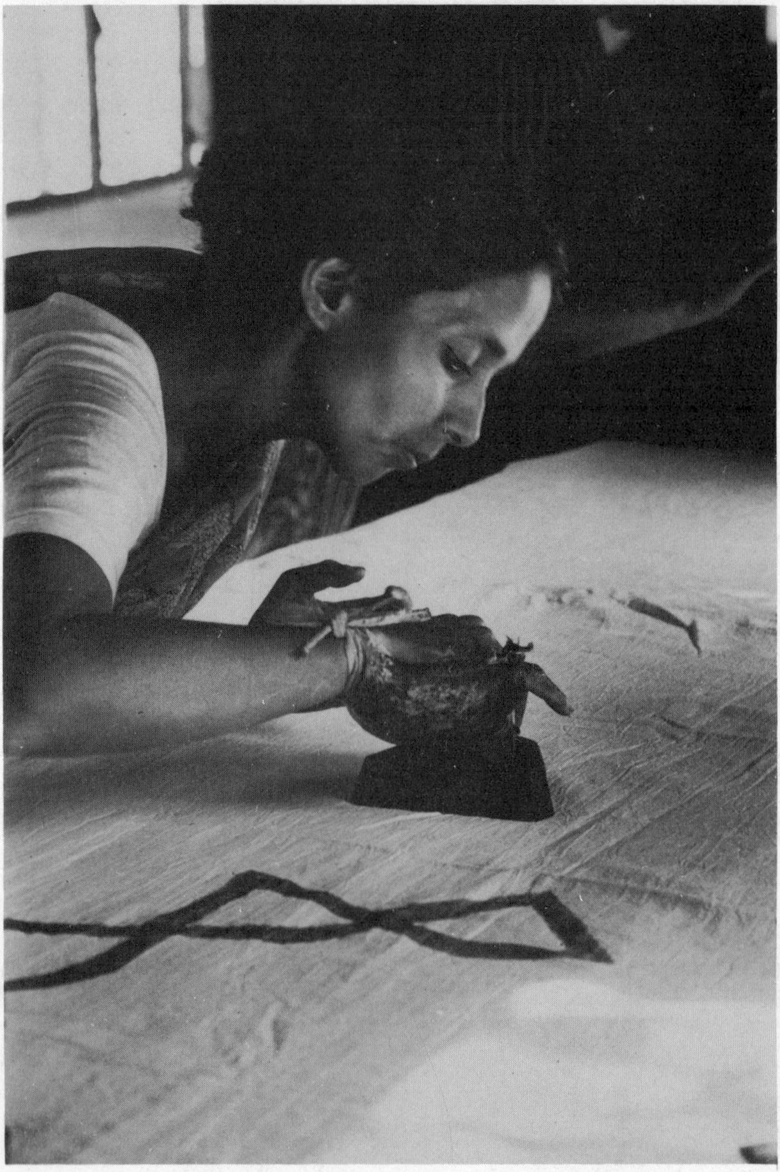

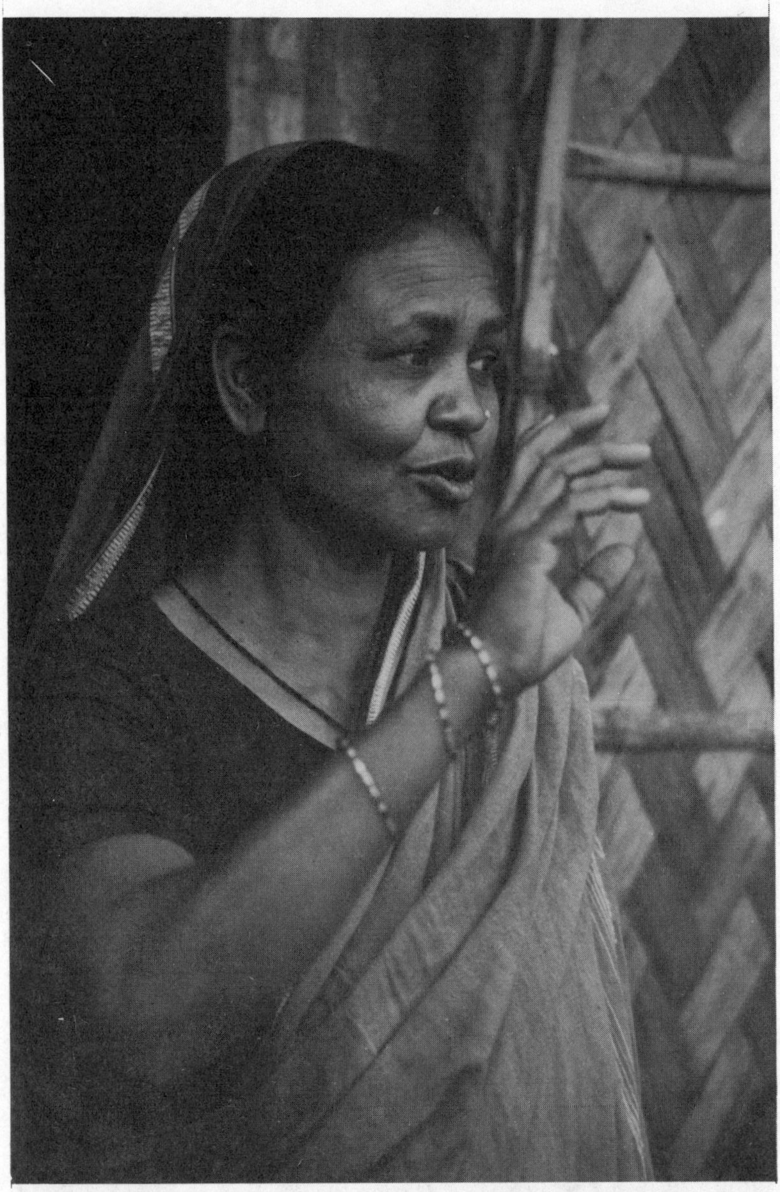

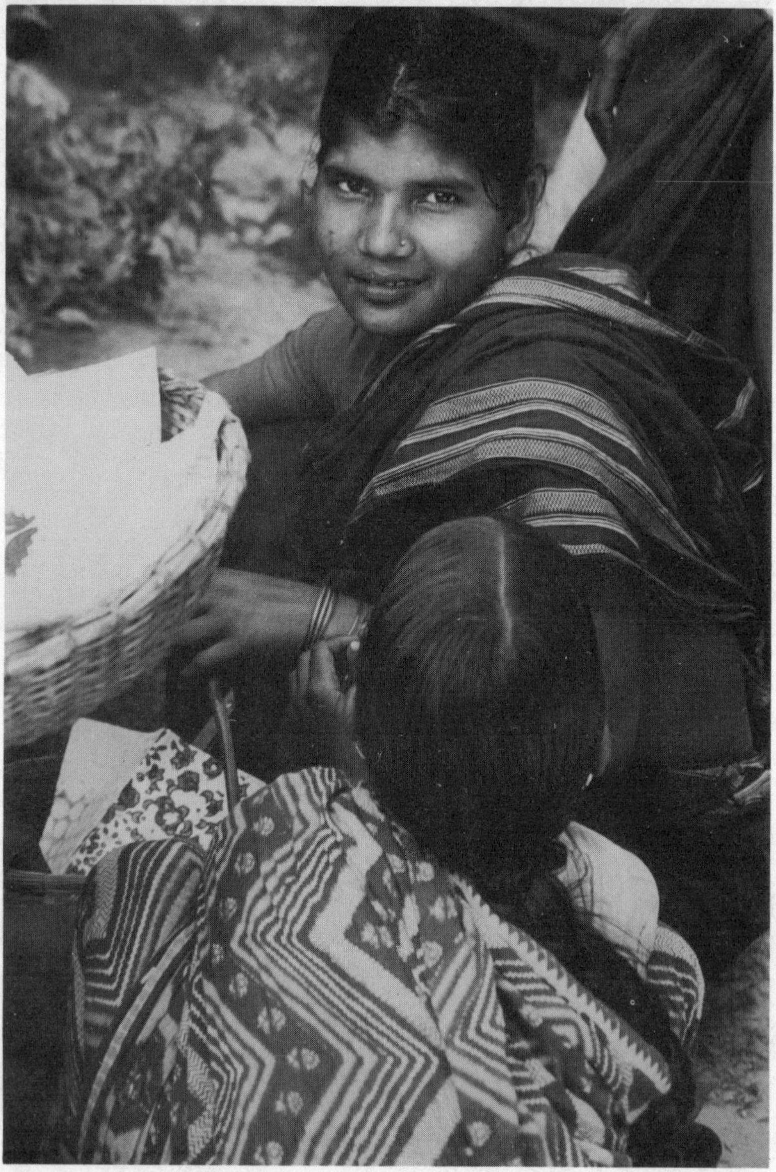

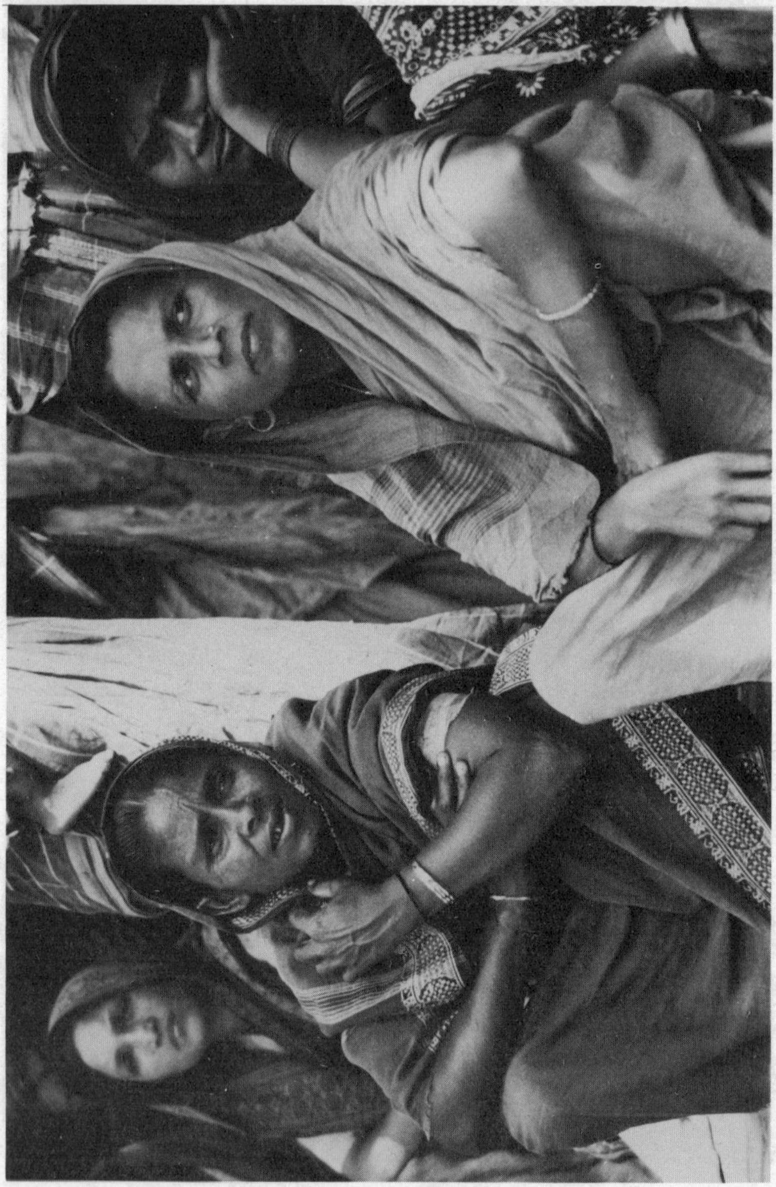

Bangladesh is for me a beautiful country. I have seen the fabled greens-and-golds of Bengali poetry. The lime greens of young rice seedlings. The emerald greens of freshly transplanted rice. The burnished golds of ripened rice. I would like to share the colors and the beauty with you. Imagine . . .

Morning. The sun has long risen but the dew lifts slowly. Concealed by wisps of clouds and the mist of rising dew, the sun sheds its light. A breeze carries with it the scent of ripened rice. It is Kartik (early November), the lushest month for rice in the fields and the leanest month for people in the villages. The stocks of rice in their homes and the demand for their labor will remain low until harvest. It is Hemanta (autumn), the season of dew-bathed and rice-scented mornings, of clear days and cool nights.

Fields upon fields. A chequerboard of fields spreading all round and fading into the distant horizon. Paddy fields broken by fields of sugarcane and jute. The colors of the fields more gold than green now. The burnished golds of the paddy. The pale yellow blossoms of the remaining stands of jute. The silken gold of jute fibre stripped from harvested stalks, tied into bundles, and put out to dry—across branches, across culverts, across the railings of small bridges.

Land and water. Fields and riverways. Fields upon fields lift out of the mist and fade into the distance. Fields laced by pools of standing water or streams of flowing water. The standing water reflects the clouds overhead. The flowing water sparkles in the sunlight. Land is peace—the source of all well-being. Water is fickle—a source of both well-being and destruction.

Rivers and boats. Large boats filled with sand low to their bows. Wide boats made wider still with crude scaffolding to hold loads of pottery. Small dugouts to ferry people and animals from stranded villages or opposite shores. Sizeable launches with inboard motors to transport people to distant places. Small houseboats that are home to itinerant traders. Sails of all sizes and shapes. Torn sails and patchwork sails. People pulling, poling, rowing.

The delta. Several major rivers divide and change their course on their way to the sea. Many minor rivers divide and sub-divide only to meet again. Countless small streams meander here and there only to join smaller channels or canals. Most streams, both large and small, overflow their banks in an annual ritual to replenish the earth.

The delta is deceptive. Seen at a distance, the land appears endlessly vast, flat, and low. Seen at a closer range, the land reveals its contours.

The waters of the delta not only replenish but also rebuild and contour the earth year after year. There is low land which is replenished by the flood waters. There is less low and less fertile land which is only partly inundated during the floods. And there is the high and least fertile land from which the rain waters siphon off the fertile top soil.

The village. Across the sea of fields and water some land stands higher than all the rest. This is where the trees grow and this is where people and animals live and more. The village sits partly on high land, contoured and raised by the water. But the village sits largely on raised land, contoured and raised by people over the years. The delta is, you see, essentially uninhabitable. The same waters that replenish the fertile soil of the delta also flood the land. Nearly all roads and homes are built on land that has been raised by people.

Earth. The movement of earth. People piling, pounding, and levelling their homestead plots. Women digging and carrying mud and clay to plaster the floors and walls of their huts. Women moulding mud to make the stove they cook on. People moving mud and clay to be fired into bricks. Men and women breaking bricks to make the ballast to make the roads. People dig, lift, and carry mud and clay in a daily ritual to redistribute the earth.

People. The patterns of life under the rising sun. Young children and old women lead cattle to graze. A boys sits on a buffalo shaded by a large umbrella. An old white-haired man and a young dark-haired boy lift water between ditches of different heights in a canvas sling which they swing between them. Men carry produce in baskets to the markets. Women carry mud in baskets to their huts. Young girls stand knee-deep in pools of water to catch fish in bamboo traps.

We follow a path heavily shaded by date palm and bamboo. Past men chest-deep in standing water stripping the steeped and rotten jute fibre off its stalks. We smell the rotted jute. Past cattle and goats tethered to stalks along the path. We smell the smoke of dung fires. Children run to stare and wave at us. Women linger in the shadows.

We turn to climb the slope of a homestead. Through an arborway of pumpkin vines, past a fenced-off vegetable garden on our right, past a lean-to covered with pumpkin vines for the livestock on our left, around a trough and some clay bowls which hold water and food for the cattle. Past large hay stacks and piles of jute straw, past mango trees with jute straw slung in the branches.

We come to a courtyard surrounded by several large mud huts with tin roofs. The hard-packed mud surface of the courtyard is spread with jute to dry. We look inside one of the larger huts at the invitation of the women. We see a wooden bed, some wooden furniture, several large mud storage bins, and tin boxes in the rafters.

The women of this homestead show us their work-place. They cook under the protection of a special cooking hut where they have constructed three mud stoves. The hut also shelters their wooden husking instrument. They own land, cattle, and poultry. They have a few luxuries—milk and eggs; plus oil, spices, and lentils to eat with their rice. Here life is *shanti*, peaceful.

We move out of that homestead, across a water channel (now nearly dry) on a narrow bamboo bridge, to the next neighborhood of the village. We come to a single, one-room hut made from jute stalks with a straw roof. The hut is about eight feet by twelve feet. A woman invites us to look inside. We see one table, a quilt of rags, and several macrame jute hangers hung from the ceiling. The woman shows us her one mud stove—in the open courtyard—which she stokes with leaves, grass, whatever she can find. She shows us a calf she has taken on sharecropping. This family of four will eat rice with some salt and chillies that day. They cannot afford oil, spices or lentils. Here life is not peaceful.

Evening. We drive home as the sun starts to set. Past elaborate bamboo scaffolds designed to lift and lower fish nets which stand like giant daddy long-legs in the shallow waters of the river. The fish nets shimmer in the evening light. Past stands of thatch which grow in the sandy banks of the river. Their feathery tips glow in the evening light. A layer of smoke from cow dung fires lifts off the fields near the villages. Men trundle home with baskets only partly refilled after a day at the market.

We drive through a market—small stalls and mats strung out along the road. The market bulges with jute—the cash crop. There are mounds of jute everywhere. There is little rice or paddy for sale. The rice stands lush and ripe in the fields but has yet to be harvested. What rice there is for sale commands a very high price. The poor have no stocks of rice and no wages to buy rice.

Poor people in a lush setting. The essential tension of life in a delta— the rich soil attracts dense settlements of poor people. All of us have heard about the poverty of Bangladesh. Some of us have seen the beauty of Bangladesh. I cannot forget either the poverty or the beauty.

Marty Chen
Author-Photographer

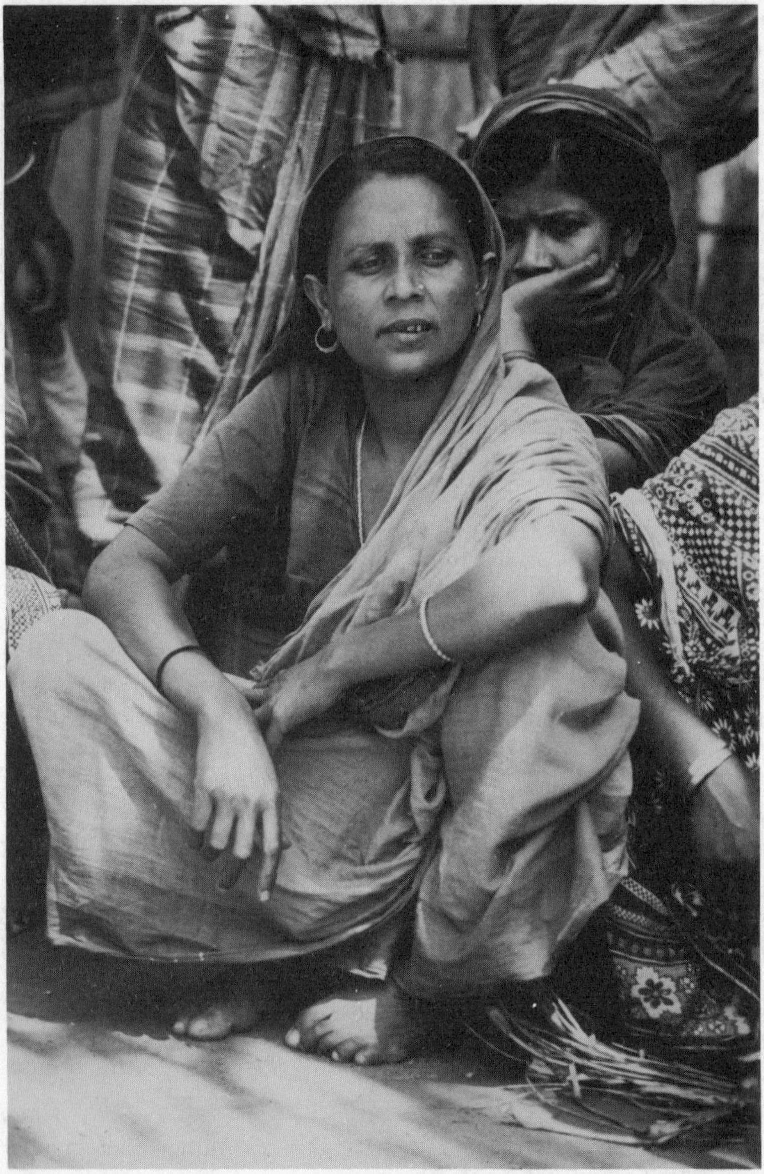

A Quiet Revolution

Women in Transition
in Rural Bangladesh

MARTHA ALTER CHEN

SCHENKMAN PUBLISHING COMPANY, INC.

Copyright © 1983
Schenkman Publishing Company
331 Broadway
Cambridge, MA   02139

Library of Congress Cataloging in Publication Data

Chen, Martha Alter.
    A quiet revolution.

    Bibliography: p. 267
    1. Women in rural development—Bangladesh—Case studies.
2. Community development—Bangladesh—Case studies. 3. Bang-
ladesh Rural Advancement Committee.
I. Title.
HN690.6.Z9C63268   1983   305.4'2'095492   83-40121
ISBN 0-87073-452-0
ISBN 0-87073-453-9 (pbk.)

Printed in the United States of America.

DEDICATED

TO THE MEMORY OF

BAHAR

Acknowledgments

This book would never have come to be written without the unfailing guidance and wisdom and the untiring support and friendship of Fazle Hasan Abed, the founder and Executive Director of BRAC, and his wife and co-worker, Ayesha Hasan Abed (known to family and friends as Bahar). I wish to express my deepest appreciation to F.H. Abed as well as my profoundest sympathy at the loss of Bahar, who died suddenly in 1981.

For their assistance, collaboration, and friendship over the years I am indebted to my many colleagues at BRAC. I am expecially grateful to Aminul Alam for his enthusiastic support, help, and advice in the design and implementation of BRAC's women's program and for his skillful interviewing of many women. I am also grateful to Khurshid Jahan for her assistance in interviewing and her continued support to the women and the program. I also want to thank Shaheed Talukdar, Anwarul Huq, Mohammed Shahjahan, Mosharraf Hossain, Ashok Kumar Chakraborty, Bhabatosh Nath, Sabbir Ahmed Choudhury, Sirajul Islam, Shushil Kumar Ghose, and Abdul Huq who assisted in the field research. My thanks also to Mahera Rahman for her steadfast assistance in all phases of our work and to Ranjith Senaratne for his patient guidance in our research.

I am indebted to the Ford Foundation, particularly to Adrienne Germain and William Fuller, for the research grant which financed the writing of this book. My thanks also go to Harvard's Institute of International Development for sponsoring the research grant and for facilitating the writing.

I am especially grateful to my husband, Lincoln, and our children, Alexis and Gregory, for their patient understanding and untiring support throughout all phases of my work and research.

Finally, it is to Rohima, Kamla, Mallika, Saleha and the many other women that I owe more than can be put into words. If they had not opened their lives to us, what I describe below would never have been possible.

CONTENTS

INTRODUCTION   xi
I. A LEARNING INSTITUTION   1
  The Beginnings of BRAC   1
  The Phases of BRAC's Program   5
    adaptive   6
    experimental   7
    expansion   9
    reassessment   10
    current   13
II. LEARNING FROM DOING   19
  Sulla Pilot Women's Program   21
  Jamalpur Women's Field Project   34
III. POOR AND A WOMAN   45
  The World of Women   46
    the economic roles of women   46
    the technological and structural constraints   52
    the social roles of women   54
    the social and cultural constraints   57
    purdah-patriarchy: problems of women as women   58
  The World of Poverty   60
    poverty and the changing roles of women   61
    the economic roles of women by class   63
    the social roles of women by class   69
    the constraints of women's work   70
    class-patriarchy: problems of women as members of
      poor households   72

IV. WHAT CAN BE DONE   77
    The Social Program   81
        women's groups and class federation   83
        methods of organizing   85
    The Economic Program   92
        on being hardnosed and softhearted   93
        the search   94
        the framework   97
V. WHAT WAS DONE   101
    Production Enhancement Schemes   103
        horticulture   106
        animal husbandry   107
        poultry rearing   108
        fish culture   112
        paddy husking   114
    Employment Expansion Schemes   119
        food processing   122
        traditional craft development   125
        silk culture   130
        agriculture   134
VI. WHAT BEGINS TO HAPPEN   139
    Changes in the Groups   141
        group development   153
        group dynamics   ???
        conflict resolution   158
    Changes in the Women   165
        changes in relationships   166
        changes in resources   178
        changes in power   183
        changes in attitudes   188
VII. THREE WOMEN SPEAK   195
    Rohima of West Shanbandha   195
    Kamala of Ramdia   206
    Mallika of Dapunia   210
VIII. WHAT SHOULD BE DONE   219
    Through Learning to Concepts   219
    From Action to Strategies   223
    Indicators of Change   236
    Prospects for the Quiet Revolution   240

Glossary   243
   Appendix I: BRAC Programs   245
   Appendix II: The Staff Structure of BRAC   248
   Appendix III: Mixing Action and Research   260
   Appendix IV: Map of Bangladesh   265
   Appendix V: List of Photographs   266
Bibliography   267

Introduction

This book describes and evaluates the efforts of one agency in Bangladesh to reach poor rural women with projects designed to increase their material and social resources. The Bangladesh Rural Advancement Committee (BRAC) is a private, non-governmental rural development institution founded and managed by Bangladeshis. Begun as a relief and rehabilitation effort in the aftermath of the Bangladesh War of Liberation (early 1972), BRAC today is an established, comprehensive, multi-faceted development institution employing over 1400 full-time staff. BRAC field ativities, with programming and administrative support from the central office, have spread to roughly 900 villages in several rural locations. In addition, BRAC disseminates and communicates the development experience gained in its field operations through its rural training center, its educational materials, its development journal, and its research and evaluation publications.*

In mid-1975, BRAC's Executive Director asked me to plan and administer a program for women in BRAC's field projects. At the time, BRAC had some limited experience but no specific concepts or strategies for working with rural women. During the next five years, BRAC field staff and I met, interviewed, and worked with countless women. We organized 6,000 women into over 250 cooperative groups through which they were able to generate higher incomes and exercise greater power and autonomy. In so doing, we learned a great deal from these women.

This book was written in order to share our learning and experience. Although there is a growing body of literature on various aspects of women in development, there are very few case studies that provide

*See Appendix I for a list of the various programs and activities of BRAC.

concrete ideas for program design or critical insights on the complex-
ities of program implementation. In writing this detailed case-study of
BRAC's women's program, I sought to identify key factors in BRAC's
women's program (those that favored as well as prevented success), to
describe our trial-and-error methods of deciding on effective strategies, to draw a picture of the economic and social roles of poor village
women in Bangladesh, and to show how the program affected the lives
of those women who participated. My hope is that information we
gained and the concepts and strategies we developed will have theoretical and practical significance for a variety of readers: policy-makers,
program planners, project staff as well as students of women, development, or South Asia.

For centuries, what is present-day Bangladesh was part of the region
in Eastern India known as Bengal. More recently, with the partition of
India in 1947, the predominantly Muslim East Bengal became part of
the new nation of Pakistan. The East and West wings of Pakistan were
united under a common name and a common religion but remained
divided by 1000 miles and by different language and race. At best, it
was an illogical union and increasingly it became an unequal union.
Eventually, the union proved untenable to those in the East wing.
After a prolonged civil war in 1971, Bangladesh was born.

Today there is the Bangladesh we are all familiar with—the media-
dramatized "international basketcase." Indeed, more than half of Bangladesh's people do not eat enough each day. Some ninety million
people live in 55,000 square miles, in an area the size of Iowa or
Wisconsin. Nine out of ten Bangladeshis live in her villages. Most of
them try to make their living from the land, but only five out of ten
rural Bangladeshis own enough land to make a living. The average
annual income is less than $100 per person.

Among the poor, the plight of women is harder still. Some 35 million
women live in Bangladesh; 31.6 million in her villages. The average
rural woman will experience 11 pregnancies but only 6 live births.
Only three out of four of her children will live to the age of five. She
herself can expect to live to 46 years of age. These village women work
long days: an average of 14 hours per day. However, unlike other areas
of intensive rice cultivation where women play very important roles in
transplanting, weeding, and harvesting, in Bangladesh village women
work almost exclusively in post-harvest activities. Under this very uniform and narrow division of labor, the only wage labor traditionally

available to women in rural Bangladesh is post-harvest and domestic work in other households. Also few Bangladeshi women engage in trade and that too at only the lowest levels of trade: petty hawking within villages but not in the marketplace.

But Bangladesh is experiencing change and there is a Bangladesh we are less familar with. During the decade of the 1970s, food production increased significanty due to expanded irrigation and the introduction of wheat cultivation. Also, during the 1970s, many agencies (both foreign and indigenous, both governmental and non-governmental) designed and implemented rural development schemes, including schemes for women. BRAC is recognized as one of the most comprehensive and successful of the indigenous, non-governmental agencies and BRAC's Executive Director was honored by the 1980 Ramond Magsaysay Award* for Community Leadership. And very significantly, during the 1970's, some village women—the very poor—broke through the traditional division of labor in search of wage work in agriculture and construction. BRAC's women's program was designed to support the courage and the search for new opportunities of such women.

This book is based on three sets of program-related data. The largest set is the collective and cumulative data gathered by BRAC field staff and myself. BRAC staff submit weekly, monthly, and annual reports on all activities. During the five years I worked for BRAC, I maintained a field diary in which I recorded notes of all meetings, conversations, interviews, and observations I attended or made. Another set of data was gathered in periodic, small-scale research projects conducted by BRAC staff. The final set of data was gathered in in-depth, tape-recorded interviews with the women participants.

The book is structured and told as a story. Each chapter represents a phase in time of the program—from the beginning and early learning phases of BRAC, through the design and implementation of the women's program, to the impact of that program on the women. The story is told either from the perspective of the women who participated in the program (I have drawn heavily from the women's own observations) or from the perspective of the staff, including myself, who implemented the program.

---

*Established in the memory of a President of the Philippines as the Asian-equivalent of the Nobel Prize.

In telling the story of BRAC's women's program, I have tried to balance a mood of analysis (to convey the concepts and strategies we developed) with a mood of involvement (to convey a feeling for the countryside and the women). I have purposefully avoided major references to the current literature on women and on rural development. To overfocus on the current debates of both these literatures would be to do injustice to the strong empirical base of BRAC's experience and to divert the reader's attention from the immediacy of the BRAC experience. I have also tried to avoid the catch-words and lingo of both the development and the academic circles. My intent is to tell the story plainly and directly.

CHAPTER ONE

A Learning Institution

The village of Derai is a commercial center. The main crop around there is rice, with some fruit. The land belongs to about 40% of the population. The rest work as farmer, labourers, or fishermen. This is an area with a majority of Hindus (60%) which explains the extent of the devastation. The Hindus fled en masse from their villages to seek protection and safety of India. All along our route, there was the spectacle of villages burnt to the ground. Only the hard earth foundations remained where the returned rufugees, who had lost everything, were trying to build straw shelters which would not even protect them from the sun, let alone the rain. I found this out for myself in Derai, when I visited a village of low caste Hindu fishermen who are particularly poor. A hailstorm, of rare violence for the season, started suddenly. We sheltered in an undamaged house but when the storm had passed I saw these poor people sweeping out the water which had drenched the inside of their houses; wet food was laid out to dry on oozing mats, indescribable desolation and the women in tears, pleading with BRAC staff to give them materials to rebuild their houses right away.

French journalist, March 1972

THE BEGINNINGS OF BRAC

Our story begins in 1972. Bangladesh had just begun to reconstruct after the upheavals of its liberation war. The ten million refugees who fled to India during that war were returning to start life anew. They returned to war-torn homes and villages. BRAC's founder and Executive Director, who had been active in refugee relief work in India, also returned to Bangladesh determined to assist the refugees. He found young nationalistic youth ready to join in his efforts. BRAC's Executive Director explains their determination.

1

"Right after the war of liberation, 10 million refugees started trekking back home to Bangladesh from India. We followed a large party of them from Meghalaya in India to the Sulla region of Bangladesh and found village after village completely destroyed. Houses—with utensils, tools, and implements left behind in terror—had been burnt to the ground, the livestock killed and eaten. We felt that the great suffering of the people of this region, because of its remoteness, would not attract very much relief assistance. This is why we chose to work in the Sulla area."

Sulla is a small town of 2000 people on the Surma river, 180 miles by paved road and then 30 miles by boat from Dhaka,* Bangladesh's capital. It takes the best part of two days from Dhaka by rail, road and motor launch to reach Sulla. The Sulla area is bordered to the north by the hills of Meghalaya which end abruptly at steep and high cliffs which separate the hills of India from the plains of Bangladesh. The hills of Meghalaya are among the wettest in the world—reputed to receive as much as 15 inches of rain in a single day. Over the years, the force and mass of the rain-water off the cliffs has dug a wide depression into the plains around Sulla. Sulla now sits in the center of several hundred square miles of depressed land and impounded water.

Imagine a saucer of land 50 miles in radius. Each year, this saucer fills to its brim with water from the hills to the north before it overflows its banks onto the plains and waterways of the south. For six months of the year this area becomes an inland sea—what the people who live there refer to as the *sagar,* the ocean. During those months their villages become marooned. Seen from the air, these island-villages look like so many logs floating in an endless sea. During the other six months of the year, once the waters recede and the fields emerge, the people grow one bumper crop of rice. This is the area known as Sulla.

Sulla may sound like an unlikely place to choose to work, and it is. Sulla is remote, inaccessible, and overlooked. There are no roads or vehicles in Sulla. During the wet months, people travel by foot along small dikes and embankments or ankle-deep through mud. A remote area with so much against it. But the people are resilient and the BRAC staff were determined. Together they began to pick up the threads of life in Sulla.

For one year, BRAC staff engaged in relief and reconstruction work.

---

*Until late 1982, the capital of Bangladesh was spelled Dacca.

BRAC's Executive Director describes how they floated more than one million bamboo down river from India to build houses:

> "The flotilla of bamboo rafts strung out for 2½ miles along the river. BRAC had conducted a survey among the homeless, refugees to India during 1971 who found homes destroyed upon their return: as to who needed homes most, how many of what types of bamboo were required, etc., BRAC staff received and distributed the bamboo. A total of 14,000 homes were built in 1972. Considering the scale of the operations, everything went smoothly."

BRAC staff imported timber to construct fishing boats and nylon twine to weave fishing nets. They provided tools (looms, wheels, hammers, saws, chisels) to the crafts-people of the area: weavers, potters, carpenters, blacksmiths, masons. They opened and ran medical centers. While dealing with the immediate needs of the people BRAC staff began to perceive the long-term needs of the area.

In early 1973, after one year of relief and reconstruction operations, BRAC launched a program of integrated community development in the Sulla region. They hoped to cover some 200 villages (a population of approximately 120,000) with an integrated package of services to each village. BRAC staff began activities in agriculture and horticulture, fisheries, adult education, health and family planning, vocational and other training programs.

Where did women fit into this integrated package? All women were to receive health, family planning and education services. One sub-group of women—whom BRAC staff called the "destitute" (widows or deserted women)—were to receive vocational training in addition. BRAC's program for women was off to a fairly conventional beginning!

The women in Sulla, like women in other parts of Bangladesh, produce and process food, raise cattle and poultry, fetch fuel and water, and more. But the BRAC field staff had not been able to observe women's traditional rounds of daily and seasonal tasks because 1972 had been a year of resettlement—of replacing homes, implements, and livestock—not a year of production. Not having seen what women do and produce, BRAC staff unwittingly accepted the current wisdom that women produce only children and "play no active economic role."

However conventional, BRAC's early programs for women provided important insights on what would and would not work. BRAC's vocational training program eventually proved unrealistic and was discontinued. In designing this vocational training, BRAC had accepted the myth that tailoring is women's work, an activity that does not interfere with their domestic responsibilities, and requires only a low level of training and investment. The truth is that commercial tailoring requires specialized skills, intensive training, a steady supply of raw materials, maintenance and repair of machines, and a market. Early on, BRAC recognized that there was not a steady supply of thread and cloth nor a ready market for tailored goods in Sulla and the vocational training program was terminated.

BRAC's functional education program, however, proved innovative and enduring. After using and being disappointed with conventional adult education materials, BRAC designed a curriculum of lessons that functionally related to the skills and problems of the people, both men and women. BRAC recruited village men and women as volunteer teachers in this program. By the end of 1973, the numbers of female teachers and students fell only slightly behind the numbers of men. Moreover, BRAC trained other village women to deliver low-cost health and family-planning services.

The failure of vocational training and the success of functional education pointed the direction for BRAC's future program for women. After an explanation of the failure of vocational training, BRAC's annual report for 1973 reads: "BRAC has, therefore, concentrated its attention on developing social consciousness of women through functional literacy and formation of women's working groups."

As early as March 1974, an English journalist who visited Sulla was to observe:

"It was in northeastern Sylhet, where the Bangladesh Rural Advancement Committee works, that I saw *the seeds of the quiet revolution* starting in village women's lives. At the meeting houses BRAC has built, the wives, young and old, are learning to read and write. Forbidden from doing marketing, they now at least can keep the accounts.

At community centres, I saw destitute widows, war victims, and wives of the landless, the poorest farmers and fishermen, learning skills like sewing, mat-making, and vegetable growing that will give them some security.

"Most of the men were very surprised at the idea at the beginning, but few object now," said a young BRAC field worker.

In one fishing village, the women have even become the bankers, saving over $2000 and lending it to their men to buy better equipment. It started in the simplest way—they collected a handful of rice a week from each family, stored it, and sold it in the market. About 50 villages in the area have thriving women's cooperatives, investing in new power-pumps or seed, and winning respect for their members."

The seeds of BRAC's future women's program had been sown. Small savings to build a group fund. Investment of group funds to increase income. Assisting women in traditional skills to increase security. Forming women's groups to develop the self-confidence, self-respect, and self-reliance of women. The seeds of a quiet revolution—a revolution within the women themselves and within their homes and villages—had also been sown. These seeds were to germinate and be transplanted, to grow and be harvested, and to be replanted season after season in many villages throughout Bangladesh. But before I tell the story of that germination and that harvest, I must describe the larger landscape—BRAC's general program—within which the seeds took root.

THE PHASES OF BRAC's PROGRAM

In development, two plus two does not equal four. Development is not a simple cause and effect process. Both the problems and the solutions change over time.   Administrator, BRAC Field Project

BRAC has been characterized as a learning institution. What this means quite simply is that BRAC "learns as it goes" through a responsive, inductive process. BRAC is not an institution setting about to prove a specific model or theory of development and its leadership has never espoused an ideology or "ism" in a dogmatic or absolutist sense. This is not to say they are not guided by an ideology, but that they do not feel their ideology has solutions for all the problems they are committed to tackling. They hope to find solutions as they set about tackling poverty and they recognize that the nature of both the problems and the solutions will change in the process.

BRAC learns so it can plan: that is, BRAC's planning involves the translation of what is learned from past and current field activities into plans for future field activities. Implementation-learning-planning are mutually reinforcing and simultaneous processes. BRAC has developed a planning methodology which takes the diagnosis of poverty in real human terms as its point of departure and which allows for flexibility in timing and in content of its plans (in recognition that plans must adjust to changing realities). During joint planning sessions, the field staff are requested to interpret poverty and village realities to BRAC administrators. While implementing the plans, the field staff are encouraged to move with the dynamic of a changing context and not be constrained by preconceived objectives and targets.

BRAC has been able to institutionalize this reciprocal process of learning and planning in large measure and is noted for its flexibility, responsiveness, and learning.* As I see it BRAC has undergone five phases of learning to date. By summarizing these phases I hope to show the evolution of BRAC's current ideology and methodology.

The Adaptive Phase (1973)

In early 1973, after a year of relief work, BRAC launched what it termed an "integrated rural development program with sectoral activities in the following areas: agriculture and horticulture, fisheries, adult education, health and family planning, vocational and other training programs." BRAC had, at the time, no specific theory or model of development to test. Rather, BRAC borrowed strategies from elsewhere and adapted them to Sulla. To be specific, BRAC borrowed the adult literacy materials and a two-tier cooperative structure from the national integrated rural development program** and the notion of demonstration plots and extension services from the community development movement.

The Sulla program covered an area of some 200 clustered villages with a population of approximately 120,000. The unit of intervention was the village. Within the village, one so-called "vulnerable" subgroup was identified—women. They were to receive fairly conventional vocational training in tailoring. One potential so-called "cadre" was also identified—educated, unemployed local youth. They were to be mobilized into social action on behalf of the community. Beyond

---

*For those readers interested in the management of rural development, I have described in some detail in Appendix II how various BRAC staff are recruited, trained, and deployed. For those readers interested in action-research, I have described in Appendix III how BRAC integrated a research perspective into its field activities and institutionalized a reciprocal process of implementing-learning-planning.

**Referred to as the Comilla Model, having been developed at the Academy for Rural Development in Comilla, Bangladesh.

and including these sub-groups, BRAC envisioned the village as a community which could define a common self-interest and whose behavior could be both harmonized and modified.

BRAC's approach at the time, much like earlier community development approaches, was based on certain assumptions:

—that the rural masses are passive and need to be conscientized;
—that the attitudes of the rural masses can be changed through education/training; and
—that village communities, although not homogeneous, can be called upon to work cooperatively and, at times, to pool their resources.

All that really is required is motivation of the village community through demonstration (in some sectors of activities) and extension (in other sectors).

BRAC's professional field staff, called "motivators," were multipurpose workers assigned to extend and demonstrate an integrated package of essential services in a specific set (averaging 5 each) of villages. They had been trained and were fairly able to listen to, to get to know, and to gain the trust of people. BRAC assumed they would also be able to motivate the community to accept change. The idea was: extend a comprehensive set of essential services, motivate people to accept them, and development will follow.

The Experimental Phase (1974)

Development, however, did not follow. The adult literacy materials proved boring to the villagers. Literacy *per se* was not a major qualification for functioning optimally in their rural environment. The women soon dropped out of the vocational training. There were neither raw materials nor markets for their new-found tailoring skills. The community centres, where constructed, did not function as the hub of development activities for the village. BRAC soon found that fostering village-wide community spirit was not as easy as expected.

BRAC entered a learning phase. The field staff began to see problems as the villagers perceived them: from the inside out, if you will, rather than from the outside in. BRAC became increasingly convinced of the latent capacities of people and, concomitantly, of a participatory rather than an extension mode of development. BRAC began to see participation not only as an end (people participating actively in their own environment) but also as a means (people participating actively in BRAC's planning and implementation).

BRAC began to refine old strategies and define new ones. BRAC constituted a Materials Development Unit to design and prepare a functional education curriculum for rural adults based on key problems in rural life; began publishing a monthly development journal with general development and more specialized articles for its rural readership; initiated a rural health delivery system utilizing two tiers of locally-recruited and BRAC-trained paraprofessionals; and developed a small Evaluation Unit to conduct baseline and sectoral surveys to evaluate its programs. A core of experienced field staff were trained to be BRAC trainers in basic development concepts and communication, leadership, and group dynamic skills. Certain of BRAC's field staff received specialized training so that they could design more meaningful technical programs.

Most critically, BRAC began to view the village not as a community but as a set of subgroups. Given this understanding, BRAC launched a cooperative program for some of the poorer sub-groups: namely, the landless, the fishermen, and women. There was nothing particularly innovative in BRAC's view of cooperative structure and activities at that time. Essentially, the cooperatives were credit institutions to be linked to the government's cooperative structure (again, the Comilla Model). But BRAC was innovative in its insistence on cooperatives for the poor and for women. The government's cooperatives had always been directed to farmers in general and not to the landless. The government's program of women's cooperatives, itself very innovative, was only just beginning.*

The BRAC cooperatives, later to be called "groups," are critical in this analysis because as they evolved in structure and function they became BRAC's key instrument for attacking rural poverty. At the time, they were simply an instrument for economic support to the poorer subgroups in the village. Side by side with these cooperatives, BRAC continued delivery of social services village-wide and advocated building "human infrastructure" in the village community. Village De-

---

*A case-study of this program has recently been published. Cf. Tahrunnessa A. Abdullah and Sondra A. Zeidenstein, *Village Women of Bangladesh: Prospects for Change*, Pergamon Press, 1982.

velopment Committees, representing the interests of all the sub-groups, were to be constituted to debate solutions for the village as a whole.

BRAC conceived the development process to lie in:

—extending an integrated package of essential services to remote villages;
—providing education and training as needed;
—fostering village-wide cooperation in solving village problems;
—forming credit cooperatives to support the poor.

In all of this, the professional field staff were seen as the "promoters" who initiated and supervised activities in a specific set of villages. Cadres of youth volunteers were also drawn into the work by way of functional education teachers and more general social workers. Women from the villages were recruited to serve as the front-line workers in health, family-planning, and female education. The recruitment of village women was critical not only because they were women, and as such could have access to problems and situations that male staff did not, but because they were from the villages to which they were assigned to work, and as such were the forerunners to BRAC's use, at a later date, of group members in the delivery of social services.

The Expansion Phase (1975–75)

BRAC continued its program of economic support to the poor and village-wide services to the community. As the skills of BRAC staff were diversified and strengthened BRAC gained recognition for its efficiency and expertise. BRAC's functional education materials and health delivery system, using paramedics and village-level female workers, were adopted by other agencies. BRAC trainers were being asked to train staff of other agencies.

But not all of BRAC's strategies were working. Some had to be discontinued. The health insurance scheme based on village-wide pooling of resources, each household at a rate proportionate to individual income and assets, had not worked. The rich were not willing to subsidize, as they saw it, the health benefits of the poor. The community centres constructed by voluntary labor on donated land to ensure, in theory, continuing interest and participation in community activities had not worked. The rich and poor alike felt they had contributed and benefited unequally. Community spirit did not develop.

Although BRAC's confidence in village-wide participation and cooperation was on the wane, BRAC's confidence in its overall approach and stategies was on the rise. The first field project, Sulla, had proved very useful experimentally. But the Sulla area not only because of its remoteness but also because of its topography (an area of impounded water which floods over during the monsoon rains to form an inland sea) was not typical of Bangladesh. If BRAC intended to develop models for development interventions, the time had come to implement its program. in an area with typical, not unique, characteristics. BRAC was ready for expansion.

In early 1976, BRAC launched its Manikganj Project* (covering the 180 villages of Manikganj thana) after searching in various districts of Bangladesh for a "typical" thana. About the same time, in an area of extreme poverty (as witnessed by the numbers of women forced to beg in the streets of the local town after the famine of 1974–75) BRAC launched its Jamalpur Women's Program covering 30 villages around the town of Jamalpur. Meanwhile, because BRAC trainers conducted increasing numbers of trainings for other agencies throughout Bangladesh, a rural campus for BRAC's Training and Resource Centre was constructed. And a Research Unit to investigate the fundamental, underlying constraints to rural development was added to the existing Evaluation Unit. BRAC had begun not only to expand its field coverage but also to analyze and disseminate its field experience.

The Reassessment Phase (1977)

Development, however, allows little time for a sense of achievement. One problem tackled throws up another. One question answered only points to further questions. The BRAC field staff, who daily encountered the realities and problems of rural life, had little time to feel confident. Their's is the frustration if a target is not reached or a strategy proves unrealistic. Moreover, BRAC was deepening its analytical understanding of the structural constraints to development both through its collective field experience and its enhanced research capacity.

BRAC began to see a number of inherent weaknesses in its earlier integrated community development approach. It is not the first institu-

---

*Refer to map in Appendix IV.

tion to understand these weaknesses, but such lessons are best, and perhaps only, understood when experienced. In assuming to bring about change in both attitude and behavior through motivation, education, and training, BRAC had not addressed the major structural constraints to change or to the elimination of poverty. It began to understand the innate conflicts in the village power structure and the inter-relationship between that power structure and the distribution of resources. BRAC's internal analysis and collective field experience had shown:

- that there is a very fundamental relationship between the rural power structure and the distribution of resources;
- that programs designed for the whole community deliver most of their benefits to the rich and tend to by-pass the very poor;
- that programs designed for the poor must address the rural power structure, which keeps not only power but also resources in the hands of a few; and
- that in order to address the rural power structure, the capacities of and institutions for the poor (and powerless) must be developed.

In light of this fundamentally new set of basic assumptions about development and poverty, BRAC reassessed its approach and strategies during 1977. The shift away from integrated community development inherent in BRAC's directing of all economic support to cooperatives for the poor was to result in a major break from the concept of the village "community" in an inter-project meeting of senior staff in November, 1977.

The following discussion at that inter-project meeting illustrates BRAC's increased understanding of the village dialectic. Prior to that meeting, BRAC had been attempting to mobilize educated youth in the village as a cadre to undertake social action on behalf of the poor. "Most typically the educated youth align themselves with a local power. When they align themselves with the government, we call them touts," stated BRAC's Executive Director. He went on to ask: "Why then do we call them cadres when they align with BRAC? Why do we need intermediaries at all, why can't we work directly with the poor?" "Perhaps the vegetable seeds we intended to distribute *through* the cadre of youth have actually been distributed *to* that cadre," someone added. Discussion continued on the issue that BRAC field staff represent more or less the same class as the youth and, for that reason,

BRAC staff should not be expected any more than the youth to align themselves with the poor. "But," the discussion concluded, "BRAC can exert some control and regulation over its staff and, more importantly, BRAC staff are outside the village power structure." This increased understanding of the village dialectic helped shape BRAC's future program.

BRAC analyzed itself more explicitly in the context both of national development strategies and of the rural power structure. To date, BRAC had been attempting to do or be something in all sectors for the rural population of certain remote areas of the country. In considering the national context, BRAC had to decide whether it was satisfied in doing a certain amount for a certain number of people; whether it envisioned Bangladesh divided into a certain number of regions serviced by as many BRAC-like projects; or whether it saw its own role (and that of other private voluntary organizations) as one of testing innovative approaches.

BRAC decided its role was not that of service-delivery in remote or neglected areas of the country, rather its role was to test what could be done with and for an overlooked segment of the population—the poor. It would test ways to better reach the poor with inputs and services and to organize the poor to guarantee their future access and control over such services and inputs. Also, for an indefinite period, BRAC would act as an intermediary between the poor and national strategies and programs; other private voluntary agencies; and resource institutions. It would also need, at least temporarily, to act as a buffer between the poor and the village power structure:

VILLAGE

POOR

BRAC

Government	Resource Institutions	Other PVO's
—mobilize services and inputs	—tap expertise	—initiate reciprocities: expertise
—demonstrate how to reach the poor	—facilitate interchange	training
—lobby for protective legislation	—demonstrate how to reach the poor	—facilitate interchange

BRAC also decided to organize small groups (averaging 20–25 members) of poor and to gradually link these small groups into a federation of the poor which could, in time, assume the roles of buffer and intermediary outlined above.

The Current Phase (1978–present)

BRAC had, in the course of its reassessment, made two extremely fundamental choices. One was ideological in nature: that development to BRAC meant empowerment of the poor. The other was methodological: that in BRAC's view organized groups of the poor were the key instrument for such empowerment. Whereas BRAC had always broadly conceived development to mean development of the poor, BRAC's assumptions about poverty and development had undergone fundamental change.

What then are BRAC's current assumptions about poverty and development?

- that the village is made up of groups with differing and conflicting interests;
- that these groups can be mobilized around issues perceived to be in their self-interest;
- that the rural poor do not participate adequately in or control their environment because they are sociopolitically and economically powerless; and
- that the poor through the power gained in collective economic and social action can more fully participate in and control their environment.

But what does this mean methodologically? BRAC had shifted from the notion of credit cooperatives for the poor to the concept of organized groups of poor—both male and female—around which all activities are to be organized and through which resources and power are to be mobilized. In the words of a recent BRAC proposal: "BRAC works in reorganizing and mobilizing the poor and disadvantaged sector of the population into cooperative groups who then plan, initiate, manage, and control group activities, both in social and economic fields. All sectoral programs such as agriculture, horticulture, pisciculture, animal husbandry, duck and poultry raising, nutrition, health care, family planning services and functional education are thus planned and implemented by the group members. BRAC supports the self-sustained growth of these group activities by providing training, extension, credit and logistics assistance."

There are three key elements in BRAC's methodology: identification of the poor, organizations of groups of poor, and formation of a class federation. Each element needs to be examined separately but also to be seen as three stages of a single methodology:

The Poor—

BRAC's criteria for its target group—the "poor and disadvantaged"—have changed over time. In the early stages of credit-cooperative formation, BRAC identified three broad, presumed to be homogeneous, groups of "disadvantaged": the landless, fishermen, and women. But BRAC began to recognize that some landless have other substantial sources of income, that some fishermen own boats and equipment whereas others are forced to hire the same, and that women of all socioeconomic classes do not necessarily, by virtue of belonging to the same gender, share all of the same problems. BRAC, therefore, refined its "economic" criteria for the target group to include: men and women of those households which do not exercise any control over the means of production and/or hire out their labor to third parties.

This definition also soon proved deficient. BRAC came to believe that those economically within the target group but with political patrons among the non-target population will be dictated to and controlled by their non-target patrons. Moreover, there are some poor without power who will not, for lingering status considerations, perform certain types of manual labor. When a group is first constituted to attend functional education classes, its members may appear homogeneous in socioeconomic status and interest. But over time many "shades" of poverty emerge: one woman is landless and widowed but receives regular remittances from her landed father. Another, a divorcee, lives in a relatively prosperous household compound of her landed brother but is forced by him to eat alone off her own means. Some women are willing to undertake heavy, manual labor; others, poor but not as poor, prefer rearing hens and goats only. One functional education teacher may genuinely emphasize with the poorest; another sees her group of learners as actual or potential "followers" in the traditional patron-client mode. Field staff must regularly discern and handle such anomalies within the groups. The poor who still negotiate notions of status or networks of power will most likely, predicts BRAC, create disunity among organized groups of the poor. Given these "shades" of poverty, BRAC redefined its criteria to include not only an economic variable but also social and political variables. BRAC currently defines its target group as men and women of:

- those households who sell their manual labor to others for survival irrespective of occupation;
- provided, they do not have political patrons among the non-target people; and
- provided, they cannot still exercise status considerations.

The Group—

The evolution of BRAC's concept of the group parallels the evolution of BRAC's ideology. Initially, BRAC believed it could tackle the problem of poverty by dealing with the village as a whole. No groups were organized. Rather, services were delivered and activities initiated across the village community. Over time, BRAC singled out certain poorer sub-groups to be organized for economic support. Currently, BRAC directs all of its support to organized groups of poor. These groups of poor are both short-term ends in themselves and long-term means for empowering the poor.

In the short run, all BRAC activities are to converge on these groups. Social services are no longer delivered village-wide, rather they are delivered by trained members from each group to the members of their respective groups. All inputs and technical services are directed to and managed by the groups. Group strength is fostered and strengthened through joint productive activities. The emphasis is on concrete productive action which necessitates daily interaction and fosters unity. In all this, BRAC professional field staff, now called "organizers," develop the individual groups to the point where they can plan and implement their own social and economic activities.

In the long run, the individual groups are to be federated to form a power base for the poor. BRAC believes the groups and the federation must be developed gradually to replace step-by-step those forces in the rural power structure which both support and control the lives of the poor. That is, BRAC believes:

- that individual behavior does not occur in a vacuum but in the context of a series of relationships;
- that to change an individual's behavior in any permanent sense one must change that series of relationships;
- that if the group is to be the key instrument of change for the poor, the group must prove a viable counter-institution to those earlier relationships;
- that the group must, therefore, provide at a minimum what the previous relationships offered individual members (varying degrees of security, resources, employment, and power)
- that a strength of unity among the members will develop to the degree the group is perceived to provide security, resources, employment and power;
- that the concerted strength of an individual group can provide the degree of power required in, for example, a successful settlement of a domestic dispute but only the concerted strength of many groups can provide the broad base of power required in, for example, the negotiation of favorable wage rates or sharecropping terms; hence, the federation.

The Federation—

The group is then only a part of something larger. One group of poor in one village, even one group of all the poor in one village, cannot exert adequate pressure to demand higher wages or more favorable share-cropping terms. BRAC plans to gradually federate all the poor in its field projects. This federation, if it is to guarantee the base of power required by the poor, must develop through step-by-step organization not through hasty mobilization. BRAC plans, and has begun, to federate individual groups first at the village level, then between villages, at the project level, and, eventually, between projects. The functions and structure of the federation at each level are to be determined by the participant groups. Eventually, the federation should become the intermediary between individual groups of poor and the village power structure, resource institutions, and national strategies and policies. BRAC would, in that event, no longer be needed.

How do women fit into these key elements of BRAC's current methodology? BRAC recognizes that poor women are at once poor and women: that is, they face at one and the same time certain problems by reason of their gender and other problems by reason of their poverty. For poor women, because of this double set of problems, the group and the federation are not simply steps in the same process of organization. Initially, BRAC organizes men and women into separate groups in order that women can address their problems of day-to-day economic survival as members of poor households and of limited social power and autonomy as women. Overtime, BRAC links the separate male and female groups into a class federation to address the long-term, systemic problems of economic domination by the rich. But before I elaborate further on these points, I would like to trace the evolution of BRAC's current concepts and strategies for women through the early years of BRAC's women's program.

CHAPTER TWO

Learning from Doing

Anandapur: a village six hours by bus, five hours by steamer, and ten
miles by foot or country boat (depending on the season) from Dhaka
city. Anandapur: a village in the vast flood plain of the Sulla region,
with little to distinguish it from thousands of other villages in Bangladesh until . . . The women of Anandapur: village women who rise
early, work hard, and sleep late, with little to distinguish them from
hundreds of thousands of other village women in Bangladesh until . . .
until in 1976, BRAC opened a camp for women staff on the outskirts of
Anandapur village and started development activities for women in the
surrounding villages.

August, 1976. I take the BRAC speed-boat from Markuli to Anandapur. The boat cuts across the ocean of water. I can see as if forever in
all directions. No tall buildings or hills, only half-submerged villages
and trees to break the view. Billowy clouds cluster at the horizon. Thin
wiffs of clouds drift slowly across the dome of the sky. Suddenly, we
turn into a narrow channel between two villages. Trees overhang the
channel. We slow down to pass country boats. I catch a close-up view
of village life; huts, hay stacks, cattle, people. Children wave. Ducks
waddle down the banks of the channel. As suddenly as we come, we
speed up and move out into the vast ocean once again.

I am going to Anandapur to meet some village women and BRAC's
new women staff. The BRAC camp sits on a small piece of land that juts
out from the village into the flooded plain. As we near, I see the cluster
of cement-walled and tin-roofed structures that BRAC has built. We
moor the boat near an open field which once in a week becomes the
village marketplace but which otherwise serves as grazing ground for
stray goats. A single shade tree stands in the middle of the field.

19

Several women come down to greet us. They are newly recruited BRAC field staff. Together we walk to the village. We visit three households and talk to the women. In one household, an unmarried daughter whose mother has died. In another, four sisters-in-law of a joint household. In the third, a married woman with no sisters-in-law or daughters-in-law to help her. We ask the women in each household to describe the tasks they perform each day and each season. They all work long days: sweeping and wetting down the floors of the huts, collecting dung and fuel, cooking and cleaning, watering and weeding vegetable and fruit gardens, grinding spices, tending animals and poultry, stitching quilts and clothing, and more. They work the hardest during harvest: preparing the threshing floors, threshing and winnowing, head-loading the grain to storage bins (they have constructed), cooking and delivering food for the hired laborers. And repeatedly throughout the year, at least once a week they process grain: winnowing, drying, storing, par-boiling, husking, again and again.

The staff and I return to Anandapur camp to discuss what we have seen. We all agree women perform a wide range of productive activities. The staff observe: "Women do a great deal of work, but their work is not valued. No one talks about what women do. Men receive seeds and credit, pumps and power tillers. But women receive no credit, no extension services, no inputs, no training, no machines." We ask ourselves how BRAC can help.

I look out across the water that surrounds us. All I can see are the higher branches of submerged tress and the single tapered spire of a submerged temple outlined against the soft pinks and greys of evening sky. And I remember my first trip to Sulla less than one year ago. And I marvel at how far we have come. We have met countless village women. Some of them are now active in BRAC-supported groups. Many of the women's groups have undertaken joint action. We have recruited and trained women staff. We have opened Anandapur Women's Camp. And, in another corner of Bangladesh, we have started the Jamalpur Women's Project. And I worry about how much further we have to go . . .

August, 1975. I joined the administrative staff at BRAC's head office in Dhaka. BRAC's Executive Director has asked me and a young Bangladeshi woman to develop BRAC's women's program in Sulla and Jamalpur. Neither of us have worked with rural women. But, at that time in Bangladesh, neither had many others. We were to learn through our experience, to learn from doing.

Perhaps no single year taught us more than the initial, experimental year of BRAC's women's program: the year that began in August, 1975. And there is perhaps no better way to recapture that year than to share my impressions. The following pages give an account of those twelve months through edited portions of my field-diary. I have selected notes for each month of that first year that highlight our learning and experimentation in both Sulla and Jamalpur. I have omitted many notes to make these pages more readable. What I hope to evoke is a number of patterns of work: patterns of development work at the village level; patterns of developing a women's program; patterns of discussion with BRAC field staff; and patterns of life for village women. Of course these notes are limited by yet another pattern: the pattern or movement and observation by a BRAC administrator and a foreigner at that! But, I was there and this is what I experienced.

I will begin with Sulla, for it is in Sulla that BRAC began . . .

SULLA—PILOT'S WOMEN'S PROJECT

September, 1975—

I have been working at BRAC for six weeks. This is my first trip to the Sulla project area. I have developed certain tentative ideas about the area and about the project—but I know these ideas are soon going to be blown away.* We take the early morning flight to Sylhet town (200 miles from Dhaka by air) a UNICEF van to Sherpur (30 miles by road); the BRAC speedboat from Sherpur to Markuli (30 miles down the

---

*In the interest of clarity and brevity, I have tried to standardize my references to BRAC personnel:
We—my colleagues and myself of BRAC's women's program. At first, there were two of us; later others joined.
Field Staff—both professional and paraprofessional field staff, unless otherwise specified.
BRAC—a combination of field and administrative staff, unless otherwise specified, to indicate when collective or institutional actions and decisions are taken.
Refer to Appendix II for a discussion of how BRAC staff are recruited, trained, and deployed.

Khushiara river). I feel caught in the juxtaposition of travelling to one of the most remote and least accessible areas of Bangladesh and yet, by BRAC standards, travelling as a VIP! BRAC field staff do this trip regularly by train, bus, and motor launch.

It is the month of Aswin—the rains are over but the water level is still high. At Markuli, the Khushiara river breaks its banks and flows over into several hundred square miles of fields. BRAC's Sulla project covers approximately 150 square miles of this vast area of impounded water. We have entered another world—a world of immense stretches of water and an enormous sky. Water everywhere and yet the peak water level has passed! I feel as if I am seeing the world through a fish-eye camera lens, as if I am standing above the horizon which swings full-circle around me.

We walk across a field and around a fish tank to the BRAC camp—a cluster of small buildings with plastered-bambooo walls, cement floors, and tin-roofs. Down the lane, BRAC's long office building and medical clinic of the same construction. Beyond them, the police station with its wireless tower and the bazaar.

Rounds of introduction to BRAC staff—some names are familiar, few faces are. Today is given to discussion with the staff. I have seen the organizational chart for the Sulla project area. A sense of the organization develops as I meet the various levels of field staff. I question individuals about their work. Discussions focus exclusively on Sulla: the area and the project. I hear no mention of Dhaka, films or politics. Even the humor takes off on field work, development jargon, or the organization. The world of Sulla is a world unto itself: both physically and spiritually.

Night is heralded by the uvulaing of the Hindu women as they light their oil lamps. Field mice scamper out of their holes. I sense the presence of nature on all sides . . .

We have come to Sulla to conduct workshops with village women's organizations in four pilot villages—two in the Markuli camp area, two in Ghungiargaon camp area. While in Dhaka, with little field experience and a few tentative ideas we have designed the workshop. Now the time has come to see which ideas seem to work, which misfire.

Daulatpur village is about four miles from Markuli. We are able to walk most of the way along an earth embankment built to prevent early flooding under a BRAC food-for-work program. The last leg of the journey is by country boat. We arrive at a BRAC-financed, village-constructed community center: one small room with packed-mud floor, woven-bamboo walls, and tin roof. A blackboard, four long benches, and a table are the only furnishings. The village's female teacher-helper arrives. She gathers other women from this Muslim neighborhood. Daulatpur is a large Muslim village. We are in one neighborhood of 200 people separated from other neighborhoods by channels of water. After half an hour about 35 women are sitting on the long benches—they range in age from young unmarried girls with bright bows in their braids to toothless old widows. Children peek through the doors and windows; infants nestle in their mother's arms.

We distribute pictures of women working at different activities in Bangladesh. The pictures cause great excitement. Some of the activities depicted are familiar to these women, others are not. We ask the women what *they* do, what things they make. They possess many skills. They send small children to fetch items they have made. Soon we have a large display. We discover their skills and interests while the women suddenly become conscious of their skills.

Next we introduce a game of Blind Man's Bluff. Everyone takes turns at being blindfolded and being led around the room. The women enjoy the fun. More than a game is involved. We ask the women when in real life they feel blinded, helpless, dependent. The women realize they share mutual problems. To end the meeting, everyone joins hands in a circle and promises to meet regularly.

Late afternoon, we conduct the same workshop in a Hindu fishing village, Omarpur, on the outskirts of Markuli. The meeting is held in someone's home. It's a busy time of day. The dynamics of the workshop differ: more interruptions, less attention. We find additional skills and interests. Moreover, there is an existant savings group of women in the village. BRAC field staff have worked with the group for some time. The groups have been able to save 7,500 taka ($500)*, putting aside handfuls of rice each day (a traditional way of saving called *mushti*). There is a Treasurer and Secretary. The groups need to organize and decide how to utilize their savings. They express interest in recovering the art of net-making (an activity previously performed by women but now taken up by men). They could purchase nylon twine from BRAC at cost price. Each woman could make a piece of net. The

---

*Between 1975–80 the exchange rate for the Bangladesh taka remained 15 taka to U.S. $1.00. This is the rate of exchange used throughout the book.

large net could then be leased out. The group agrees to meet every Thursday with the BRAC field staff to discuss this possibility further.

October, 1975—

We take an early morning speed-boat ride from Markuli to Ghungiargaon past innumerable little island-villages. I observe certain details of their water-logged existence: cattle are kept yoked at all times: enormous hay stacks (of rice straw) provide fodder; embankment walls of bamboo poles at the narrow end of each village have been built to brace the soil against erosion from the waves. Resources seem so scarce: little land, few trees, only water. Our tentative ideas for women's economic activities appear so inappropriate to the setting: fish breeding (there are no tanks); composting (there is no extra land); pickle-making (there are no fruit trees); crafts (there is no bamboo, jute, or cane)!!!

Two workshops today. Group dynamics, interest, resources differ one village to the other. Each group must define its own interest, problems, and solutions. We hope to start a participatory process whereby individual women learn to think as a group with shared problems and shared talents. The women must set their own goals, define their own project. BRAC male staff accompany us to these village workshops. Their acceptability in the village, even with the women is self-evident. They will meet weekly with the women's groups— provide suggestions, encourage activities. We have a great deal to learn from them . . . and the women . . .

November, 1975—

The month of Agrahayan—the water has receded. It is the month of migratory birds; intensified fishing; fish-drying. Fish nets dry on tall pullies. The smell of fish pervades the atmosphere—fish drying on special racks atop bamboo stilts, fish drying on mats covered with nets to keep birds away.

We awake to the sound of pigeons in the rafters. We return to Daulatpur along the BRAC-financed embankment to conduct a second workshop. This workshop is designed to encourage discussion on alternative activities the women's groups might take up: what interests the women, what problems are associated, etc.

At dusk we take a country boat downstream to the channel dividing Hilalnagar, a nearby Hindu village. It is *puja* (festival) time in the Hindu villages. Cattle are coming home, children run with *bola-bulis* (straw scare-crows on long broom handles to be burnt at dusk and thrown into the river to forestall illness). We join a group listening to *kirtans* (devotional songs) in the courtyard in front of the village temple. An old woman and her daughter perform in the middle of a circle of men who accompany them with drums, gongs, cymbals, and an harmonium. Interested village women lurk in the shadows outside the circle of men. The old woman—a natural story-teller—half narrates, half sings the story of Lalita and Krishna at a river crossing. With her husky voice, her animated yet serene face, and her natural movement of limbs she is a most powerful, compelling figure . . .

We conduct two more workshops the next day and, in the evening, a staff meeting on women's programs. Sixteen BRAC male staff, the female teacher-helper from Daulatpur, two women from Dhaka, and ourselves attend. The purpose of the meeting is to brainstorm on ways to integrate women into BRAC's programs. The group lists and then ranks the felt and unfelt needs of village women. The staff describes existing programs for women. The group evaluates these programs according to village women's needs. Additional potential programs for women are discussed. Everyone agrees special impetus should be given for women's programs. Special staff should be employed. Books and journals on other women's programs should be sent to the field. The mandate for us in Dhaka is to network ideas from other projects to the BRAC field staff and to work out the staffing requirements for women's program development in Sulla.

December, 1975—

My job has already been redefined. There is little need for us to try to conduct a pilot village cooperative long distance from Dhaka. The male field staff in Sulla are quite prepared to carry on with the women's program there given encouragement and ideas. In any case, my colleague in the women's unit has assumed responsibility for the Jamalpur women's project.

BRAC's Executive Director and I decide my job is to help plan women's programs in Sulla and the soon-to-be-started Manikganj field projects; and to plan and administrate the Jamalpur women's project. I will try to help all three field projects develop a strong women's component. The Sulla field staff requested I network ideas for women's economic programs from other programs and countries. I send out my first circular to this effect.

Notes on Ways to Further Integrate Women in
BRAC's Development Activities

AGRICULTURAL ACTIVITIES:
1. Employ women as agricultural labor in a demonstration plot using improved methods of farming and/or growing experimental crops.
2. Encourage both women and men to let women participate in weeding and transplanting activities; these are traditionally women's work in many developing countries.
3. Hold discussions with other staff and with village women and men on improved methods of post-harvest activities for women.

HORTICULTURE, COMPOSTING:
1. Engage women in growing and marketing seedlings.
2. Engage women in preparing and maintaining compost pits using cow dung, night soil, etc.
3. Engage women in collective vegetable or other crop growing on fallow land or small plots. These plots may be worked cooperatively by women. Every effort should be made to encourage more intensive use of both uncultivated and cultivated land surrounding the villages.
4. Encourage women to dry vegetables (cut into very thin strips) to be stored and reconstituted for consumption in off-seasons.

FISH CULTURE AND POULTRY:
1. Engage women in fish-breeding where ponds available.
2. Encourage improved poultry raising (home-centered) through: (a) improved housing for poultry—ventilation and perching roosts needed; (b) cock-replacement scheme—improved breed; (c) twice-yearly innoculations or use of sulfa dioxide; and (d) improved feed utilizing rice husks, crushed egg shells, oil cake.
3. Prepare and market chicken feed and sell chicks and eggs.

PRODUCTION ACTIVITIES:
1. Food Processing: paddy to rice; paddy to *cheera/muri* (crushed and puffed rice); dried fish; shelled and cracked betel nuts.
2. Vegetable and Fruit Trees: grow and sell seddlings (papaya, vegetables); tend and harvest fruit trees and vegetable gardens.
3. Handicrafts and Carpentry: manufacture mats, tables, stools, chairs, or brooms; split, weave, finish cane and bamboo.
4. Bakery: bake and market bread and biscuits.
5. Local small public works to contract female labor.

January, 1976—

Minutes from a weekly staff meeting in Markuli Camp read:

"Omarpur Women's Group submitted a requisition for nylon twines for netmaking. We have given a second thought to it as the requisition is too high (i.e. 600 lbs.). By next week they will submit a new requisition for 100–150 lbs., which we will distribute on cash payment . . .

Daulatpur Women's Group is also organized and they are now generating their group fund. They have collected 350 taka ($23.33) so far. They are interested to start a sewing center. Accordingly, we are getting ready to supply them one sewing machine on loan."

Three other camps report the beginning of women's groups in nine new villages.

February, 1976—

Despite these efforts to further involve women in BRAC's Sulla program, we are not satisfied. For one thing, there are no full-time paid women staff in the Sulla project. For another, there are so many program ideas yet to be explored.

How can we accelerate this process? We discuss the possibility of converting one of the camps in the project area into a women's camp. Women staff would be the ideal media for designing, extending, and stimulating new activities and ideas with the village women. Perhaps in an all-female environment some of the housing and social problems in recruiting full-time female staff might be overcome. We already know from the Jamalpur experience that women can work as a team in field work.

We discuss the Anandapur Camps as a possible site. There is already a BRAC-run medical center with a doctor and a paramedic. Female paramedics could be hired and trained there. There are a cluster of 10 to 12 villages within a short radius of the camp. Staff from adjacent camps currently carry out BRAC's general program in those villages. Women field staff could assume the responsibility for general programs and develop specific programs for women in those villages.

The decision now rests with my colleague in the women's unit. She must choose whether to remain with the Jamalpur project or start the Anandapur Women's Camp. We discuss her options. In Anandapur she would have direct responsibility for BRAC's programs in ten villages plus indirect responsibility for developing women's programs in the 200 villages of the Sulla project area. In Jamalpur, she has helped train a team of women staff and initiate development activities with women in 28 villages. She decides the Jamalpur team can continue their work without her. The challenge lies in Anandapur.

March, 1976—

Anandapur Women's Camp opens. We have been able to recruit seven women staff: two from the Sulla area and five from elsewhere in Bangladesh. We conceive the roles of the women staff as follows:

> "The staff of the camp will carry out the female segment of BRAC's ongoing activities: functional education, public health, family planning, cooperatives. They will also experiment with and demonstrate potential economic activities for women: poultry and duck farming, food processing, intensified horticulture, manufacturing of utility items, etc. Eventually, it is hoped they might design extension services and appropriate technologies to improve women's grain processing, fuel processing, water collection, etc.

> Anandapur Camp will also serve as a training center for prospective female leadership from other areas. Each camp's staff members (there are eleven other all-male camps in the Sulla project area) are being encouraged to locate a core of motivated and interested women from their camp areas to facilitate some of the development activities now being facilitated by male staff. Anandapur camp will serve both as an experimental laboratory (in which various ideas for women's development activities can be tested and evaluated) and as a training center (for female leadership)."

April, 1976—

Minutes from a project-wide meeting of staff held in Markuli in early April read:

> "The meeting reviewed the efforts of each camp towards creating human infrastructure in their respective areas. It was noted that the male section was covered in some areas. It was reminded to give similar efforts to bring both male and females under this program . . .

> All camps were going ahead with women's programs. Each camp had its own ideas and system towards organizing women's groups, but the direction was the same . . .

Derai camp had a problem with its Barmonpara women's group—in respect of storage facilities for their potato crop. It was felt that unless BRAC helped with storage this time, the heavy financial loss to be incurred would discourage the group seriously . . .

All camps were advised to give much thought before undertaking economic programs for women's groups in the future."

May, 1976—

We catch the 5:30AM passenger launch to Derai town. It is Baishak—the month of harvesting. Two hours of early morning views along the Khushiara river: hired laborers for the rice-harvesting (from far-away districts) on their boats; other boats overhung with pottery for barter with rice. In Sulla, surplus rice is bartered for lentils, pots, jackfruit from other regions.

I meet additional BRAC staff in Derai town. We walk four miles across fields, through villages, into a jungle to reach Dayergaon camp. It is the hottest day of the year (105 degrees recorded in Dhaka). We take a half hour rest then walk another mile to Baushi village. Fifteen women from six villages have gathered to discuss women's cooperatives with BRAC staff.

We discuss the purpose and principles of cooperatives. The women mention the need for exchange of knowledge and ideas and for helping each other. They then ask: "How can a cooperative be formed?" Some women want BRAC to call meetings. A BRAC staff answers: "But you called us here, we didn't call you." One woman agrees by saying: "Unless we can do things on our own and understand what we are doing, no amount of outside assistance will help us." All agree to initiate meetings with women in their own villages to explain the purpose of cooperatives. They plan to meet again in two weeks.

We spend an afternoon with Omarpur women's cooperative. The responsible field staff has been meeting regularly with the women. Seventeen members attend. They have been engaged in net-making (as planned last November). They discuss the rent for the nets they make and lease. They discuss what to do with the unhusked paddy they have saved: whether to sell it when the price doubles (the price is lowest during havest) or process it into husked rice and sell it for a profit now. They express interest in building a tank in which to breed fish. Omarpur is a fishing village. The women dry and store fish in earthen jars. The jars are sealed when full and the *shutki* (dried fish) sold. If they had more fish they could sell more *shutki*. They express interest in resuming functional education classes in the village. They must select new learners and a new teacher (as the former teacher had left to be married).

June, 1976—

BRAC's women's activities are still relatively new and exploratory. But we are confident that they indicate the potential for such activities. We are asked to prepare a paper for a national seminar on the role of women in socio-economic development in Bangladesh. In the first half of the paper, we challenge certain "myths" about rural women in Bangladesh with the realities we have seen. In the second half of the paper, we outline what seems to work or not work, and what needs to be done for rural women.*

What seems to work:
1. Rural women can be motivated to design and implement development activities—functional education, public health, family planning, cooperatives—both inside and outside their own villages (there are 90 village-based family-planning helpers and 30 village-based teacher-helpers in the Sulla project).
2. Urban women can be motivated to design and implement development activities in villages (the Jamalpur teachers are from the town but work in villages).
3. Relatively inexperienced women, given sufficient and appropriate training, can plan, design, implement, and monitor a development program (the Jamalpur teachers designed and are implementing their own program).
4. Social constraints can be overcome if female workers work in pairs or in teams (the female staff of Anandapur Camp live together in a hostel).
5. Rural women will leave their homesteads to attend central meetings for functional education, mothers' clubs, cooperatives, or whatever.
6. In such gatherings, rural women voice opinions. They are usually free, open-minded, and receptive to new ideas.
7. Rural women will join and form cooperatives. They can cooperatively accumulate a limited capital through *mushti*-savings** (cooperatives in Sulla and Jamalpur have done so).

---

*Kabir, Khushi, Ayesha Abed and Marty Chen. *Rural Women in Bangladesh: Exploding Some Myths*, Ford Foundation, Dacca, 1976.

**A traditional method of savings whereby women put aside and store [often secretly] a handful of rice weekly or daily from the domestic stock.

8. Rural women will travel outside their own locality to receive training they perceive to be beneficial (several women from Sulla and Jamalpur are currently in Sylhet town for six-weeks duck-farming training).

What seems not to work:
1. Programs that address welfare needs but offer nothing economic or
tangible. Interest and motivation slacken and attendance drops in such
programs.
2. Programs which fail to take into account the felt needs of the
participants.
3. Programs which are imported or imposed ready-made without
evolving from the participants.
4. Programs which fail to take into account problems of training,
supervision, management, procurement, marketing.

What needs to be designed and tested:
1. Innovative ideas on ways to integrate women into development
programs and on new economic opportunities for women.
2. Ways to instill and maintain cooperative spirit.
3. Ways in which savings of cooperatives can be economically invested.
4. Ways to teach women how to do their routine work more
efficiently and productively.
5. Appropriate technologies to improve the tools and techniques
women use in their agricultural work.
6. Appropriate technologies that permit women to lessen the time
and strain of routine chores.
7. Appropriate extension services, credit facilities, cooperative training to reach women.

The very fact that new empirical lessons have been learnt about the
role of rural women in the socio-economic development of Bangladesh
argues for further experimentation. Action programs designed
specifically for women should be developed as an integral part of any and
all rural development programs. Rural women can and must participate
in the planning, designing, and implementation of such programs.
Through further experimentation strategies for the integration of rural
women in development can be refined and improved.

July, 1976—

Interest in the program at Anandapur has spread. I am asked to help
write a story on the steps taken by the women staff to involve village
women:*

*Brehmer, Margaret, Marty Chen, and Eikbal Hussein, "Anandapur Village: BRAC
Comes to Town" in *World Education Reports*, No. 13, November 1976.

"... The Anandapur staff have to feel their way as they begin projects with rural women. Few action programs for women have been conceived of, fewer yet tested or evaluated. New program ideas need to be developed which address the felt needs of and are acceptable to rural women. The Anandapur field workers tackle some basic—and universal—problems as they try to involve rural women in a new project ...

The first task of BRAC field workers is to overcome the villagers' suspicion of strangers. They go from door to door, patiently explaining what they intend to do and urging women to join. They assure the villagers the meeting will be interesting as well as relevant. The field staff talk with the village *mashima* ("aunty")—an old widow, socially mobile and acceptable throughout the village. She helps to spread the word about the meeting.

Who selects the women that attend? The women select themselves. They listen to the *mashima* or the field workers. Those eager—or just curious—show up. But not all. A newly-wed bride in the village shows interest in the meeting but her mother-in-law angrily rejects the ideas. The girl should not attend any public meeting—her place is at home. The young bride is disappointed but she obeys.

An open area between houses is chosen as the site for the meeting. Women begin to gather around the *mashima*. These women encourage others to join the group. All ages come. It turns out to be a good meeting with nearly the whole village crowding into the open space. Village leaders seem pleased.

Rural women lead busy lives and bear heavy responsibilities. They doubt that these strangers could understand their needs. They doubt their own ability to change the course of their lives. What is there that they can do? Life in the village has changed little in their lifetimes. What could change it now? BRAC field workers believe the women can bring about change. But first the women must become "conscious" of what they already do. These village women possess many skills. They must be made to feel these skills are valuable. Then the women must decide for themselves what they can and want to do.

BRAC staff distribute photgraphs to the crowd and give everyone a chance to look and see for themselves. The photographs depict women in Bangladesh engaged in a variety of activities (some familiar to these rural women, some not). It is important for the villagers to draw their own conclusions about the relevance of the pictures to their own lives. One group studies a picture of women growing potatoes. Their questioning begins. Who are these women? What are they doing? What tools are they using? BRAC staff also probe. Are all these women in the pictures from Bangladesh? Yes. Can you do all the things they are doing? Some, not all. Would you like to learn what you now cannot do? Yes.

BRAC staff discover what skills and interests women from the area possess. The women themselves gain a "consciousness" of their skills. Their sense of self-esteem grows. They slowly realize they are not merely reactors to but creative agents in their own homes, in their village. The discussion has started women thinking along new lines.

The photo discussion is one way of helping villagers to feel self-confident. Everyone's comments are important here. Everyone has something to contribute. Suddenly the villagers *are* involved. They are learning and they are themselves contributing to the learning process."

August, 1976—

I attend a full-day project workshop chaired by BRAC's Executive Director. The meeting opens with the question of representation from each camp. The representatives must be able to transmit back to respective camp staff not only policy decisions but also the rationale behind these decisions. Each BRAC program (health, family planning, cooperatives, and women's programs) is reviewed in terms of BRAC's approach to development, current progress and problems, and future goals.

The discussion begins with rural work's programs—poor women coming forward for such work are breaking through a taboo. "How else can change be effected?" Certain social actions can be taken: to encourage primary school education for all girls; to motivate males to family planning; to encourage widow remarriage; to discourage polygamy. Economic change is also needed. Duck raising seems potentially economic for women of this area. Two female trainees from Sulla have received training; two more are to go on September 1. The trainees sent from Sulla to Sylhet town for duck-rearing training should be responsible, independent, and intelligent. Women, as well as landless men, should be considered for agricultural schemes. Each camp is requested to submit at least one agricultural scheme for women. Weaving on a pilot basis is also considered. One camp expresses interest and will submit a scheme (including information on raw materials, loan, trainer, market). Each camp has developed at least two women's cooperatives. Our pilot village approach of last fall has long since been expanded by regular BRAC staff. Now, we must all come up with economic break-throughs for village women.

Much has been learned and so much remains to be done in Sulla. Meanwhile, in Jamalpur town, five hours drive north from Dhaka, similar seeds have taken root.

Jamalpur Women's Field Project

Jamalpur District was severely affected by the floods of July and August 1974. UNICEF's Nutrition Unit staff visited the area to see the condition and observed large numbers of women begging in Jamalpur town. Largely as a famine-relief measure but also to demonstrate the possibilities of cultivating sandy soil, UNICEF decided to employ women to grow sorghum and sunflower on the banks of the local river.

UNICEF through local government committees initiated a food-for-work scheme [i.e., wheat as wages] in February, 1975. The number of women willing to participate in agricultural work under this food-for-work scheme was higher than expected. One hundred women had been expected; 840 participated. By June, harvesting was completed, the monsoon had begun, and the UNICEF Nutrition Unit approached BRAC with a request to provide functional education to the 840 women until the advent of the next agricultural season.

On request from UNICEF, BRAC's Executive Director and functional education coordinator accompanied by UNICEF staff paid a visit to the Jamalpur project site in early June. During their visit they met with the local government officials involved in the Jamalpur project and discussed BRAC's proposed functional education program for these women. They decided to hire 15 teachers and to hold classes in the Jamalpur stadium.

One hundred women applied for the 15 teaching jobs. Those selected (through interviews) were given a five-day training by BRAC staff. The training was designed to be very practical and to familiarize the trainees with functional education methodology. The trainee group was active and intelligent; they easily grasped the ideas the training was designed to communicate. Only two of the teachers seemed shy in talking in the training circle. My colleague in BRAC's women's program was posted as supervisor to the Jamalpur program.

BRAC's functional education course started in mid-July. The 840 women were divided into 30 groups—about 28 women in each group. The 15 teachers had two groups each: one group attended classes on Mondays, Wednesdays and Fridays; the other group on Tuesdays, Thursdays, and Saturdays. Women belonging to the same village were grouped together with one exception (a group of women with some degree of literacy).

The shifts did not work too efficiently at the start since few of the women arrived at the correct time. Women whose class started at 12:30 would come at 8:00 in the morning and demand to have class held immediately; others whose class was to begin at 8:30 calmly arrived at 11:00 only to become upset over not being able to attend classes. Unfortunately there was no way to accommodate all 15 classes together. Scheduling, however, improved considerably during the next month.

In July, attendance was very poor. On certain days only three learners attended class. One factor was the heavy rains—some learners had to walk over 5 miles in the rain in order to attend class. Another factor was that wheat payments had been due to the learners since June. For most of the women this was the only income they had; survival became more difficult each day. The average attendance in July was 18 out of an average class size of 28.

August, 1975—

During August attendance in classes was slightly higher than in July. It did not rain as heavily as before; and it was expected wheat would be distributed any day. By the third week of August some wheat was distributed. Attendance became more regular from then on. The learners still seemed suspicious of the functional education classes. Their motivation to attend class was due more to the wheat payments than to any interest in learning. The system of wheat payment was based on attendance in class—each learner got wheat for the number of days she came. The learners blamed the teachers for the delay in wheat payment and argued with them that some learners were being paid less than others. The educational materials did not seem to have much of an impact on the learners.

But between the teachers a feeling of unity began to grow. The supervisor conducted a one-day workshop with them in mid-August to reinforce functional education methodology, to create a more harmonious working atmosphere, and to help bring about a feeling of unity. The discussion centered on problems they felt in their work situation and how best to solve these. The discussion method used was the same as used with the learners in class: first a brain-storming of the problems faced; next small-group discussions on solutions; and lastly a group consensus on solutions.

BRAC started a child feeding/day care centre. Sixteen of the better learners were chosen to work as cooks and helpers at the center. The chief cook got a small salary; the rest got a share of the meal cooked. The feeding center was intended only for children five and under. Each child was issued a card. Upon presenting the card each child was given a bowlful of *khitchuri* (a mixture of wheat, soyabeans, lentils and spices). Children were fed after the mothers finished attending class so that each mother could supervise her child's feeding.

While mothers attended class the helpers organized the children into groups and held informal classes. Once each month the children were weighed and their weight recorded in a special weight-card. Once a month the local Health Visitor from the government's Maternity and Child Health Center visited the center to check the health of the children and dispense medicines as needed.

The child feeding/day care activities reinforced the BRAC functional education program. Wheat was being supplied more regularly than before. Most learners had learned to write their own names. A few could also recognize certain words. These factors helped raise the morale of the learners. By the end of September a marked change was noticed in the learners. Their earlier resentment had gone. The learners felt close to their teachers and free to talk with them about their problems.

BRAC began considering the possibility of a replacement for the supervisor in the event the functional education program continued after November. The teachers proposed that a supervisor should be chosen from their own group; an outsider, they reasoned, would not understand BRAC's functional education approach. The teachers then chose unanimously the person they felt most able to handle the role. In late September, the original supervisor left Jamalpur for three weeks. In her absence the teacher chosen as future supervisor was left in charge of the program. This was to be a test and training period for her. All the teachers were to submit a report when the original supervisor returned.

October, 1975—

Attendance in October was very regular. When the supervisor returned to Jamalpur, she noticed the learners' total acceptance of the functional education program and a high degree of warmth and closeness shared between learners and teachers. Classes were going well. The learners were active and alert. There was an increased interest in literacy and numeracy.

November, 1975—

Initially, functional education was to end when the food-for-work resumed in early December. Upon hearing that the functional education program would end, the learners requested the teachers to continue classes. The teachers held discussions with the learners and found a general desire among the learners to continue attending classes even on a voluntary basis (earlier wheat-payments were used as an incentive for class-attendance). They decided jointly to approach BRAC with a proposal for the continuation of the functional education program.

After several discussions with learners and two work-shops with the teachers, BRAC reconsidered its position and decided to seek financial support for a continuing program if the teacher-team could design a concrete plan for the next phase.

December, 1975—

The teachers worked out a tentative plan of action to continue functional education classes and to expand into village-based women's development work in the learners' villages. BRAC agreed the teachers would spend an initial trial month (December) investigating the field area while continuing the functional education classes in Jamalpur town.

January, 1976—

The teachers came to Dhaka for a five-day intensive training. We set fairly ambitious targets for their training:

—to help the teachers design their own program by: setting goals; translating goals into action terms; phasing out project activities over one-year; designing a feed-back monitoring and record-keeping system and a work schedule; etc.
—to develop a group dynamic by: demonstrating the process of consensus reaching in a team; discussing the merits of team work; illustrating the importance of group cohesion.

—to make the teachers conscious of their role as "catalysts": the qualities of a good change agent (especially, acceptibility and self-motivation)

—to acquaint the participants with the different concepts and modes of communication: how to identify felt and unfelt needs, interests, problems of rural women; how to translate unfelt needs into felt needs; how to communicate; how to move from known concepts to unknown concepts

—to make the teachers aware of the importance of proper leadership: their leadership as responsible change-agents and the leadership of rural women who could serve as change-agents in their own villages

—to make the teachers more analytical and systematic in their thinking, planning and action

Together with BRAC trainers, we designed a series of exercises around each of these goals. What evolved out of the training was a year's plan of action designed by, directed towards, and to be implemented by women—the Jamalpur Women's Project. The group of part-time teachers have matured into a team of full-time development workers.

The objectives of the project, as formulated by the teachers-turned-field staff during the training, are:

1. to make village women conscious of the root causes of their problems and to help them seek solutions;
2. to control population growth through family planning motivation and delivery of services;
3. to encourage joint savings and cooperative economic activities by village women;
4. to educate village women in hygiene and nutrition;
5. to encourage horticulture and poultry raising by women;
6. to encourage village women to utilize fallow land surrounding their respective villages;
7. to initiate women's organizations in the villages; and
8. to educate village women.

February, 1976—

The teachers are now working by pairs five days a week in the twenty-eight villages (with a total population of 36,000 in 6,400 families). Each pair of teachers is responsible for four villages. Their team leader is a roving field worker. Fourteen village functional education classes have opened. Women members for women's groups are being identified. Each teacher has developed and will expand a clientele of successful oral contraceptive users. Each Saturday, the teachers meet to report on and discuss the previous week's activities and to plan for and discuss the next week's activities. The teachers have formed their own savings society and opened a joint bank account. Their spirit and hopes as a team of development workers are high.

March, 1976—

Two members of BRAC's Material Development Unit are in Jamalpur working on revision of the women's lessons of BRAC's functional education curriculum.

Picture twenty women sitting in a circle on the floor of a one-room Union Council office. A few children and a young man are also seated in the circle. The young man has just told the women a story entitled "Siddique's Mother". The moral of the story is "oppression"— oppression of a young mother by her husband, by her employer, by society. The young man queries: 'We women are often oppressed by men, are we not?'

The young man playing the role of the functional education teacher is a member of BRAC's Materials Development Unit. Together with another long-term BRAC field staffer and a BRAC artist he is developing new lessons for BRAC's functional education curriculum. Some of these lessons are designed to meet the specific needs of individual learning groups—such as the lesson for women he has just tested on a new group of female learners in Jamalpur.

April, 1976—

As administrator of the project, I visit Jamalpur at least once in a month to observe village-level activities and to hold a monthly staff meeting. My minutes from the April meeting read in part:

> Income Generation: The village women already know some certain skills. Ideas based on these skills include: processing *cheera* (pounded rice) and *muri* (puffed rice); fish cultivation; potato cultivation; pottery and bamboo-work. These are done traditionally but could be expanded and upgraded with credit and designs. No action taken as yet, only ideas being discussed.

Women's Groups: The objective is to form working groups from savings-and-loan groups. The staff decide a President and Secretary should be elected yearly.

Coverage: The staff do not want to take on additional villages yet. The main activities include functional education, family planning, and vegetable seed distribution. The suggestion is made that women could be selected to grow and sell seedlings.

Loans: The principle is that if the society saves 200 taka ($13.33) then BRAC will match the savings with a loan of 200 taka. This amount is to be utilized to finance a group activity. The BRAC loan is to be paid back in monthly installments. The plans as to how to utilize the loan must be drawn up before the loan is given. Additional ideas include cooperative banana or papaya cultivation.

Functional Education: Fourteen village centers with 280 learners have opened.

Mother's Clubs: Mothers express concern over their children's ailment such as: worms, scabies, edema, pneumonia, rickets. It is not feasible for them to supplement breast milk. Idea: scabies eradication program. Posters on health, family planning, and sanitation are needed.

Trainings: I report that composting and poultry raising trainings are being arranged. I will discuss with the trainers whether the whole team or selected staff should take the training.

May, 1976—

At the monthly staff meeting in May, we discuss the process of field work, the changes the staff have observed, and the problems they face. My minutes read in part:

Changes: Poultry raising, vegetable cultivation, and family planning practice have increased. The women ask the teachers about different aspects of their lives: marriage partners for their children, etc. In the villages where there are graduates from the earlier cycle of functional education (that is, from the days of the stadium) progress comes quicker. The graduates understand better and respond quicker. They are trying to lead better lives and to earn some money. In the villages where there are no graduates, the response to the general program is not as high.

Field Work: The staff go to the villages about 9:30AM. The functional education classes start at 12:30 noon. During the morning, the staff go round to different houses: to discuss family planning, poultry rearing, kitchen gardening, etc. They initiate and work with Mother's Clubs and women's groups.

Functional Education: To test the learners, the teachers have them read a letter that describes a problem. The learners are then asked to discuss the problem. In each village there are about 25 learners. After 10 lessons, the women can read. They can break the word into phonemes and then pronounce it. They begin to acquire a group feeling. The literacy games—like word dice—are very popular. Everyone is interested in them. The teachers are also keen on the games because that is how they can interest the learners. Many new students understand quickly because often their relations have been graduates. They are familiar with the concepts and have even sometimes been tutored by graduates. Their grasp of the lessons comes more quickly and easily. The other women in the village who have not yet participated are now very eager to join the class. At first, they were only eager to earn the wheat. But now, they are really interested in learning new things: about a new way of life, savings, earning, cooperation etc. Women from other villages also want to learn, but they are unwilling to come to neighboring villages to join the class. Idea: the older students in the villages could be given additional training and be appointed teacher-helpers in other villages. The staff would only need to provide supervision.

Problems:
—the papaya seeds did not germinate
—there are not enough posters for the number of Mothers' Clubs
—the staff feel the need for the back-up services of a doctor or a paramedic
—the side-effect of the oral pills are: headache, heavy bleeding, or no bleeding

Savings: Thirteen groups have been formed to date. Each group on the average, has accumulated savings of 50 taka ($3.33)

June, 1976—

We call the staff to Dhaka for a four-day workshop to review the project.

After six months of experience, the staff are more familiar with the realities and constraints of field work. They review the original plans for the year in light of these realities:

Functional Education: The problem here is supply not demand. They have started the 14 village centers planned. The staff worry about the graduates who, having been motivated, need further encouragement and support. The staff decide to engage the new graduates in small income-generating schemes (poultry raising, goat rearing, paddy husking, sweet potato cultivation, etc.).

One problem remained outstanding even after the review workshop. As planned, functional education centers had been opened in only half of the villages. But what about the demand for functional education in the other villages? Could the staff assume the load? Or should village volunteers be trained as teachers? (The Jamalpur staff decided to train village volunteers as teacher-helpers only in November 1976. It seemed that having started out themselves as teachers, it was difficult to conceive of village women performing the same role).

Family Planning: A major constraint to family planning acceptance is the concern of mothers for their living children. The health care of living children is of more immediate concern and stands in the way of planning for future children. The staff decided in light of that and other constraints to cut their family planning target for the year by half: from 1500 to 750 acceptors.

Mothers' Clubs: The Jamalpur Women's Program was designed to include a preventive health component (the Mothers' Clubs) but not to offer curative health services.* The staff were trained to provide certain basic services: blood pressure checks and iron supplements for pregnant mothers, recording of child weights on "road-to-health" cards. The staff, however, did not feel equipped to provide these services and answer the mothers' concern for the health care of their children. Despite our efforts to assist—a paramedic was seconded to Jamalpur from Sulla for four months to help further train the staff in these preventive health measures—both the women and the staff feel the Mothers' Clubs prove repetitive in their message and offer too few tangible incentives for the women to attend regularly.

Women's Groups: The staff decided that cooperative societies should have 20–25 members. Below 15, there are not enough members to make the group viable. Above 25 members, the group runs the risk of disagreements and quarrels. The staff have received preliminary training in cooperative organization and management. They recognize that the women need the same training.

Our experimental year was over. The pilot women's program in Sulla and the women's field project in Jamalpur were both one year old. We had met and talked to many village women. We had listened to their needs and problems. We had tested ideas and strategies with the women. We had hired 22 women staff to work with rural women. They were working in teams in two separate corners of Bangladesh. Together with field staff, we had organized roughly 800 women into 40 working groups. All of the members of these groups had attended BRAC functional education classes. Most of these groups were pooling

---

*BRAC had decided against a curative health component because:
1) financial and management costs too high for a project of this size; but, more importantly,
2) as the villages are near the municipality the approach should be to avail of and lobby for the existing services.

their savings into a group fund. Some groups had decided how to invest their funds: in paddy husking, fish net making, poultry rearing, fish culture, potato and vegetable cultivation.

And so on that pink-and-grey evening in Anandapur I was to marvel how far we had come and to worry about how much further we had to go. We had faced some obvious and (with hindsight) avoidable problems. I felt confident we would avoid these in the future. First, all women do not necessarily face the same degree or type of problems; BRAC needed to decide on which women it wanted to benefit in what ways. Second, all women will not necessarily work well together; BRAC needed to ensure the working groups were developed from members with like needs and interests. Third, the problems of women's lives are complex and interrelated; BRAC needed guarantees that each women would benefit from a comprehensive set of programs. And fourth, women will not remain interested in programs that do not offer concrete solutions or tangible results; BRAC needed to provide concrete and tangible programs.

We had also faced some less obvious and (even with foresight) unavoidable problems. I felt we could work on these. The womens' groups could generate small savings, but would they be able to manage and invest large amounts of credit? The staff had been trained to develop and supervise BRAC's more general programs, but would they be able to provide the technical and managerial support required when the groups take up more complex production activities?

But we had also faced some more subtle and more intractable problems. The women face and tackle these every day. If we were determined to help the women, we would need to tackle these as well. Would we be able to identify and design viable economic projects to ensure each member of the group reasonable income in a subsistence economy with extremely limited demand for commercial goods and services? Would we be able to identify and develop adequate strategies to ensure each member of the group a reasonable voice in an hierarchical socio-political structure with extremely limited options for the poor, especially women? But before I tell of our search for viable schemes and for adequate strategies, I must describe what we learned from the women about their traditional work in that subsistence economy and their traditional roles in that hierarchical structure.

CHAPTER THREE

Poor and a Woman

Anwara is busy from before sunrise until after dark. She rises early to clean the dishes and utensils from the previous day, to sweep and wet down the floors of her hut, to prepare breakfast (tea and puffed rice) and to bathe before the rest of the family wakes. After breakfast, Anwara tends to the cattle and poultry, cleans the stalls, collects cow dung and sticks, fetches water, and puts the pillows and mattresses out to dry. She grinds spices before cooking the main meal of the day—rice, pumpkin, lentils cooked with some oil and spices. After the noon-day meal, she prepares and dries dung sticks for fuel, sweeps and waters down the courtyard. Some part of each day she processes paddy. Threshed paddy must be parboiled and dried. Usually, she spreads the paddy on a bamboo mat in the open courtyard to dry. During the rains, she dries the paddy by baking it over her mud-stove. Sometimes, the house needs replastering with mud and dung; a new mud-stove must be built; or new storage bins must be constructed from mud and straw. At other times, quilts and clothing must be stitched or repaired or new mats to dry the paddy must be woven out of palm leaves. In the late afternoon, Anwara bathes her four children, feeds and waters the cattle, and waters her fruit and vegetables. At dusk, she lights the oil lamps and heats left-overs for the evening meal. Anwara finds little rest during the day and goes to bed late.

Anwara and her husband own 2½ acres of land, two heads of cattle, a few hens. They live in a one-room hut with bamboo walls and thatch roof. They are able to subsist off what they produce. Anwara says she is busiest during harvest when she must wake earlier to prepare the threshing floor, gather fuel, and parboil, dry and husk paddy. They cannot afford to hire labor to help them but if they work hard they are able to feed their four children on what they produce. After harvest, she can relax a little. Otherwise, Anwara sees life as a never-ending succession of long and hard days much like the one she described to us. "I cannot stop working," she explains, "because I would not then be able to feed my children. If they should die, life would have no meaning."

We learned about Anwara's busy day because we talked to her directly. If we had consulted any other source, we would have gotten a different picture. If we had talked to Anwara's husband, he would have said: "My wife does some work around the homestead." If we had listened to conventional wisdom, we would have heard: "Rural women do no productive work." If we had consulted the statistics on Bangladesh, we would have read that most rural women, like Anwara, are "housewives."

And so we went directly to the source, to the women themselves. Over many years, we observed how women do things. We asked detailed questions—in informal interviews and small surveys—about their work and their skills. We discovered they were not only producers but also technicians and specialists in their own right. The women explained how skills are passed on from one generation of women to the next. They described their overlapping and continuing tasks and responsibilities. And they told of the persistent problems and constraints they face.

What follows is a "typical" picture of the world of Muslim women in small farm households in Bangladesh*—it is not an exact description of Anwara's world but a distillation of what we learned from many similar women in very similar situations.

THE WORLD OF WOMEN

The Economic Roles of Women

Under the traditional division of labor in rural Bangladesh, women perform a wide range of economic tasks. There are five main

---

*We talked with and worked with Hindu as well as Muslim women, but Bangladesh is predominantly Muslim and what we describe holds true predominantly for Muslim women.

areas of *income-generating* production undertaken by most farming households in Bangladesh: grain production; jute production; tree, vine and vegetable cultivation; animal husbandry; and craft manufacture. There are also several areas of *income-conserving* production generally overlooked because they are carried out by women: household maintenance and repair; fuel and water collection; and labor force reproduction and maintenance.

1. Rice Production

Rice is the predominant crop in Bangladesh. Rice is seen as a "male" crop as men control field operations and marketing. But the division of labor is as follows:

a. *Field operations* are the domain of men. Land preparation, seedbed preparation, transplanting and planting, weeding, and harvesting is done, almost exclusively, by men. Selection and storage of seed from the previous harvest is a female speciality. If a seed-bed is near the homestead, women are sometimes deployed or hired to prepare the bed and plant and tend the seedlings.

b. *Threshing* is carried out jointly by men and women. While men cut, stack, and transport the paddy from the fields, women prepare the hard-mud threshing floor near the homestead. They must clean and smooth the floor and bind the dust. Women occasionally thresh grain. If bullocks are used to thresh, women unbind the bundles, spread the stalks and turn the stalks as it is threshed. If a barrel or feet are used, the women may do the threshing. Women gather and stack the straw after threshing and dry the straw. Women clear the threshing floor.

c. *Winnowing* and *sieving* of grain is carried out by women. Grain is winnowed and/or sieved several times (after threshing, after husking, and after polishing) to separate grains of rice from particles of straw, dirt, husks, and unhusked grain. After threshing, the straw and kernel are separated by sieving. Two or three sieves of different degrees of fineness may be used. After husking and milling, rice needs to be winnowed two or three times. Winnowing is done in several ways: by tossing the grain in a flat horseshoe-shaped basket *(kula)*, by dropping the grain from a raised-tipped basket to be cleaned by a breeze; or by using the *kula* to fan the grain.

d. *Drying* of grain is carried out by women. Grain is dried several times: post-threshing and pre-storage as paddy seed; post-parboiling and pre-storage as paddy; pre- and post- husking; and, intermittently, during the storage period. The courtyard must be specially prepared (with a cow dung-and-water mixture to bind the dust) and swept before drying. The paddy is spread on the courtyard to dry. The work is not heavy but someone must guard the grain from animals or birds and turn the kernels at regular intervals. Women do this activity in and around other tasks or ask small children or old women to tend the grain. Women turn and gather the kernels using a rake-like instrument *(harpata)*.

Drying proves difficult if space or time is limited. Several families may share a single courtyard. During the rains, drying is very problematic. A dry place must be found. Someone must be ready to move the grain quickly if rain threatens. Sometimes, grain cannot be sun-dried and the women must devise other techniques (such as baking the paddy over their mud-stoves). On a metal road the drying process is twice as fast as on the mud courtyard. During the rains, the roads are dotted with rows of drying grain. Although vehicles drive over the grain and toss it about in the wake of their exhausts, the women have calculated that loss against the advantage of quick drying.

e. *Parboiling* is done exclusively by women. Parboiling is a process of partially boiling the paddy in large drums over slow fires. Paddy which is treated in this way is easier to husk, retains additional nutritional value, and is preferred for its taste and size in Bangladesh. This process is very time-consuming. All paddy for sale or consumption as rice is parboiled. Some paddy is reserved (without parboiling) as seed or for sale as paddy.

f. *Husking, polishing,* and *milling* is done by women. These processes are very labor-demanding. After parboiling the grain is husked. The husk is removed but not the mesocarp because storage is better if the final polishing is not done. Before consumption, the final polishing is done. Most typically, paddy is husked in a foot-operated hammer-action implement, known as the *dekhi.*

Picture a heavy wooden beam pivoted on a wooden stump. At one end of the beam there is a short wooden pestle. This pestle drops into a wooden mortar fixed in the ground. The mortar is filled with the paddy to be husked or polished. One (or two) women step on the opposite end of the beam to lift the pestle two to three feet above the mortar in a crude see-saw motion. The woman suddenly releases pressure on the beam and the pestle drops into the mortar. The force of the pestle hulls the paddy. Another woman stirs paddy in the mortar.

Milling is also done in the *dekhi.* Rice is milled to prepare a special rice cake.

g. *Storage* of domestic and market stocks of rice, paddy, and seed is women's work. Women prepare the storage bins and supervise the storage of the grain. It is women who can judge rice, paddy, and seed for its quality and moisture before and during storage.

Storage of seed paddy requires the greatest care and longest time. The seed patty must be dried more carefully and longer (for "three suns") than paddy for consumption. The plastered baskets in which seed paddy is stored must be hermetically sealed with a mixture of cow dung and mud.

h. *Preparation* and *cooking* of rice and rice products is done by women. In addition to boiled rice which is (if available) eaten every day, the women prepare the following rice products:

Muri (puffed rice)—the preparation involves the roasting of twice-parboiled rice.

Cheera (pounded rice)—the preparation, a more arduous process, involves husking and then pounding once-parboiled rice. *Cheera* is stored and fried before serving, most typically with spices and onions.

Peetha (rice cake)—the preparation involves steaming cakes of rice flour which have been molded or etched into different shapes or designs.

i. *Marketing* is carried out exclusively by men, except for very small-scale barter a woman might conduct within the village or from the homestead.

2. *Jute Production*

a. *Land preparation, planting, weeding,* and *harvesting* is all done by men. With jute, as with grain, women are involved in post-harvest operations.

b. *Steeping* of the jute is most typically done by men. After cutting, jute is steeped in water for several days so that the fibre will rot on the stalks.

c. *Stripping* of the jute fibre from the stalk is done by both men and women. Men will often stand waist-deep in the water where the jute has been steeped to strip the fibre. Women squat on the banks of the ponds to strip the fibre.

d. *Storing* the jute stalks is carried out by women and men. The stalks are used as fuel in richer households and as building materials in poorer households.

e. *Processing* jute fibre into rope and macrame wall hangers is done by women.

f. *Processing* jute stalks into fencing or siding is done by men and women.

g. *Marketing* of jute fibre and products is carried out by men through a government-regulated system of depots and controlled prices.

3. *Wheat Production*

Wheat was first introduced in Bangladesh after 1972. With intensified irrigation, wheat production has expanded significantly. Wheat is grown during the dry winter months on land that cannot sustain a winter crop of rice.

a. Wheat is seen as a "male" crop as men dominate the *field operations* and control the *marketing*. Extension workers and agricultural experts have spent long hours convincing male farmers to grow wheat in an area where wheat was traditionally not grown or eaten.

b. As with rice, women take over in the *threshing, processing, drying,* and *storage* phases. Few extension workers or agricultural experts have addressed the constraints women face in the post-harvest operations of this new crop. Usually, wheat is threshed using bullocks. But many households in Bangladesh do not possess or have access to a bullock for threshing. Women in those households have had to devise methods of threshing wheat. Wheat is more difficult to thresh than rice. I have seen women struggle with small bundles of wheat stalk in the mortar of the *dekhi* (designed to contain kernels not stalks) and with the pestle wrapped in cloth to cushion the blow. The women explained that the wheat will not thresh using a barrel or their feet. Others have taken to threshing wheat using a sickle.

4. *Winter Crop Production*—Mustard, Millets, and Lentils

a. Men dominate the *field operations*, although recently women have been hired to harvest these crops (presumably because they are less valued and assumed to require less skilled labor).

b. Women take over *post-harvest:* they thresh, dry, and store the mustard seeds, lentils, and millet grain.

5. *Tree, Vine, and Vegetable Cultivation*

a. *Plot preparation* is carried out by women. Mud must be dug, carried, and piled up to level the plot, typically at the rear of the hut along the slope of the homestead mound. Women construct trellises for beans and pumpkins or allow them to grow up the side of the hut and over the roof.

b. *Planting, weeding, watering,* and *harvesting* are all carried out by women. They grow a variety of tropical vegetables plus tomatoes, eggplants, cauliflower and various kinds of beans. The most common fruit trees are: banana, papaya, jackfruit, and date nut palm (which, in Bangladesh, is tapped for its juice, not grown for its dates). Women are able to hawk small amounts of their own produce (and control that income), but women must rely on men for bulk sale.

6. *Animal Production*

Care of all animals is women's domain. They are responsible for tending the animals as well as collecting fodder.

a. *Chickens* and *ducks* are kept in clay coops at night to protect them from weasels and snakes. But they are scattered to forage as best they can during the day. Small children are sometimes deployed to herd ducks to the nearest water and food source.

b. *Livestock*—cows, a few sheep, more often goats—are kept tied to stakes near the homestead or under shelters by night and along roads and fields by day. Older women and young children are deployed to graze livestock. Women clean the coop and stalls, arrange additional feed as necessary and if feasible—chopped grass and water troughs for the large animals. Women often milk the cattle. Women collect droppings for composting and fuel.

Again, women can exert some control over the income from small sales of milk and eggs but the large volume of trade is done through the men.

7. *Craft Manufacture*

Women manufacture a great many of the items and equipment used in and around the home. Women make the clay stove they cook on, the bamboo tray they winnow with, the mats they sit and sleep on, the mattresses and quilts they sleep on and under, the jute macrame hangers they store supplies in, the fans they use to keep cool and to keep flies away, and more.

8. *Hut Construction and Repair*

Men erect the walls and thatch the roofs of the huts. Women help lay the foundation and prepare the floors. Women carry loads of mud and clay up from the fields to replaster the mud floor of their huts and to level the homestead plots. Women slice and weave bamboo to make fencing and walls.

9. *Household Maintenance*

Women perform a great number of household maintenance tasks. They scavenge for tinder, wood, and other fuels. If cow-dung is available, it must be collected, moulded into cakes or around sticks, and set to dry. Women compost small droppings and waste. They collect ash to replenish the fields. They fetch water each day from either a private tube-well, a communal pond or a near-by river. In addition, women daily clean the huts, stalls, and homesteads; wash the dishes and utensils; cook and serve meals; and run numerous errands.

10. *Labor Force Maintenance*

It is women who reproduce and maintain the labor force.

a. *Children* are women's domain: feeding, tending, bathing, supervising and putting to bed.

b. When male laborers are hired to work alongside the men, it is the women who must rise that much earlier to prepare that much more food and to serve the laborers. Women in the Sulla report the following cooking and serving schedule during harvest:

3:00 a.m.	rise to cook for the laborers
4:00 a.m.	feed men of the household, send food to laborers in the fields
9:00–10:00 a.m.	breakfast for the children and older women
1:30–2:00 p.m.	lunch for all
9:00 p.m.	dinner for all

All of this preparation and handling of food on top of preparing the threshing floors and winnowing, drying, parboiling, husking grain during that peak period of activity.

11. *Artisan Production*

Women play integral production roles in the different artisan or occupational communities. In the fishing communities, women weave the fish nets and dry and sort fish both for consumption and sale. They prepare bamboo racks to dry the fish on. They must protect the fish from birds and other prey while drying. Women also prepare the earthen jars in which the dried fish are stored and sold. In the weaving communities, women spin and prepare the bobbins. And, in pottery communities, women model clay items.

12. *Marketing*

Marketing is the domain of men. The men do all the shopping for household items. Most critically, they do all the major selling of the household's agricultural and non-agricultural produce. Although women exert some control over the income from small-scale trade they are able to negotiate through their children, all large-scale volume of trade is carried out by men.

The Technological and Structural Constraints

Nearly all village women work long and strenuous days. But this simple fact has not been fully comprehended. We began to see why. First, under the census only what is directly paid is regarded as work. Second, to most outsiders women's work remains "invisible" because it is not carried out in a work-place, not even in the fields, but in and around huts scattered throughout the village. Moreover, women's "productive" work is done in and around their so-called "domestic" work (housework, childbearing, and childrearing) so much so that the productive work of women appears as a "natural" manifestation of their domestic roles. Third, women produce as much to conserve as to generate income. And even when women's produce is marketed, the marketing is done by men so that women's production remains unrec-

ognized. Fourth, women's and men's economic roles are often so complementary that women's contribution is subsumed under men's work.
The result is that Anwara's husband, and others like him, whose
main occupation is to raise grain for their families, are listed in the
census as "full-time workers," while Anwara, and others like her, who
raise and tend the domestic animals; thresh, parboil, dry, store and
husk the grain; grow fruits and vegetables; clean and maintain the huts
and homestead; give birth and raise the children; and, occasionally,
produce craft for the markets, are listed as "housewives" even though
their tasks are as critical to the welfare of their families and to national
production as are the men's.

Micro-studies have begun to show that nearly all rural women work,
but macro-data obfuscates this simple fact. The census in Bangladesh
tells us:*

—a total of 31.6 million women (92% of the total female population)
  live in the villages of Bangladesh
—a total of 20 million of these rural women are above the age of 10;
  and of these 20 million
—a total of 15½ million are "housewives" and over 3½ million are
  "inactive;" some 740 thousand are "employed" (in paid work) and
  26 thousand are "looking for (paid) work."

Clearly something is wrong with this data. Our observations told us
that at a minimum the 15½ million "housewives" should be considered
"full-time workers." Even if we were to accept that housework, childbearing and childrearing are not work but only domestic tasks, we
know that nearly all village women are full-time workers in agriculture
and animal husbandry. Clearly the definitions of work and of rural
production systems in Bangladesh need to be reanalyzed.**

But why? Shouldn't women be seen and studied as a part of the
family unit? Shouldn't women's work be seen and studied as part of a
family farming enterprise? Not necessarily. If BRAC wanted to assist

---

*Institute of Statistical Research and Training, *Statistical Profile of Children and
Mothers in Bangladesh*, University of Dacca, Dacca: March 1977. The figures are based
on the 1974 national census.
**The first national survey to highlight the long and strenuous days of women was:
Farouk, A. and M. Ali, *The Hard Working Poor: A Survey of How People Use Their Time
in Bangladesh*. Dacca: Dacca University, Bureau of Economic Research, 1976. Some of
the micro-studies which document rural women's work are listed in the bibliography.

women in their numerous roles, we needed to understand women and women's work from a number of perspectives. After all men are part of that same family enterprise, but men receive credit, inputs, training, technical assistance, and extension services. Shouldn't both men's and women's contribution be recognized and supported? What if the man should take ill or die? What if the man should abandon or divorce his wife? What are her options?

Since most of the detailed information on women's contribution under the traditional division of labor has only recently begun to appear in micro-studies, very little social and economic value has been placed on women's work in development policy and intervention. Women contribute substantially to national production, but they have to date received very few of the support services that men have. Assessment should be taken of the wide range of productive activities by women with a view to enhance their output or productivity and to transform subsistence-level productive activities to a commercial level.

The Social Roles of Women

A son is future; a daughter is nothing. She goes to her husband's home, and there is nothing.

Woman Field Staff, Jamalpur

Both the mother-in-law and the wife are dependent on the same man and, consequently, the mother-in-law becomes angry if her son buys saris for his wife.

Women at BRAC-Organized Workshop

The economic world of women—a world largely determined by the traditional division of labor by sex. The social world of women—a world largely determined by the traditional division of social spheres by sex. Women are excluded from the public sphere—fields, markets, roads, towns. Women are to remain secluded in the private sphere—hut and homestead—and to move about only at prescribed times in the village.

Within the prescribed space of hut and homestead, each woman at different stages in her life plays different social roles, that of: daughter, bride, mother, wife, widow. Each role is determined by the dominant male in that stage of her life. Very often, women are not called by their given names but referred to as so-and-so's daughter, bride, mother, or wife, and (even many years after a husband's death) as so-and-so's widow. A woman is seldom granted respect and rights as an individual. Her rights and respect, her status, derive from her male relationships. With one notable exception. As mother-in-law (the one social role defined by a woman's relationship to another woman or women), a woman can exercise some status, authority, and mobility in her own right.

Let me describe briefly a woman's varying treatment at different stages in her life:

Infancy—

A girl is branded at birth because she is not a boy. Since daughters usually join a different family upon marriage, it is sons who provide free labor throughout life and security in old age to their parents. The family will, therefore, put more expense and care into the health and nutrition of a boy than a girl. For this reason, infant girls die more frequently than infant boys.

Childhood—

A small girl enjoys relative freedom. Both boys and girls are socialized into adult labor roles at young ages. A boy because he is to be around and should learn. A girl because she is not to be around and should contribute while she is. But during childhood, a girl's freedom is gradually limited.

Young girls are thought of, and often called, "guests." The meaning is clear: she will eventually leave her paternal home. Implicit is the thought that too much trouble will not be taken in her upbringing. There is little incentive for the family to invest in girls over boys for education, specialized treatment, responsibility, or leadership.

Her legal right as a child is to inherit one-half the amount of property or goods her brothers inherit. In practice, few girls claim this inheritance.

Pre-Marriage—

In late childhood, a girl is restricted and denied contact with boys. Her family, especially her male guardians, want to get her married and keep her married. The family invests in the girl's marriageability: she is schooled in the "womanly" virtues of chastity and fidelity and trained in "womanly" skills of embroidery, crochet, etc.

Marriage—

A young woman is contracted in marriage without her consent, often at a young age. Traditionally, marriage is universal and early marriage is preferred. Upon marriage, a young wife usually moves to her husband's home. Her husband and his family assume responsibility for her protection. Her legal rights in marriage involve the right to be economically supported and the right to *mahr* (dower: a sum of money or property the groom promises the bride in case of divorce). In practice, however, few wives collect the *mahr* before divorce. And, increasingly, grooms demand dowries from the bride's family. The marriage is often tentative until the birth of the first child, preferably a son. Many women face the possibility of divorce or the prospect that her husband will take a second wife. Few women want to be divorced. Economically, they would be left unsupported. Socially, it is more acceptable to be a co-wife than a divorced woman.

Early Marriage—

The first years of marriage are often lonely for a woman. She is a stranger in her husband's household. She has to prove herself—to the women of his household and to his kin.

The natural lines of affection and support lie with the kin of her birth. She will see them only on once-a-year visits to her father's home. These visits, called *nayor*, are poignantly significant to the young bride. One exercise of dominance by the husband or his family is to threaten and/or actually deny the *nayor* or to demand gifts from the paternal home upon the wife's return from the *nayor*. A few husbands marry into their wives' village and these women may enjoy the warmth and support of paternal kin all their lives.

Motherhood—

A young wife gains some status and autonomy with the birth of her first child—especially if she bears a son. Most women give birth at home. Local midwives advise during the prenatal period and assist at childbirth.

Mothers-in-Law—

In general, older women dominate younger women. The mother-in-law dominates daughters-in-law. The elder brother's wife dominates the younger brother's wives. The older women ally themselves with the men. Mothers-in-law share much of the formal status and authority vested in the elder man of the household. It is essentially power over other women. The mother-in-law makes most of the decisions in matters relating to women, young children, cooking, daily religious observances and the like. She exercises not only authority but also considerable domestic respect with this seniority.

Older Women—

Older women, especially widows, have the most autonomy and mobility in the village. They are free to come and go as they like.

The Social and Cultural Constraints

Despite the varied treatment women receive at different stages in their lives, the world of women is almost uniformly a private world. Women do not share the meagre pleasures or small adventures of the man's world. Women do chat and gossip by the lamplight in the evenings and attend feasts and festivals and ceremonies of various kinds. But women are not permitted to go to the markets or to the towns. They cannot loiter in markets or alongside the roads or visit other villages. There is a prescribed time and space for women's activities. Women have few choices. They find little time or opportunity to confide one woman to another. Many women turn to the midwife to discuss any physical problems associated with marriage. But few women find friends or allies (especially in their husband's village) to whom they can turn for their emotional needs and support.

What would women talk about if given the chance? How do women perceive their world? We tried to provide as many opportunities as possible for women to meet together and to discuss their problems. Often, a BRAC meeting or workshop is the first time women have discussed their mutual problems and needs. At one BRAC-organized workshop for women, the participants were asked to list their problems as women. They listed the following in no particular order:

—oppression by mothers-in-law
—differential feeding as a child

—no education
—no inheritance
—religious constraints
—no choice in marriage, remarriage, or multiple marriage
—treatment according to husband's whims
—beatings by husband
—no freedom of movement
—dowry
—differential feeding as an adult (literally, "eating last")
—blame for sterility (typically, women are blamed and punished
   when a couple is sterile)
—treated for fertility (more women undergo tubectomies than men
   vasectomies)
—few options and low wages for paid work
—societal interference

Problems imposed by the woman's own family: differential treatment; few property rights; marriage without consent. Problems
threatened or imposed by the woman's husband and his family: threat
of actual beatings; divorce; a second wife. Constraints posed by "religion" and "society": little freedom of movement. And more. Few options for paid work. Low wages for paid work.

We needed to understand the constraints faced by women if we
wanted to work with and assist them. We wanted not only to know
what constraints and problems they face but also to understand how
and why these forces operate to affect women. How and why does the
traditional division of social spheres by sex operate? How do these
systems affect women? To what degree do they support women? To
what degree and in what ways do they constrain women? We asked
these questions of others, of ourselves, and of the women. We heard
different explanations.

Purdah and Patriarchy: The Problems of Women as Women

When people describe the status of women in Bangladesh, more
often than not they refer to the custom of *purdah. Purdah* means,
literally, curtain. *Purdah* is used, figuratively, to mean the veiled seclusion of women. In the narrowest sense, *purdah* involves the seclusion of women within the four walls of their homes and the veiling of
women when they move outside the homes. In a broader sense, *pur-*

dah involves the exclusion of women from the public "male" sphere of economic, social and political life. In practice, most rural women in Bangladesh remain confined to their homesteads but, at prescribed times for prescribed reasons, move out without a veil. As people try to understand the economic and social roles of rural women, more and more they refer to the system of *patriarchy*.* In Bangladesh, patriarchy describes a system of male dominance over women with economic underpinnings. Men are said to exert power and authority over women because they control property, income, and women's labor. Under this analysis, *purdah* is seen as one instrument (together with the Muslim laws of inheritance) of patriarchal control.

Whereas *purdah* is useful in describing the status of women, patriarchy is more useful in analyzing how and why men control and dominate women. The custom of *purdah* which, in theory, both restricts and protects women, does not explain, for example, why girl infants are fed less to the point, at times, of starvation. The system of patriarchy, based as it is on economics, offers a plausible if not acceptable explanation. Boys and men are fed first because they are considered the primary "bread earners."

As we met and worked with women in the villages, we observed that the domination of the patriarchs through the custom of *purdah* was being relaxed—at least in some households. Some men allowed their women to leave the secluded female world of *purdah* to enter the public male world. We met women who sought paid work—in the fiields, on the roads, in the towns. These women complained they were denied paid work or were paid low wages. Who denied them? Who paid them poorly? Clearly not the patriarchs of their own households. If not, who? Seemingly some other forces were in operation. If so, why?

We asked the women to explain. This is what some of them said: "It is the strategy of the village leaders to keep us working at low wages in their homes. If we work outside, without *purdah*, then the rich people will not be able to advance credit to us poor women at exhorbitant rates of interest. If we women work outside, we might be economically better off."

---

*Cain, M. T., S. K. Khanam, and S. Nahar, "Class, Patriarchy, and the Structure of Women's Work in Rural Bangladesh," Center for Policy Studies, Working Papers #43 (May 1979), The Population Council.

Work in other people's homes, work outside the village. Poor women, village leaders. We had entered another world. The world of poverty—a world largely determined by the traditional division of households by class. A not unfamiliar world, but one we had not previously seen through the eyes of women.

THE WORLD OF POVERTY

Purdah does not feed us.
                    Women's Group in Dapunia Village, Jamalpur
The pain of hunger pushed away their veil.
                    Memo from BRAC Field Staff, Sulla

Poverty is everywhere in Bangladesh. It is inescapable. We saw it wherever we turned. Within each village, some households are richer and other households are poorer. BRAC had begun to work exclusively with poor households. We knew that all households did not own cows or poultry or land. We knew that some families ate infrequently at best. But we had not yet understood the particular and often devastating impact of poverty on women.

When people discuss the poverty in rural Bangladesh, they invariably refer to the growing number of landless households. The figures are alarming. One third of rural households own no cultivable land, and, if one includes those who own less than half an acre, nearly half (48 percent) of rural households are "functionally landless." People point out that the rise in landlessness has not been matched by a rise in employment opportunities. Then they calculate the number of wage laborers, sharecroppers, and unemployed—all men.

But few people discuss poverty in terms of women. Some reference is made to poor women who work in rich households for low wages. And some reference is made to "destitute" (widowed or deserted) women who must fend for themselves. But few have calculated how many poor or "destitute" women seek work and whether, given the dramatic rise of landlessness, they find enough work within the village.

But the women themselves make their own calculations. And, during the post-famine conditions of 1975, they began to leave their villages. Suddenly, there were women in the towns, on the roads, in the fields. They were looking for work; and there was not enough work to be found. We asked them why they had left their villages. They said they had no paddy to process, no animals to tend, and no food to cook. The wealthier households were not hiring them. They needed to find work. "*Purdah* does not feed us," they explained bitterly. They told us how they used to work at night in the fields so as not to break out of *purdah*. But now, after the famine, there was not enough work at night or in the villages. Were these women all "destitute" women or were some women from poor households? Where were the male earners of their families? How many children did they support?

When BRAC decided to work exclusively with the poor, we needed to understand what it meant to be poor and a woman. Over several years, through a mix of action and research, we were to learn a great deal about women from poor households. Various BRAC staff and I participated in an informal survey of the 800 women who participated in food-for-work in Jamalpur; a formal study (with both questionnaire and in-depth interviews) of 300 women who participated in food-for-work in several districts of Bangladesh; a village study which incorporated data on the resources of different households by class; and the organization of some 6000 poor women into 250 groups.

What follows is a distillation of our collective knowledge and experience of what poverty means to women in rural Bangladesh.

Poverty and the Changing Roles of Women

The first lesson the women taught us about poverty is that poverty is not static. The reality is not simply that some are rich and some poor. The reality is that poverty has a dynamic in which the poor and rich interact. Most often this dynamic leads only to increased poverty for the poor. Typically, disaster conditions (man-made or natural) or illness or unemployment force the poor to sell some land. Chronic unemployment, coupled with this loss of land, eventually forces them to sell any remaining land and their meagre household possessions. Further illness or unemployment or disaster forces them to go into debt. Women at a BRAC-organized workshop describe this downward spiral:

> "During a drought, a flood or etc. when the poor have no work, they have to go to the rich for loans which are given at a very exhorbitant rate. Afterwards, they can only repay such loans by selling their homesteads and whatever household articles they possess. If they do not repay the loans through these measures, they are forced to work as labourers in the homes of the rich throughout the year and for which they do not get fair wages. In addition, they have to go to the rich for money in the event

of illness, death of a family member, or during the marriage of their daughters. The rich take advantage of these opportunities to cheat the poor and make fortunes for themselves. . . . ”

The second lesson the women taught us is that poverty forces women to work outside their homes. As households get poorer, all family members try as best they can to find work, to help eke out an existence. Women will seek employment from other women in wealthier households. They will care for animals, fetch water, weed the gardens, husk the grain, cook the food for more wealthy families. However, there is no fixed rate of payment and no fixed schedule for this work. These women are more often paid in meals and clothes than in cash. Whether in cash or kind, they are badly paid. A woman will earn about 20 cents for a long and strenuous day of work only to go to sleep unsure whether she will find any work the next day.

If the woman's husband or father or son were to fall ill, be injured, or die, the woman's situation is worse still. She has not been conditioned to fend single-handed. She has never had access to formal credit or to markets. Take the case of this woman, a member of a BRAC-organized group in Jamalpur:

> My husband was a rickshaw-puller. He fell ill. Then I sold our land for 2500 takas to have him treated. The balance of the money was spent on family expenses. My husband died. Then, I fell into hardship. No one gave me a loan. They said: "She had not got a husband, if we give her a loan, how will she repay the loan? She should not be given any loan." Villagers were harvesting pulses. I went and worked with them. Some of them gave me cooked rice. I brought the rice home and ate it with my five children. I had 15 bricks. I sold them. I had a bamboo bush. I sold that for 30 takas. I sold the branches of trees for 40 takas. I started a small business. I went to the house of a rich man where I used to work. I bought one maund of paddy. I told them: "Before your eyes we are dying for lack of food." They gave me one maund* of paddy. With this and the other 70 takas I started a paddy-husking business. My money increased to 300 takas. I paid off the one maund of paddy loan. The balance of the money I spent on food. Then I worked in the rice mill. A few days passed with great difficulty.

Women have been conditioned to be financially dependent on fathers, husbands, or sons. They have always worked hard but within the

---

*One maund equals 82 pounds.

confines of their homes or villages. As families get poorer, women often face a frightening financial independence.

The third lesson the women taught us is that poverty erodes the traditional family support systems. As families get poorer, the traditional family obligations begin to break down. The first victim is the extended family ties. The second victim is the immediate family ties. Ideally, if a women is widowed or divorced her sons or brothers should look after her. Under economic pressure, sons and brothers sometimes do not offer this support.

Take what the women tell us is happening to marriage. Earlier, when a marriage was registered the *mahr* or dower (the amount of money or goods which the groom promised to pay in the event that he divorced his wife or died) was settled upon. This bridewealth was seen as the property of the wife and the amount was registered at marriage. In practice, women seldom received that amount upon divorce. Increasingly, when a marriage is being negotiated a dowry (the amount of money or goods which the bride's family promised to pay the groom) is being settled upon. Moreover, what is being demanded is not a dowry upon marriage which is the bride's own but rather substantial goods before betrothal in order to negotiate the marriage. And, in practice, there are an increasing number of instances of quick divorces by grooms who hope to get multiple dowries.

So the world of poor women has become increasingly complex. As her family gets poorer, she must seek more and more work. If her husband should fall ill or die, or should divorce or desert her, she must learn to fend for herself. At the same time, due to similar economic pressure, fewer households are able to hire her labor. And at the same time, due to the same economic pressures, her extended family cannot fulfill their traditional family obligations. She is often forced to seek wage labor outside the village, to cross the boundary into male space.

The Economic Roles of Women by Class

See, she is rich. Her brother has got a tin shed house. She eats better, she drinks milk, etc. But we are very poor. If we eat now, we worry for the next meal.

Tohooron of Mithura Village, Manikganj

There are two broad classes of women commonly known to all the rich and the poor—which means there is one class of women whose husbands are richer and the other whose husbands are poorer. There is, of course, another class who are destitutes—different from the aforesaid two classes—they are a bit independent, though not out of social jargon— they are involved in the struggle of life—the pain of hunger pushed away their veil; but as ill luck would have it be, there is not sufficient scope for them. So any programme to be designed for this class should provide sufficient scope for their training and simultaneously scope for their employment too. Any programme not providing direct return to them is supposed to become futile.

BRAC Field Staff, Sulla

When people discuss the households of Bangladesh, more often than not they divide them into different socio-economic classes. If we were to talk about and work with women, we recognized that we could not think in simply rich-poor-destitute terms. We had to understand what being a woman in each class of household actually meant. We began to look at women in the context of the different classes of households. These classes of households are generally defined in terms of men's labor and income:

—*rich* households; in which the men can support their families well by cultivating their own land using hired labor or sharecroppers.
—*middle* households; in which the men earn enough to support their families adequately by cultivating their own land and, at times, hiring others to work for them.
—*marginal* households; in which the men cannot support their families adequately off their own land but must also work as share-croppers or wage laborers.
—*poor* households; in which the men work as wage laborers or sharecroppers but (as they own no cultivable land) do not earn enough for the family to subsist.

Do the economic roles of women differ from class to class? Do all women in rural Bangladesh possess the same skills? Do they all per-form the same kind of work? We found that almost all women perform the same set of traditional tasks. The sexual division of labor is more or less inflexible across class. Most women possess roughly the same set of skills, although women from richer households find more time and materials to perfect "leisure-time" skills: embroidery, crochet, and etc.

But within the limits of a set of traditional tasks and a set of tradi-tional skills, we found that women from different classes pursue these tasks under different conditions. Some women perform the given set of tasks only as unpaid labor within their own household. Others perform the same tasks both within their own households and as paid labor in other households. Some women hire other women to perform the same tasks in their stead. Some keep more busy and some less busy at the given round of tasks each day and each season.

The following brief sketches of four women, one from each class of household, illustrate these differences:

Rich Woman—

Subora rises early to wash dishes, fetch water, and prepare breakfast. In the morning, she tends to the cattle and poultry, cleans their stalls, sweeps and cleans the courtyard, and cooks lunch. After lunch, she husks paddy, bathes her children, and sweeps the house. Later she brings more water from the pond, prepares supper and bathes the children. During harvest, Subora contracts other women to help her thresh, husk, and store paddy. At other times, Subora contracts other women to help tend the animals, process grain, or repair her hut and homestead. Subora does not bother to raise vegetables or fruit. She says that she has no fixed time for her work. Although at times she feels bored, she never thinks of her daily work as a burden. In her free time, she reads books or gossips with her neighbor.

Subora and her husband own 4½ acres of land and several cows and bullocks. They live with their five children in a well-constructed, two-room hut with bamboo walls, tin roof, and front verandah. Subora has two mud stoves. One sits in the open courtyard. Another is sheltered in a small lean-to along with her *dekhi* (paddy-husker). She uses the open one during the dry season, the sheltered one during the rains.

Middle Woman—

Anwara, you will recall, is busy from before sunrise until after dark. She too rises early to clean the dishes, sweep the floors of her hut, to prepare breakfast and to bathe. After breakfast, Anwara tends to the cattle and poultry, collects cow dung and sticks, fetches water, and puts the pillows and mattresses out to dry. After the noon meal, she prepares and dries fuel, sweeps and waters down the courtyard, and husks paddy. In the late afternoon, Anwara bathes her four children, feeds and waters the cattle, waters her fruit and vegetables, and heats left-overs for the evening meal. Anwara finds little rest during the day and goes to bed late. Anwara is very busy during harvest and cannot afford to hire labor to help her.

Anwara and her husband own 2½ acres of land, two heads of cattle, and a few hens. They live in a one-room hut with bamboo walls and thatch roof. Anwara comes closest to the image of the "ideal typical" woman from the self-sufficient farm household.

Marginal Woman—

Vimala, unlike Anwara, is not busy from before sunrise until after dark. But she would like to be. Vimala's is an enforced idleness. She and her husband own no agricultural land and no livestock. Vimala cares for animals, fetches water, weeds the gardens, husks the grain in the homes of more wealthy women. But this work is occasional and badly paid. During the rainy season, Vimala makes hand-fans, mats, and other handicrafts.

The river washed away Vimala's land and hut. Somehow she and her husband were able to purchase a small piece of land on which they built a flimsy, jute straw hut with straw roof. Vimala says they have no space to dry the paddy (they earn) or to grow vegetables. Their three children have no place to play. Vimala's husband suffers from asthma. Periodically, he has difficulty breathing for days at a time and cannot work. Vimala tries to feed the family off what she earns.

Poor Woman—

Kamala's grandfather had no land. Her father was a day laborer and her mother worked in other people's homes. But, Kamala remembers wistfully, they used to own fruit trees and a cow. Somehow they got along by selling fruit and milk.

Kamala's husband owns no land or fruit trees or cow. Although he and his brothers each inherited tiny plots of land, only one of the brothers was able to hold onto his land. The others were forced to sell off their land. Kamala's husband had to sell their land because he falls ill each rainy season. During the other months of the year he can work only a little. Kamala worries constantly about how to feed her two children, a two-year old son and a five-year old daughter. She used to work in other people's houses or do cane work or stitch quilts or do whatever work she could find in the village. But more recently Kamala has begun to look for work outside the village.

Kamala and her husband live in a delapidated one-room bamboo hut with thatch roof. Their hut backs onto the compound of her more-prosperous brother-in-law. Against the advice and with the ill-blessing of this brother-in-law, Kamala and some other women decided to cultivate paddy on a plot of land they were able to lease. Kamala explains her decision: "If I stay hungry, no one will feed me or my children. Hence, I do not work because anyone forces me to. I work because of my own zeal. I do not take anyone's advice."

Although the division of labor by sex remains remarkably rigid across class, we found that some women produce more for home consumption and others more for cash. The data we collected in one village, Dhankura, illustrates these differences.* Almost all women in Dhankura engage in some subsidiary agriculture: poultry, dairy, or horticulture. But not all of this production is geared for a cash income. Some households consume most of what the women produce.

The decision to pursue these tasks in order to conserve or to generate income relates to the realizable options being pursued by each class of households. Subsidiary agriculture depends in part upon land available (especially for horticulture) but also in large part on one's capital and risk-bearing capacity (especially for dairying). We found out that subsidiary agriculture also depends in some part on the individual household's ability to conserve women's labor.

We found in Dhankura that the rich maximise poultry and dairy production over horticulture. This reflects in part their investment capacity and their ownership of cows and poultry. But certain normative factors also operate. All of subsidiary agricultural production is the preserve of women, but horticulture requires the most labor. The rich, for reasons of status, try to conserve their female labor. And, for reasons of status and because they can afford to, the rich consume all that women produce in poultry and dairy. The consumption of these items carries high status and the rich are not forced to sell these items to purchase grain.

The marginal and poor households maximise horticulture as they have less capital to invest and own few cows and poultry. The constraint to their cultivation of fruit and vegetables is the amount of land

---

*Who Gets What and Why: Resource Allocation in a Bangladesh Village, BRAC, 1979.

they own. The marginal and poor households sell more than they consume of what their women produce. They cannot afford to consume these products as they need cash to buy grain.

The Dhankura data and the sketches of the four women illustrate the differences in volume and mode of work by women from different classes. Women from rich and middle households work only as unpaid family labor and produce mostly for consumption. Women from marginal households work as both unpaid family and paid village labor* and produce for both consumption and cash. Women from poor households produce whatever they can for cash, work as paid village labor, and seek wage employment outside the village.

In order to counteract the tendency to discuss village life from the perspective of men only, we have redefined the classes of rural households in terms of women's labor and women's income:

—*rich* households; those which can preserve (for status reasons) their women from some unpaid family labor and which consume most of what women produce.
—*middle* households; those which can subsist given the unpaid family labor of their women and the income from what women produce.
—*marginal* households; those which cannot subsist without the paid village labor of their women and the income from what women produce.
—*poor* households; those which cannot subsist even given the paid village labor of their women and must deploy all members of the family to seek wage labor outside the village.

These four classes of households can be distinguished one from another by the degree to which women's paid or wage labor and income from women's produce are required to provide food to the family. Generally, the more dependent a household is on the income and labor of women the poorer the household.

---

*For the purposes of this analysis I have classified:
1) unpaid family labor to include all agricultural and productive labor women perform in and around the family homestead;
2) paid village labor to include agricultural and non-agricultural labor for cash or kind *inside* the village and, therefore, traditionally female; and
3) wage labor to include agricultural and non-agricultural labor for cash or kind *outside* the village but including the fields of the village and, therefore, traditionally male.

The Social Roles of Women by Class

Poverty not only determines the options women pursue within the traditional set of economic roles but also influences the social roles of women. Poverty affects both the relationships between men and women within a household and the composition of the household. Generally, so long as the household remains intact, the poorer the household the more egalitarian the relationships and responsibilities between the sexes.

All girls are put to work as all households use girls as free labor. But in poorer households, girls and boys are treated more equally. Neither receive an education. Both are deployed to find whatever work can be found. In poorer households, the older girls often work side-by-side with their mothers at wage work: construction, harvesting, or whatever their mothers can find for them to do. The marriageability of poorer girls is often compromised because of this work, because they have worked outside the village and sometimes, worse still, among male laborers. Rumours fly about their lack of honor and chastity. The groom demands a higher dowry.

Listen to this discussion between BRAC staff and earth-digging* women from Chandor village in Manikganj:

BRAC Staff: What about your marriage? Earth-digging girls, can they get married?

Women: See this girl, there had been proposals of marriage for this girl. But now only because she cuts earth, we can't give her in marriage. They say: "We will not take an earth-cutting girl." There are more girls in this situation. See, there is one, there is one. Here is one with Shahida, and our Muli is one.

BRAC staff: Why don't the girls get married? Is it that they cut earth or also that you can't give money as a dowry?

Women: Both are reasons: lack of dowry and digging earth.

BRAC Staff: Suppose you cut earth and your daughter also digs earth. You want to give your daughter in marriage. The bridegroom demands 4000 taka ($270). Suppose you are able to give 4000 taka. In this case, is the marriage possible?

Women: Yes, in that case they will take the bride. But we can't give that amount. That's why the girl does not carry any honor.

---

*The literal translation from Bengali is "earth-cutting," which refers to the digging, lifting, and carrying of earth in the building or excavating of roads, dykes, embankments, ponds, etcetera. Because women did not traditionally work at construction sites, those who are now forced (out of economic necessity) to do such work have been given this "title" by other villagers.

BRAC Staff: On the one hand, they cut earth only because they are poor and can't give anything as dowry. And, on the other hand, if they cut earth it is not an honorable job.

Upon marriage, the poorer the groom the more likely the bride is to enter a nuclear household. Her new home may back onto the compounds of her in-laws households, but they will probably not share their food or responsibilities. The poorer the household the less likely it is to remain a joint, extended household. A woman who married into a poor household will, therefore, have more autonomy. Her mother-in-law, even if they live side by side, cannot exercise authority if they do not work together or eat from the same stove.

The poor woman, like other women, gains some respect and position with the birth of the first son. But in poorer households, notions about the gender and number of children are subject to change. As sons no longer prove dependable in their old age, a mother's preference for sons may go down. As mother and daughter work side-by-side, the affection between mother and daughter is often strengthened. The trade-off between an extra pair of hands to work and an extra mouth to feed is not so obvious when there is neither food or work.

Poor women seldom exert the kind of power as mother-in-law that richer women do because they seldom live in joint households. Their sons often separate their homesteads from their parents. Daughters-in-law are, therefore, more autonomous. And poor women seldom enjoy the relative freedom and autonomy of old age that rich women do. Poor women must continue to find work even in their old age as they cannot depend on others for their survival. They are not released from the day-to-day task of survival.

As poverty erodes the basic composition of both nuclear and extended families, a growing number of women are becoming heads of households. The social and economic constraints faced by these women are largely the same as those of women from poor households. They also seek paid village and wage labor.

Constraints on Women's Work

There is a growing number of women in rural Bangladesh who require employment in the wage sector: the poor and head-of-household women. In the female-headed and poor households, the traditional pattern of production, the traditional division of labor by sex, and the traditional kin and family support systems no longer assure day-to-day survival. All members of these households require access to wage labor.

Estimates of *de jure* female-headed households (households headed by widowed or divorced women) range from 6.4% to 16% of rural households. Estimates of *de facto* female-headed households (households in which the men are absent or infirm or otherwise not bringing in an income) range even higher. A national survey found that one third of rural households own no cultivable land. Given these figures, we estimate:

—a minimum of 1.3 million (6.4% of rural women over the age of 10 years)
—more likely 6 million women (30% of rural women over the age of 10 years) seek wage employment in a labor market that has, to date, excluded women.

The census, you may recall, tells us only 26 thousand rural women are looking for "paid" work.

The main constraint on women's employment is the level of demand for their labor. Under the traditional division of labor by sex, Bangladesh women are excluded from wage employment in field activities and assigned tasks related to grain processing at the village level. Until recently, the segregation of male labor (in the fields and outside the village) and female labor (in the homestead and inside the village) had been strictly maintained. So much so that very few women have ever competed with men in the wage labor market.

Women from poor households and female-headed households are now, out of necessity, entering that competition. But they carry the double disadvantage of being poor and women. One study shows that female heads of households find wage labor for 17% of total person-days, compared to 41% for male heads of households. For all types of income-generating work, women find work for 63% of person-days; men for 83%.* Policy makers should recognize that these women need access to wage labor as much as men, because they share or carry equal dependency burdens.

Other constraints on women's employment have been brought about

---

*Cain, M. T., S. K. Khanam, and S. Nahar, "Class, Patriarchy, and the Structure of Women's Work in Rural Bangladesh," Centre for Policy Studies, Working Papers –06743 (May 1979), The Population Council.

by certain capital intensive development interventions. The introduction of rice mills threatens to deprive a large number of women from one of the few traditionally "female" paid employment options. Rice processing as paid village labor by women has provided a critical margin of income to many poor households. But that margin of income will be, and is being, taken away by the introduction of intermediate and high technology rice mills. The issue is not simply that the machine displaces women's labor and is controlled by men. The critical issue is that the mill displaces the labor of marginal and poor women and is controlled by men from rich households. Moreover, capital intensive interventions in the textile industry threaten the handloom sector which supports a very large number of households, second only to the agricultural sector.

The constraints stem from the "blindness" and bias of development planners and policy-makers,—the urban patriarchs, if you will. But the poor and head-of-household women face constraints to their wage work from the village patriarchs as well.

Patriarchy and Class: The Problems of Women as Members of Poor Households

The real constraint, as the women see it, is that the rich control the paid labor opportunities within the village and dictate the norms that prohibit women from seeking work outside the village. If the rich disapprove of what poor women do they can always threaten to or actually cut off their work within the village. Or, if the rich disapprove of poor women working outside the village, they can put pressure on the woman or her family through the religious leaders.

The women at a BRAC-organized workshop describe the strangle hold of the rich in this way:

> "Women work whole days in the homes of the rich: boiling paddy, drying paddy, cooking rice for them. In return, they are given only watery rice, boiled wheat or one quarter or half seer rice for a whole day's work. They also have no fixed working hours which men have. The women start working early in the morning and until night . . . It is the village leaders' strategy to keep them working at low wages in their homes. If the women work outside, without *purdah*, then the rich people will not be able to advance credit to poor women at exhorbitant rates of interest. If the women work outside they might be economically better off . . .

The rich in their own interest have made norms and laws. To suppress the poor, the rich, the *matbors* (village elders), and the *mullahs* (religious leaders) formulate religious policies and impose on them certain religious injunctions . . . "

I picked up the women's line of analysis in discussions with field staff. I wanted to know how the rich managed to control the options for women: both the paid village labor and wage labor outside the village. What is at issue, the field staff explained, is the definition of what is *purdah* (within the norms of *purdah*) and what is *bepurdah* (literally, non-*purdah*; outside the norms of *purdah*). *Purdah* as practiced is no longer the "ideal" of veiled seclusion. The limits of *purdah* shift and change.

"But how and why?" I asked. "At the convenience of the rich and the elders," explain the field staff. "What is necessary for their wives to do is sanctioned as *purdah*." The staff cited an example. When the women from rich households need to go to the town to appear in court, even to remain in town for 3–4 days at a time, this is sanctioned as *purdah*. When women from a BRAC-organized group want to go to town for one night, or even for a day, to attend a workshop or meeting, they pay a tremendous social price when they return home. Their action is condemned as *bepurdah*. The norms of *purdah* that may be relaxed for the wives of the rich can just as easily and quickly, be clamped down on the women of other households.

"But," I ask, "how can the rich or elders dictate these norms? Don't the *mullahs* (religious leaders) have a say in what is *purdah* or *bepurdah*?" They do invoke the norm, I am told, but at the behest of the rich and the elders. The elders sit on the local mosque committee which elects the local *mullah*, sets his tenure, and determines his stipend. The *mullahs* have some say about religious norms, but the elders have the final say about them. The *mullahs*, upon request from the elders, will start the rumour that such-and-such action or behaviour is *bepurdah*.

In this way, the rich and elders (through the religious leaders) can determine what work is suitable or not suitable for women to perform. In fact, few activities are without social stigma. The only work outside the village which might increase a woman's standing, that of a teacher or a government extension worker, require education and are, therefore, options taken primarily by women of rich households. Some wage work available to women in rural Bangladesh has an ambivalent effect but most has a slightly or significantly negative effect on women's status.

I have listed the range of paid work open to women and classified each activity as to how it affects a women's status. What is at issue is the social price a woman pays in taking on different income-earning activities:

EFFECTS OF INCOME-EARNING ACTIVITIES ON WOMEN'S STATUS

		Inside Village	At Fields	Outside Village
INCREASE	Teacher			X
	Government Extension Worker			X
AMBIVALENT	General Housework	X		
	Paddy Husking & Processing	X		
	Food Processing	X		
	Feeding Cattle	X		
	Raising Animals	X		
	Raising Poultry	X		
	Craft Manufacture: rope, brooms, fans,	X		
	Quilt-Making	X		
SLIGHT DECREASE	Carrying Paddy		X	
	Gleaning Grain		X	
	Grazing Cattle		X	
	Weeding		X	
	Harvesting chilli, potato, peanut		X	
	Stripping Jute			X
SIGNIFICANT DECREASE	Earth-work Labor			X
	Construction Labor			X
	Rice Mill Labor			X
	Agricultural Labor		X	

Poor women take on these social risks because they must work. They know in so doing they can jeopardize their chances to be married or remarried, to find work or receive loans, but they must work.

Norms and rules dictated by one class and imposed on another.

Purdah is an instrument of the patriarchy, of men. But the question is "which men?" Men interpret the religion and impose religious injunctions. But, again, which men? However useful patriarchy was in explaining the dynamic between men and women within households, can it explain the dynamic between households within the village? Class analysis is more useful in explaining the dynamic between rich and poor within the village, in explaining the dynamic between male village leaders and poor village women. Patriarchy (the hierarchy of men over women) explains women's subordinate position within the households, as a woman. Class (the hierarchy of rich over poor) explains the oppressed position of certain women within the village, those who are poor.

We pursued this line of analysis for several reasons. First, we wanted to ensure our policies and strategies fit the actual situation of poor women and, in order to do so, we needed to understand the recent trends in household composition and dynamics. Secondly, because we wanted to be able to predict the resistance by village leaders to BRAC's programs for poor women, we needed to understand the village dialectic and dynamic. Thirdly, because we wanted to increase the productivity and expand the employment of women, we needed to understand the constraints on their productivity and employability.

Consider these examples of how what we learned and analyzed affected our program:

—once we recognized which wage-earning activities decrease a women's status, we used that labor itself as a screening device; that is

—once we knew that only poorest women will participate in wage labor outside the village, we selected those women as a primary target group for our activities

—once we recognized women have little access to credit, training, inputs, extension services, we began to design schemes to provide these to poor women

—once we recognized how many women are managing the day-to-day requirements of their families, we began to lobby for women's entry into the wage labor market and to counter the "queue" argument which dictates that in situations of widespread unemployment women should wait in line behind men (who are assumed to be the primary "bread earners")

—once we recognized that those women who find wage work earn less than men, we began to lobby and to organize women to demand equal pay for comparable work

—once we recognized the differences between women of different classes, we were able to forestall latent conflicts by organizing women into more homogeneous groups

—once we recognized the different constraints posed by the patriarchy and the class hierarchies, we were better able to decide when gender or class issues were of priority in our women's program.

Given what we had come to know, what did we decide could be done and what did we do?

CHAPTER FOUR

What Can Be Done

Picture women. . . .

—discussing a problem posed to them by BRAC trainers: divorce as experienced in their own lives and villages. The women are being trained to be volunteer teachers to other poor women in their respective villages. Only two years before all of these were themselves functional education learners, previously illiterate and unaccustomed to attending weekly meetings. Now they will conduct weekly meetings and teach others.

—walking to the local government medical clinic to demand one of their group receive medical attention. One hour earlier this same women went to see the doctor only to be told, after a long wait, that he was too busy to see her. Now the doctor pays attention as the group of women announce they have the right to free medical care.

—marching to a local government office to request tubewells be installed in their neighborhoods. Previously the rich of their village were allocated tubewells to which the poor were denied access. Now the women insist on and are granted two tubewells for their own neighborhood.

—seated in a circle with half a dozen men. They form the local judicial council (called a *shalish*) which has been convened to arbitrate in a dispute between the women and a rich landlord over the rights to some government land. Previously women were never directly represented, much less sat as judges, in these local councils. Now the women sit as judges, represent their own case, and win the right to the land.

—surrounding and blocking (in local idiom, "gheraoing") the office of

77

the local member of parliament (MP) to demand that they be allowed to participate in a food-for-work scheme in their locality. Previously women had not been hired under such schemes. Now the women demand their right to wage labor and the MP promises to take the necessary action.

These are but some of the social actions undertaken by BRAC-supported groups of women. Between 1972 and 1980, BRAC organized more than 6,000 women into 250 groups which have undertaken joint social and economic action.* I cannot tell the individual stories of all the groups nor do I wish to tell the story of only one or two groups. Instead I will try to compress the multiple stories into a composite story to outline a model of the programs we have developed and to present the framework of concepts and guidelines we have used. In so doing, what was a synchronous and often cyclic process of testing and implementing ideas in different villages will be presented as phased schemes. And in so doing, what was often only implicit in our thinking will be presented as explicit concepts. This is not to say we were without schemes or concepts from the beginning but that what is now definite and explicit in our thinking evolved during our experience of organizing women.

In this chapter, I will begin by answering a few basic questions. Which women did BRAC choose to support, and why? How does BRAC perceive the problems of these women? And what does BRAC propose to do about these problems? I will then describe in some detail BRAC's methods of social organizing and our general strategy for deciding what economic schemes could be undertaken. In the next chapter, I will describe in detail selected individual economic schemes which were undertaken. And, in chapter six, I will describe how BRAC's social organizing works in practice.

BRAC currently defines its target group households as those households in which the men sell their manual labor to others for survival (irrespective of occupation) provided they do not have political patrons or do not exercise status considerations. Even BRAC classifies households by men's work and income. BRAC's definition of its target group

---

*As of December 1982, BRAC had organized 8265 women in the three field project areas described in this book and another 9955 women through its recently expanded credit and outreach programs.

includes the poor and the marginal households* which together constitute if you will recall, nearly half (48 percent) of all households in
Bangladesh.
In working with field staff, we have reclassified these households in
terms of women's income and labor. BRAC works with both:
—marginal women who seek paid village labor and sell whatever
they produce; and
—poor women who seek wage labor or paid village labor, whatever
work they can find.
In organizing the women, we found it was important to keep both
groups separate. The marginal women are not yet quite as needy as the
poor women and are willing to undertake only certain types of labor:
what is traditionally "female" labor, preferably within their homesteads
but also within other people's homes. However, the poor women are
willing to perform any type of manual labor to survive—including road
construction; well, canal, or pond digging; harvesting, whatever they
can find.
BRAC is committed to working with the poor and marginal in Bangladesh. No one struggles harder to feed, clothe, and house the members of poor and marginal households than the women. And no one
faces greater constraints or receives less support than the women.
Typically, these women have been excluded from the wage labor market and have received little if any credit, inputs, training, technologies,
or extension services to increase their production. But these women
cannot afford to adhere to the strictures of the society or be denied
support services. They are more than ready to be supported in their
day-to-day struggles and to be organized around issues perceived to be
in their self-interest.
Given the range and degree of constraints faced by poor and marginal village women, BRAC has had to ask itself what it can do for these
women. What are the priority problems? What problems can BRAC
deal with directly? Which problems are best left for the women to face
directly? What sequence and combination of activities would benefit
the women?
The first and most immediate problem faced by the poor and mar-

*By any standards both categories of households are poor and should be more accu-
rately termed as marginally poor and absolutely poor. However, in the interest of
succinctness, I have chosen to use the terms marginal and poor.

ginal women is their day-to-day struggle to feed, clothe, and house their families. To focus our program on these women meant perforce to focus, at least initially, on economic activities. We observed that programs which neglect the economic component almost invariably exclude the poorer sections of women, who cannot afford to attend meetings or classes which do not address their economic needs or fit their work schedules. As one of BRAC's senior field staff put it: "No activity—whether functional education, cooperatives, family planning—will be of convincing importance without some scope for generating income".

The second problem these women face is their lack of social power and autonomy in their own right. To our way of thinking, the lack of social power and autonomy not only affects these women slightly less directly than their lack of economic resources but also is partly rectified as the economic base of women is strengthened. That is, we believe women's control over and access to material resources is a necessary precondition to women's exercise of social power and autonomy. We believe that village women are powerless to the degree they depend on the men of their households to allocate their productive labor and to market their produce and on the men of their village to allocate their paid village labor and to sanction their wage labor outside the village. If their productivity can be enhanced or their employment expanded, women will automatically exercise greater power and autonomy within their households. And if women's employment can be expanded and revalued, they can begin to negotiate greater autonomy both within and outside the village.

Finally, BRAC does not see women's economic or social independence as ends in and of themselves but insists that all economic and social action be undertaken collectively and that the organization of poor women be seen as part of the larger struggle to organize the poor, both men and women. On the one hand, BRAC does not want individual women to acquire power and autonomy without being united with other women. On the other hand, BRAC does not want women to become so independent that they do not unite with men of their class in their common struggle as the poor.

BRAC organizes poor and marginal women into groups of 20 to 25. These groups are identified from the learners of functional education classes conducted by BRAC in each village. Each group chooses one or two representatives who receive training in group management and in class awareness. Each group also chooses one member to be trained as a health and family planning helper to serve their respective group. Each group decides on and undertakes a series of joint economic activities: schemes that either enhance the productivity of what women traditionally do or expand employment for what women traditionally do or develop new skills. Each group also undertakes a series of joint social actions: schemes to demand higher wages, to settle marital disputes, to demand rights and services, and more.

THE SOCIAL PROGRAM

> BRAC works in organizing and mobilizing the poor and disadvantaged sector of the population into cooperative groups who then plan, initiate, manage, and control group activities, both in social and economic fields.
>
> BRAC Project Proposal

This will lead the group to become a viable group which is the final stage of growth. We expect the following things from a *viable group:*

1. Unity—a growing sense of group identity and cohesiveness;
2. Leadership—strong, but not dominant or exploitative, leadership;
3. Joint action—collective production and economic activities;
4. Improved economic condition—increased production and income;
5. Critical consciousness—high awareness of social, political and economic conditions;
6. Self-reliance—ability to undertake and manage social and economic action;
7. Power and autonomy—increasing control over their own destiny;
8. Federation—linkage with other groups.

> BRAC Staff Hand-out on Group Formation*

Organizing the poor. Developing groups. Building a federation. These are not simply BRAC catchwords. BRAC has organized over 13,000 poor men and women into some 500 groups of poor and has

---

*BRAC administrative staff have prepared a series of hand-outs as part of the field staff orientation and training. These hand-outs cover most aspects of BRAC's field work:

economic support and its dimensions
group formation
family planning services
basic principles of accounting
basic concepts of management
role of development agent
voluntary effort in employment

begun to link these groups into a federation. BRAC directs all of its support to these organized groups because it sees these groups as both short-term ends in themselves and long-term means for empowering the poor. Let me explain.

In the short run, all BRAC activities converge on the groups. Social services are delivered by trained members from each group to the general members of their respective groups. All inputs and technical services are directed to and managed by the groups. Group strength is fostered and strengthened through joint productive activities. The emphasis is on concrete productive activities which necessitate daily interaction and foster unity. At various stages of its development, the group serves one or more of the following functions to its membership:

—savings society
—rotating credit society
—cooperative society (to receive services, credit and inputs)
—collective labor society
—class association

In all this, the BRAC professional field staff develop the individual groups to the point where they can plan and implement their own social and economic activities.

In the long run, the individual groups are to be federated to form a power base for the poor. BRAC believes the groups and the federation must be developed gradually to replace step-by-step those forces in the rural power structure which both support and control the lives of the poor. The group is then only a part of something larger. One group of poor in one village, even one group of all the poor in one village, cannot exert adequate pressure to demand higher wages or more favourable share-cropping terms. BRAC plans to gradually federate all the poor in its field projects. This federation, if it is to guarantee the base of power required by the poor, must develop through step-by-step organization not through hasty mobilization. BRAC plans and has begun to federate individual groups at a series of levels:

—at the village level
—between villages
—at the project level
—between projects

The functions and structure of the federation at each level are to be determined by the participant groups. Eventually, the federation should assume from BRAC the role of intermediary between the individual groups of poor and the village power structure, available resource institutions, and national strategies and policies.

Looked at from the point of view of the poor, the groups are the first step in this federation. But looked at from the point of view of the women, the group is not only a first step but something more as well.

Women's Groups and Class Federation

Poor women are at once poor and women. Simple as this may sound, the reality for the women is far more complex. They face at one and the same time the problems posted by patriarchy and class. They can no more deal with their problems as women (those posed by patriarchy) while ignoring poverty than they can deal with their problems as poor (those posed by class) while ignoring sex disparities. For poor women, because of this double set of problems, the group and the federation are not simply steps in the same process of organization.

Initially, BRAC organizes men and women into separate groups in order that women can address their problems of day-to-day economic survival as members of poor households and of limited social power and autonomy as women. Overtime, BRAC links the separate male and female groups into a class federation to address the long-term systemic problems of economic domination by the rich.

Through the organized groups, poor women address the problem of economic survival and begin to exercise social power and autonomy within their homes. Initially, BRAC organizes women around economic action: economic action to guarantee survival and to provide the economic base from which to exercise power and autonomy within the home. Gradually with the social power gained in group interaction and the economic power gained through joint economic action, the women begin to exert greater power and autonomy within their homes. Participation in BRAC programs affords the women much that has previously been denied to them. Very often, BRAC meetings are their first opportunity for social contact outside of family or home and BRAC functional education classes and trainings their first opportunity to be educated. Moreover, BRAC's credit, training, and support services are usually the first access these women have had to public resources. And the income the women earn from joint productive activities is often the first income over which these women exercise some control.

Through the federation, poor women begin to address the problem of economic domination by the rich and to exercise social power and autonomy within their villages. Representatives from both men's and women's groups attend the workshops, trainings, conventions and other tools of federation. Through the power and unity gained in collective social and economic bargaining with other poor, the women begin to participate in and more adequately control their village and environment.

The basic objectives (resources, power, and autonomy as women and as the poor), the basic tools of organizing (the individual groups and the class federation), and the individual strategies (collective economic and social action) of BRAC's programs for women are perhaps best presented in the form of a model:

POOR AND A WOMAN IN RURAL BANGLADESH

Resources, Power and Autonomy as Women: by Organizing Women's Groups which undertake -
  —collective economic action as women
    eg: schemes to enhance productivity or expand employment: poultry rearing, silk worm rearing; paddy husking; block-printing; etc.
  —collective social action as women
    eg: in one village, the husband of a group member wanted to marry for a second time. The group took action against that man by telling his prospective in-laws that he was already married. In the end, he could not remarry. Due to the group's pressures, he is still living with and supporting his first wife.

Resources, Power, and Autonomy as Poor: by Linking Men's and Women's Groups into a Class Federation which engages in
  —collective economic bargaining as poor
    eg: in one field project, men's and women's groups acting together have been able to negotiate better wage rates and sharecropping terms
  —collective social action as poor
    eg: in another field project, the poor were vocal in their demand for fair representation in local government. Sixteen groups of poor were able to occupy all the seats in their respective village councils. In one instance, they selected a woman from one of the women's groups to be the village "headman!"

But how does this model translate into action? What exactly is a BRAC group? What steps are involved in organizing a group? What activities are actually undertaken? Let me describe as best I can what goes into organizing a group of women and the federation of the poor.

Methods of Organization

The task of organizing rests with the BRAC professional staff each responsible for organizing the poor in six villages. The field staff live as teams in simple office-cum-dormitory complexes together with the paramedics and field accountants for that area. The field staff walk or bicycle twice a day to one or another of their respective villages: in the morning to hold discussions and to supervise activities and in the evening to attend meetings and classes. They visit each of their respective villages at least once a week.

Entering the Village—

When they first start to work in a village, the field staff walk around the village talking to individuals, observing neighborhoods and households, establishing contacts with the poor. They make informal rounds of all neighborhoods. They observe the households (patterns of work, occupation, assets, etc.) and make mental notes as to who has what, who does what, who talks with whom, etc.. They try to establish friendly contact with all households while assessing which households fall under BRAC's criteria for its target group.

Establishing Personal Contact—

The field staff invariably establish stronger contacts with certain individuals—either those who offer themselves or those whom the staff seek out as informants. These informants provide critical insights about the village. The staff are cautioned to understand the implications of their associations with different classes of people and to establish as wide a network of relationships as possible, especially with the poor.

Use of Survey—

Prior to initiating work, BRAC field staff invariably conduct if not a formal socio-economic survey at least an informal survey of the area: of village institutions, physical infra-structure, etc. In Sulla, this survey took the form of household counts of what had been lost or destroyed during the Liberation War. In Jamalpur, the staff conducted an informal survey (about attitudes, skills, and problems) with the 800 women who participated in the relief phase of the program. In Manikganj, a formal socio-economic survey was conducted in addition to informal surveys of local infrastructure and development interventions. After these area-wide surveys, the field staff conduct their own informal village surveys in each of their respective villages.

Preliminary Action—

Sometimes the organizers will undertake a preliminary activity by way of introducing themselves and BRAC to the village: for example, small-scale food-for-work schemes enlisting village representatives to plan the scheme and the village poor as labor.

Group Discussions—

After a few weeks, once the field staff feel familiar enough with the village to know which of the poor could be drawn into a group they suggest a meeting be held at someone's house. At that first meeting, the field staff briefly introduce themselves and BRAC. Those attending the meeting are encouraged to talk about themselves and their problems.

At some point during the discussions the field staff interject to ask: "How many of you would be interested to attend an adult education class? BRAC will provide the lessons, blackboards, notebooks, and pencils. Would you be able to locate a volunteer teacher? Where could we hold classes?" If the group is interested to attend and is able to identify a local volunteer teacher (someone slightly educated from that group or village), BRAC trains that teacher-helper for one week in BRAC's functional education curriculum and methodology.

Functional Education—

Functional education, as developed by BRAC, revolves around village problems and a problem-solving dialogue. A separate problem is presented, discussed, and analysed during each class. Towards the end of each class, the words (broken down into phonemes and letters) and numbers pertaining to that problem are also taught. The curriculum and materials—a set of 60 lessons with charts and a teacher's manual—were developed by BRAC staff.

Separate male and female classes meet in village homes. Village men and women are recruited on a part-time voluntary basis as teacher-helpers. These teacher-helpers receive an initial training and continuous in-service supervision and training from the BRAC field staff. The classes are often the first time the poor have sat together to discuss and analyze their environment. They begin to look at themselves, each other, and that environment in a new way.

Traditional "teaching" is replaced by group discussion where the learners become the participants and the "teacher" assumes the role of facilitator or guide to introduce new ideas or information into the discussion when necessary. The method of discussion is that of problem-solving dialogue. The purpose is to initiate a two-way process of communication. This type of dialogue, the basic methodology of functional education, is used by all BRAC staff in all field work.

Through such dialogue, BRAC field staff begin to learn not only about village problems but also about the underlying root causes to these problems. By observing and supervising the functional education classes, they are able to identify groups of poor with like interests to be organized into working groups. The field staff then work closely with those groups which grow out of the functional education classes.

Group Formation—

Towards the end of the functional education course, the field staff begin to discuss future action with the viable groups. Most typically, the group discusses a joint economic activity. The group may decide to undertake collective farming or fish culture or a rural industry. The field staff together with the group discuss all the details and potential problems in such a scheme. Meanwhile, the group members are encouraged to accumulate savings and shares as a sign of their intention to work together and to build and maintain a group fund.

Economic Action—

No set rules for group financial and production transactions exist. Each group discusses and decides on its individual production and financial plans. The field staff help them review the plans for their cost-effectiveness and feasibility. Each group member must purchase a small share (averaging $1.00) per year. Each member is also encouraged to save a minimum (average 5 cents) per week. The accumulated savings and shares constitute the group fund. The field staff assist in the maintenance and recording of these funds.

These funds are used on a rotation basis to finance either small loans to individual members, who otherwise are forced to take loans from money-lenders at exorbitant rates of interest; or group capital for small-scale joint productive schemes upon submission and approval of the production plan by the group. As required, BRAC provides credit, inputs, and support services to back the productive activities. BRAC loans carry an interest rate of 12% per annum. Generally, each member is required to repay a minimum (average 15 cents) per week from his/her earnings against the group loan. The types of economic schemes range from jute, paddy, or sugar-cane cultivation to animal husbandry or poultry rearing to weaving or mat-making.

Social Action—

Groups also discuss and undertake collective social action. They may decide to use their group funds or joint labor to assist each other or other poor in the village: in the case of illness, death, property loss or damage. They may decide to negotiate the terms and conditions of labor: to demand minimum or delayed wages or contest maltreatment. They may decide to lobby for public goods or services which are their due: licenses; power pumps; lease of public lands or ponds; medical services; or rations. They may begin to circumvent the local money-lender by building group funds [to finance small individual loans] through savings, shares, and the profits from joint economic schemes.

Group Development—

When a group is first constituted to attend functional education classes, its members may appear homogeneous but over time many "shades" of poverty emerge. Field staff must regularly discern and handle such anomalies within the groups. A group may decide on one set of principles initially but challenge the rules or each other when loss occurs. Loss and conflict are not uncommon. Resolution of loss and conflict, skillfully handled by group members or the field staff, can strengthen a group. The groups that undergo and learn from loss and conflict are often the strongest in terms of sympathy one for another and eagerness to undertake further collective action, both socio-political and economic.

When the groups carry out their activities, they are regularly confronted by the village "establishment" (the rich, elders, religious leaders, and/or local politicians). Much of the skill required in group organization and much of the cohesion within the group stems from and relates to devising tactics to deal with these conflicts and obstacles. On principle, mass confrontation and violent tactics are avoided. BRAC reasons that only a strong federated base of power will be adequate to deal with a mass confrontation. But small-scale conflicts are the everyday fare of the groups and their organizers.

Leadership Development—

BRAC field staff plan regular workshops and trainings to develop the leadership and capacity of each group. One member from each group is selected to be trained as that group's primary health and family planning worker. These health-helpers are trained and supervised by BRAC paramedics. General members receive technical training as needed to undertake joint economic schemes.

A minimum of two group members are trained in cost-accounting and group management. They remain the informal leaders to perform key functions of the group. The group is formalized, with an election of officers and adoption of constitution and by-laws, only if and when the function of the group necessitates. For instance, groups must be formally registered to avail of certain governments' inputs or to receive training from certain agencies.

Active and strong groups are chosen to organize other poor in their own or neighboring villages. Representatives from these "core groups" are selected as "cadre." BRAC bring the "cadre" together to share the problems and experiences of their respective groups and to develop their class identity. BRAC conducts various workshops to develop the understanding, awareness, and solidarity between core group and regular groups. All groups are to be linked together gradually: first at the village level and then at the field project level.

Group Federation—

BRAC planned to first organize one male and one female group in each village and then gradually expand the number of groups to include all the poor in each village. But existing groups are themselves beginning to organize other poor in their own villages. "Otherwise," as one group leader put it, "we're only 20 out of 700 in our village." There is a significant spread-effect as non-group poor observe the activities of a group in their own or a neighboring village. As the number of groups grows, BRAC holds inter-village meetings with representatives from each group to discuss mutual problems and share lessons learnt in the joint action.

Through such workshops and trainings of group representatives, the village-wide groups of poor are linked into project-wide federations. A common identity is growing. The groups have chosen the term Working People's Force for this federation (the Bengali original for 'working people' literally translates as "those who live off their labor"). All female groups are called Working Women's Groups. All male groups are called Working Men's Groups. And each individual group carries before the common title the name of their respective village. Together the groups constitute the Working People's Force.

A Convention of the Poor—

A convention of the Working People's Force in one project area drew 5000 participants. Representatives from the groups in that project area had been meeting regularly. They felt that without a demonstration of their consolidated strength and voice, they could not adequately lobby for government inputs and services. They decided to hold a convention of all the poor in that project area. They met with the BRAC organizers to plan the convention.

It was decided that the convention was to forge a sense of common purpose and resolve between all the groups and to impress upon the outside world the strength in numbers and rightful demands of the poor. It was agreed that all the members of BRAC-organized groups of poor in that project area should attend the convention. A consolidated speech covering the problems and issues raised by the different groups would be prepared.

The coordinating committee decided to raise their own funds and not seek outside funds to cover the costs of the convention. They agreed that each delegate would provide either 2½ kilos of rice and pulses or 15 taka ($1.00). This would take care of the major expense: food. Another sum of 22,000 taka ($1,466) was raised through contributions from group funds to cover the costs of accommodation, facilities, and the public address system. The delegates would be housed and the convention staged at the campus of the local college. BRAC agreed to provide all the necessary logistical support.

The coordinating committee decided to invite the Minister of Local Government and Rural Development to address the convention. The presence of the Minister would ensure more active participation and cooperation in the convention by the local officials. More importantly, the presence of the Minister would help ensure the officialdom took serious note of the issues and proposals put forward at the convention.

On the evening of the convention, the delegates converged on the convention ground. They came in procession from all directions chanting slogans—demanding their rights as poor—and bearing placards giving the names of their groups and home-villages. That evening the town took on a somewhat festive air as the delegates were shown a popular film—a village tale depicting the inequities of village life—at the local movie house. Early the next day, over 5,000 delegates seated themselves by groups on the grounds of the college where a stage had been erected for the convention speakers.

The delegates were addressed by the Minister and several of the local government officials. The keynote address, prepared by the coordinating committee, was read out by the leader of one of the male groups. In that address, six problem areas requiring the attention of public policy were presented:

1. the fixing of a minimum wage rate for agricultural labourers;
2. changes in the sharecropping terms;
3. involvement of the disadvantaged in the planning and implementation of food-for-work and other public works schemes;
4. facilitating loans for the landless and disadvantaged from the existing credit institutions;
5. more equitable distribution of public inputs and services (power pumps, fertilizers, seeds, medicines, public lands, derelict ponds, etc.);
6. greater opportunities for women through village-based small-scale rural industries.

After the convention, as most of the delegates returned home to their villages, the coordinating committee met again to formulate ways of maintaining the momentum. The coordinating committee would select a Convenor to head the Working People's Force. The post of Convenor would be rotated every six months. The Coordinating Committee will meet regularly to formulate a time-frame and strategies for tackling the six problem areas presented at the convention. An advisory Council of non-group members interested in assisting and advising the poor was to be constituted.

The convention was the first of a kind: a convention for the poor convened by the poor. But the convention must, BRAC contends, become only the first of many. Eventually, the Working People's Force will be federated across BRAC field projects. Already, representatives from each project-wide federation attend intra-project workshops at BRAC's Training Centre. The convention was a significant step in a long-term process of federation.

What principles of organization has BRAC learned to date?

- people generally act on the basis of self-interest;
- the poor can, if they perceive it to be in their self-interest, be organized into groups;
- to guarantee their interest, the poor should initially be organized around immediate and tangible activities;
- in so doing, the groups of poor must increasingly take the initiative in the organization process.
- over time, as the organization of poor strengthens they can move to more complex, abstract, long-term and systemic issues.
- because theirs is the risk in such action, the poor themselves must decide which systemic issues using what tactics should be tackled when.

Given these principles; we decided to organize women, at least initially, around immediate and tangible economic activities.

THE ECONOMIC PROGRAM

The only way to generate non-agricultural employment on a significant scale in rural areas is through import substitution. Survey

your rural markets. See what is brought in, what is bought by the rich of
the village. Set a target: 'Twenty percent of what is coming from outside
must be locally produced'. Then begin to mobilize public opinion. Encourage purchase of local products: 'Buy your own village goods, keep
our money within the village'. Exhibit new village products at public
meetings and bazaars. For weeks no one will even notice your products.
Do not get discouraged. Eventually some interest will be shown. Also,
of course, study the national import strategies. Collect and analyze data
on what is being brought into the nation from the outside. But, remember, it is much simpler to substitute for national imports. That is what
the large-scale industrialists do. But it is far more difficult and risky at
the village level. To work at the village level requires a certain
"madness".

Rural Industry Consultant

Voluntary agencies are, by their very nature, 'soft'. That is to say,
their main characteristics are unbounded goodwill, a desire to help and a
lot of compassion. Also, they are constitutionally unable to be hardnosed
in their dealings with the 'beneficiary' groups—even when the dealings
are fundamentally economic but mistakenly viewed as 'developmental'.
The 'soft' world of voluntarism cannot mesh with the 'hard' realities of
the world outside where millions are competing to make a living or a
little money here and there.

BRAC Staff Handout on Voluntary Efforts
In Employment Generation.

On being Hardnosed and Softhearted

We decided to launch an economic program for the women because
we had observed how poverty affects their lives. They had told us what
it was like to not know where the next meal was to come from, to be
husbandless or burdened with a chronically-ill husband, or to need to
supplement a husband's meagre earnings. We had learned that there
were few options open to women for paid work and little support
offered to women in their traditional work. The women proceed on
faith and hard work because they have no choice. We decided to do the
same and to try to help them find ways to earn a better income or to
find additional employment.

We knew that in launching an economic program we were up against
the limited capacities of both ourselves and the women. We knew that
the capacity to save money among the organized groups of women is
small so that their group funds would never be sufficient to finance
anything more than the most modest economic schemes. We recognized that although the survival skills of these women are significant

they had not been conditioned to develop many entrepreneurial skills (e.g., women in Bangladesh are seldom in trade and never in the marketplace). We also recognized that the BRAC staff were strong on commitment, communication, and organizing skills but weak on technical and management skills. We knew that even the most technically and financially sound scheme requires a level of management and supervision not always within the competence of the BRAC field staff. In order to develop economic programs for the women, we would need to develop the technical, financial and management capacities of both BRAC staff and the women.

More fundamentally, we knew that in launching an economic program for women we were up against the subsistence economy of rural Bangladesh. We had learned that there was little effective demand for commercial goods and services in the villages of Bangladesh. We recognized that to identify and design viable economic projects which would ensure a reasonable return to each member of a group would be difficult and that to do so for several thousand women in several hundred groups would be extremely difficult. And we recognized the need in Bangladesh for overall development with equitable distribution. These limitations notwithstanding, we decided to proceed.

And so we had to proceed with the "soft-heartedness" of the voluntary sector (who come in contact with the hard realities of poverty) but also with the "hard-nosedness" of the private sector (who understand the hard realities of the commercial world). We were committed to finding options for the women but also to meeting as many conditions of feasibility as possible before any scheme was adopted. We tried to balance the pessimism that not much could be done with the optimism that hard work could deliver some options for the women. In the final analysis, we decided no one can predict with certainty if an economic scheme for poor women will be feasible because very few have tried to reach quite the same people in quite the same way. And so we erred on the side of optimism rather than pessimism and decided to follow the women's example of faith and hard work.

The Search

We launched an on-going search for potential schemes and existing skills. We conducted surveys, interviews, and discussions with the women. At some point in every discussion with women we asked: "What do you know how to make or to do?" If they pleaded unskilled, we questioned further: "What did you make or do yesterday? What food items do you prepare? Which food items can you store for some length of time? What skills are you expected to know in order to impress a prospective groom's family? Who made that fan, this mat, that quilt? Didn't your grandmother or your old aunt make many things? Can you show us?" We instructed field staff to keep their eyes and ears open: "Poke around and find skills or come up with ideas." We were fairly relentless in our search.

What skills did the women confess to and the field staff identify? Most rural women know tailoring, embroidery, or crocheting: embroidered clothes, crocheted prayer hats, gold embroidery, rag dolls, and the stitching of quilts (both simple quilts and the celebrated embroidered quilts of Bengal). Many know bamboo, cane, or palm craft: mats, fans, fish traps, baskets. Most know how to work jute fibre into rope and macrame jute pot-hangers and how to process various food items: pickles, chutneys, snack foods. Moreover, women in pottery communities model clay; women in weaving communities spin thread and prepare bobbins; and women in agricultural households process grain, cultivate fruits and vegetables, and rear poultry and livestock.

We read and talked about feasible schemes. We talked to staff from other programs and agencies. We read whatever case material we could find on successful schemes elsewhere. Some of us toured other projects and other countries. We came up with a long list of possibilities, which I have divided into certain broad categories of economic activity:

1. Agriculture and Horticulture
   —cultivation of:

paddy	soybeans
sugar cane	tobacco
onions	peanuts
potatoes	pulses
vegetables	wheat
fruit trees	

   —growing and selling seedlings
   —composting
   —provision of agro-services
     seed preservation and storage
     commercial storage: rice, paddy, and seed
     insecticide spraying
     tube-well installation and maintenance
     agricultural implement manufacture

2. Food and Grain Processing
   —grain processing
      paddy husking
      pulse grinding
   —food processing—handling traditional crops
      oil pressing
      molasses preparation
      gathering and selling tamarind
      shelling and cracking betel nut
   —processing and bottling:
      pickles and chutneys
      vinegar
      mustard seed dressing (*kasundi*)
      clarified butter (*ghee*)
      rose water
      lime juice
      tomato puree/sauce
   —processing and packaging
      mango cheese (*am sutto*)
      shredded coconut
      coconut preparations (*sandesh* and *cheera*)
      lentil balls (*bori*)
      lentil and rice flat bread (*papads; papri pitahs*)
      molasses candy (*batasha*)
      crystallized fruits and vegetables (*halwa* and *murabba*)
      snack mix (*chanachur*)
      ground spices
      medicinal herbs
      baked goods (bread, cookies, biscuits)
      crushed rice (*cheera*)
      puffed rice (*muri*)
      natural cosmetics: soap and shampoo and masques

3. Textiles
   —spinning cotton or wool
   —lace-making and crochet
   —sewing and tailoring
   —embroidery
   —natural dye manufacture
   —natural fibre processing (pineapple, banana)
   —seri - and ericulture: spinning, rearing, and weaving
   —block-printing
   —batik
   —embroidered quilts

4. Small Industries
   —cigarette rolling

—jute handicrafts
—rope-making
—net-making
—package-making
—envelope-making
—bamboo and cane and palm products:
 mats, fans, baskets, furniture
—match-making
—incense-making
—soap-making
—hand-made paper
—hand-printed stationery
—paddy and wheat straw cards
—printing
—book-binding
—office-files
—leather goods
—coir products
—brick-making
—carpet making [wool or jute]
—furniture
—jute seat-backs

5. Poultry
 —chicken rearing
 —duck rearing
 —feed preparation

6. Fish Culture
 —pond excavation
 —fish cultivation
 —fish processing, drying, and preserving
 —fish-net making

7. Animal Husbandry
 —goat and cow rearing
 —veterinary services

The Framework

In our search, we were willing to look at any or all skills and schemes. But in our programming, we had to be more selective and systematic. First, we had to look beyond nifty schemes which might employ 30 women here or another 50 there. We needed to help thousands of women in hundreds of villages. Consider these figures for one moment. In its three field projects, BRAC works in some 300 villages. Each village in Bangladesh averages 1,000 residents. BRAC aims to reach and benefit the poorest third of each village. Each household in Bangladesh averages six members.

300 villages × 1,000 = 300,000 people
300,000 ÷ 3 = 100,000 poor people
100,000 ÷ 6 = 16,666 poor households

If we wanted to organize one woman from each of the poor households, we needed to organize and support some 16,666 poor women. So we had to determine which schemes might work for large numbers of women.

Secondly, each group of women must decide which scheme or schemes they want to undertake. The schemes have to fit the needs and requirements of the individual group: their current patterns of work; the seasonality of their current work and the proposed scheme; the relative importance of quick small returns over long-term larger returns. And just as women often pursue multiple strategies to survive, some groups of women choose multiple, small schemes to ensure a steady (if not large) income over several seasons. Each group of women discusses their choice of schemes in light of these factors: long term versus short-term returns, steady versus seasonal work, supplemental versus primary income.

Thirdly, we wanted to evolve a framework to expedite our economic planning. We had learned a great deal from the search itself and from early implementation of various schemes. As a first step in developing a framework, we asked ourselves which skills and schemes were potentially major sources of employment for women in Bangladesh:

—traditionally "female" occupations that were or had been major sources of employment for women:

   post-harvest agriculture
   pre-weaving processes
   pre-and post-fishing processes
   animal husbandry
   poultry rearing
   tree, vine, and vegetable cultivation

—traditionally "female" skills that were potentially major sources of employment for women:

quilt-making
craft-manufacture
embroidery and lace

—traditionally "male" skills and occupations that are potentially major sources of employment for women:

pre-harvest agriculture
weaving
block-printing

We began to try to transform these skills and occupations into viable employment schemes for women.

CHAPTER FIVE

What Was Done

Imagine women . . .

—transplanting paddy seedlings to the fields (they have leased and tilled) under the watchful eye of two men (they have contracted to instruct them how to transplant)

—arranging bottles of pickles in neat rows to sun in an open courtyard

—kneading, rolling, and cutting dough to make *chana-chur* (a snack food) in a newly-built workshop

—seated in a small hut amidst piles of colorful used clothing: remaking some, repairing others for resale at a local market

—staking out and digging rows of a demonstration plot to sow soybean and ground-nut

—lifting and carrying earthern pots filled with water to irrigate their plot of cabbages

—seated in a semi-circle in an open courtyard discussing the cost-benefits of paddy husking

—seated in a row behind spinning wheels learning to spin silk thread from cocoons they have reared in their own huts

—seated on mats in a small room stitching colorful motifs onto embrodiered quilts

—sprinkling feed into a large pond (they have excavated) to feed the fish (they are cultivating).

These are but some of the economic schemes undertaken by BRAC-supported groups of women.

Having identified many existing skills of women in Bangladesh and having explored the feasibility of several economic schemes for women, we were able between 1972–80 to engage over 2,500 women in viable employment schemes.* For some schemes, we needed to provide the type of support given "male" agriculture: that is, inputs, technologies, credit subsidy, prices, and markets. For other schemes what was required was the type of support provided in industrial "job creation": that is, skills training, fixed and working capital, management and supervision. We decided, given these two broad types of requirements, to classify all potential schemes either as:

—those which *enhance productivity* of what women already do; or
—those which *expand employment* from what women already do or have never done

In this chapter, I discuss those schemes through which we engaged significant numbers of women over several years. I will try to present these schemes within the framework we evolved; to summarize each type of scheme in phases (six-month phases unless otherwise noted); and to highlight what was required during each phase by way of research, training, technological transfer, management, and organization. In so doing, I will stress the organizational and managerial aspects of the process over the financial and technical aspects.** discuss the potential for and problems in each scheme, and present the critical bottlenecks faced and subsequent changes in plans made while developing each scheme. My purpose is to provide a sense of process: that is, of how we addressed the problems confronted, how we reshaped plans, and what measures we took in implementing each scheme.

---

*As of December 1982, BRAC had engaged 4600 women in viable economic schemes in the three field project areas described in this book and another 6000 women through its recently expanded credit and outreach programs.

**One note on the financial and technical aspects of each type of scheme. This is not the time and place to present the technical lessons learned. BRAC developed and acquired technical expertise in each area as it went along. Records of technical information and training are maintained in BRAC files. And, for some schemes, we prepared a technical manual. I will not go into the specifics of each technology here but try to convey the important steps taken in technology transfer. This is not yet the time to discuss the financial aspects of the schemes. Most schemes take a minimum of four to five years to mature to the point where they are running at reasonable enough levels of production and efficiency to be analyzed financially. At the time of writing, most of the schemes I describe were only three to four years old. BRAC research staff plan to conduct a financial analysis of each scheme only after five years.

PRODUCTION ENHANCEMENT SCHEMES

Women in rural Bangladesh produce food, process food items, and manufacture craft items. Yet their contributions to the economies of the household and of the country have generally been disregarded or undervalued. In part, women's contributions have not been recognized because they produce mostly for consumption and not for the markets. This disregard has meant that women produce without the support or services offered to men in their production and that, on occasion, women's labor is displaced by machines. In order for women to produce more efficiently these trends need to be reversed.

We have, therefore, undertaken schemes which aim:

—to transfer subsistence production into commercial production
—to increase output and efficiency
—to prevent or reverse displacement
—to improve terms and conditions of production.

Transforming Subsistence Production into Commercial Production—

Many of the productive activities of women can be transformed from subsistence to commercial production (that is, to reach the markets and bring home an income) with small amounts of working capital. Some women have managed to do this on their own. As reported by one woman in Manikganj:

"My mother used to husk paddy. We used to husk paddy with her. A *madrassa* (Islamic school) was built in our village and my mother enrolled us in the *madrassa*. She paid the *madrassa* fees out of her paddy-husking income. After that our mother reared goats. Then mother said: 'You all rear goats. Whatever you earn from goat-rearing, we will spend on your education.'"

But not all women share this innate entreprenurial capacity and few women have access to working capital. This is where BRAC and others can help.

To transform subsistence production into commercial production does not necessarily require fixed capital, skills training, or marketing. The market for such products is generally the local markets, which the women negotiate through family members. What is needed is small amounts of working capital. BRAC has helped many women transform agricultural, horticultural, food processing, poultry, and animal husbandry production to a commercial scale with small amounts of credit ($20 or under).

Increasing Output and Efficiency—

Women's output and efficiency could be improved if they were to receive the same package of extension services offered to men: credit, inputs, technology, training. Early on, BRAC provided extension services to both men and women in horticulture and in animal husbandry (both traditionally "female" areas of production). Gradually, BRAC targeted these services more specifically to women and offered extension services in other "female" areas of production (poultry, grain processing).

BRAC field staff were asked to investigate which investment would "give the most increased marginal productivity." BRAC field staff found output and efficiency could be increased with any, preferably all, services:

—inputs
    wholesale rates for raw materials
    improved seed varieties
    animal and poultry vaccines
—technologies
    to reduce the drudgery of domestic activities
    to increase the output of productive activities
—training
    in improved techniques
    in additional, related skills
—credit
    to purchase raw materials and equipment
    to increase working capital

Preventing or Reversing Displacement of Women's Labor—

Until recently, Bangladesh has had a reasonably vital base of rural industries. Many rural industries are still carried out in pre-factory conditions: in individual courtyards or huts using traditional implements and engaging significant numbers of women and men: the husking and processing of paddy; the preparation of sweets and molasses; the making of bricks; the spinning and weaving of textiles; the weaving of mats, fans, baskets, or fish-nets; the drying and curing of fish. A real bustle of activities not yet coopted by machines or centralized into workshops.

However, recent policies have encouraged capital-intensive over labor-intensive investments which threaten this base of rural industry and the rural labor force. A classic example of taking away with the left hand what one promises to offer with the right: namely, employment to the millions of under- and unemployed men and women.

BRAC became concerned that rural labor, especially women's, in handloom and post-harvest sectors were being threatened by recent investment in mechanized mills for paddy and cotton. BRAC decided to lobby for policies that would protect women's labor from displacement by machines. In order to lobby effectively, BRAC conducted a field study to measure the output of women's labor and the dependence of women on returns to that labor in post-harvest operations and, based on the findings, drafted a policy paper on "appropriate technologies under pressure" to advocate an employment-oriented set of policies at the national level.

Improving the Terms and Conditions of Women's Production—

So long as women do not own or control the means of production, so long as women's work is so interdependent with men's as to be overlooked, so long as women are dependent on men for credit and services, the measures listed above will have only limited effect. Once women are in control of their own labor, the returns to that labor, and the means of production, their productivity will increase dramatically.

BRAC believes it is important that women be organized into working groups which can exert control and resist exploitation. Once organized, women can work together to improve the terms and conditions of their work. Groups of women can invest in the means of production: land or equipment. Groups of women can be trained to maintain, repair and manage the means of production: hand tubewells, small-scale rice mills, insecticide sprayers. Groups of women can be trained to perform all stages of production, rather than just one, in those activities where their work is otherwise interdependent with that of men (e.g. agriculture, weaving, pottery). Groups of women can begin to resist and eliminate various levels of exploitation: the moneylenders and middlemen (often one and the same). In such organization, the group is not just a vehicle to reach women and provide services to women but also an end in itself: the base from which women can evolve a collective voice and the unit to which control of resources should devolve.

1. Horticulture

All of horticulture production is the preserve of women. Most women engage in horticulture, but few women receive extension services in horticulture.

Early on, BRAC launched what it termed a "blanket" scheme in horticulture extension: that is, a scheme intended to reach all households, not specific households or individuals. In cooperation with the Mennonite Central Committee (a U.S. voluntary agency active in improving the productivity of small farmers in Bangladesh) vegetable seeds were imported and distributed each year to thousands of families and to local primary and secondary schools. Vegetables new to the area as well as traditional varieties were grown. Instructions on seed-bed preparation, transplantation and care of plants were provided by BRAC field staff. BRAC also encouraged the growing of fruit trees and regularly transported thousands of seedlings and saplings of coconut, banana, mango, papaya, and guava. All of these inputs were sold at cost to interested households.

Currently, BRAC has redirected these horticultural services to more directly reach and benefit women. Women who do not possess much land or who want to pool their labor are encouraged to take up collective fruit and vegetable cultivation on leased or sharecropped plots of land. One group of women, by way of example, planted 60 lemon trees (each of which cost 3 taka): a total investment of 180 taka ($12). They harvest roughly 30 taka worth of lemons per tree per year: an annual return of 1800 taka ($120; or ten times their investment). Women are also organized to plant and rear seedlings and saplings for sale.*

---

*As of December 1982, over 800 women were engaged in horticulture.

2. Animal Husbandry

Animal husbandry is the preserve of women. In those households that can afford animals women tend them, but few women receive extension services in animal husbandry. Regrettably the nation as a whole has not put too much emphasis on the livestock sector, but it is hoped that when they do recognition is given to women's role.

Early on, BRAC planned to train its paramedics to function as "paravets" as well. BRAC recognized that in order for livestock to prove more productive for draft and milch purposes better care and feed were required. Although some training and research was arranged in cooperation with a government dairy farm, BRAC did not progress very far in this area.

Currently, BRAC provides credit to groups of women who possess few if any animals and who wish to rear animals cooperatively. Many women's groups with loans from BRAC buy young animals which they rear and sell for a profit 10–12 months later. A calf purchased for 500 taka ($33.33) will sell 10 months later for 1000 taka: a profit of 50 taka ($3.33) per month without much cost or labor.

By way of example, a group of 15 women borrowed 7,500 ($500) from BRAC in January, 1978. They purchased 15 calves. Each member of the group was responsible for rearing one calf. The rearing costs were negligible and involved no cash outlay. After one year, 14 calves were sold (one calf had not been properly tended so that woman continued to rear it to an optimum size for sale).

Purchase price for 14 calves: 7,000
Sale price for 14 cows: 14,814

The women repaid the loan to BRAC a few months behind schedule but only because they waited for a high market price for their cows. BRAC charged an interest rate of 15 percent per annum on their loan; the total interest came to 1050 taka.

Sale price for 14 cows: 14,814
Purchase price plus interest: −8,050

Net income: 6,764

Fifty percent of the income was distributed equally among the 14 members of the group: an individual profit of 242 taka [$16] per woman.* The other fifty percent of the net income was deposited in the group fund.

Some groups prefer to take smaller loans and purchase only a few animals.** The group then decided which members of the group have the facilities (space and feed) to rear the animals. The initial investment is made by the group and the rearing costs are borne by the individual. The individual woman realizes half of the profit and the other half is put in the group fund. If a loss is incurred, that loss is borne by the group. So the group keeps pressure on the individual women to rear the animals properly.

It should be noted that these animal husbandry schemes are designed more to maximize a profit than to enhance production. No extension services have been offered and not much cost or effort is invested, the only BRAC inputs are credit and field staff supervision. BRAC hopes to expand its activities in animal husbandry to include training and inputs (vaccines, improved feed) to enhance production.

3. Poultry Rearing

Q: Does everyone rear chickens in the village?

A1: Before I did not know how to rear chickens but now I know.

A2: Not everyone. For lack of money everyone cannot rear chickens.

A3: Where to rear? I have no place.

Q: Do you have place now?

A3: No. Now everybody rears chickens through our group and no one says anything if chickens stray into each other's houses. Before it was not like this. There was no unity before the group. There were quarrels everyday with one's neighbors over goats, poultry; even children. Now everyone's things are the group's things. If anything is lost then we feel for each other.

Interview with Dapunia Women's Group, Jamalpur

Most, but not all women, keep a few chickens or ducks (depending on the terrain) to scavenge around the homestead. But there are problems in so doing: lack of skills, money, space and neighborliness. We

---

*It should be remembered that the average annual per capita income is less than $100 per year and that these women come from the poorest households where the income average is lower still.

**As of December 1982, over two thousand women were rearing cows or goats.

decided that something could and should be done about these problems.

Year I: Research and Training

After preliminary discussions with existing programs, we initiated in 1976 a poultry program designed:

—to expand the free-ranging/scavenging system of rearing (the alternative—poultry farms—requires procured feed and proves uneconomical in an economy where there is already tremendous demand on limited supplies of grain);
—to improve the quality of poultry through:
  a. training: on improved breeds, feed, and housing: disease control and cures;
  b. mass vaccination (using government vaccines and a BRAC-designed training-extension system)
  c. cock-replacement (using stock purchased from government farms and a BRAC-designed distribution system)
—to lobby for and obtain access to government stocks of vaccine (the option to import vaccines for BRAC's purposes, although tempting as a short-term solution, was rejected because it would not serve to stimulate long-term solutions to the vaccine problem)

During that first year we collaborated with several agencies on training and supply questions. We organized the first duck-rearing training for women in Bangladesh in collaboration with the International Voluntary Services (IVS). Together with the women's program staff of the government's Integrated Rural Development Program (IRDP) we lobbied for vaccines. We purchased high-bred cocks from the Mymensing Agricultural University. Pilot poultry schemes were initiated in several villages.

Take the case of Bonpara village near Jamalpur. During 1976, the villagers engaged in discussion on improved varieties and were persuaded to castrate all local varieties of cocks. Twenty white-leghorn cocks were supplied to the village. Thirty poor women of the village, who did not possess poultry, were provided local-variety hens on a loan basis. Within a few weeks the whole village was buzzing with the news of newly hatched "white babies." The new cross-breed poultry should yield more eggs. Village volunteers were trained in vaccination and a mass vaccination of the village poultry was completed. Improved feed and housing techniques were also discussed. The interest in this pilot scheme was high.

Year II: Pilot Schemes

1977 was a year for feed-back from the pilot village schemes. For example, I met with the poultry group in Bonpara village in October. My minutes of that meeting read as follows:

> We meet in a courtyard of a home having stopped on our way to inquire about the care of milch animals (a speciality of women and children in Bangladesh). The 12 members of the poultry group are assembled. The women of Bonpara report an increase in egg production of 50% with the cross-bred hens:
> —local varieties yield 60 eggs, on the average, in 3 months
> —cross-bred varieties yield 90 eggs, on the average, in 3 months.
> But there is no one story. We hear of both failures and successes.
> What are the problems?
> —disease
>   vaccines were not always available or administered
>   cross-bred chicks are less hardy (if they get wet or damp, for example, they more easily catch a chill and die)
> —predators
>   small fox and weasels, from a near-by graveyard, prey on the chicks
> —scanty feed
> What are the solutions?
> —mass vaccination campaigns
> —improved housing; to provide protection, ventilation, and a perch
> —supplementary feed; waste by-products (fish scales, bones, rice husks, oil cakes, etc.) should be given to supplement what the chickens glean by scavenging.

Certainly with hard work and special care some women had increased egg and meat production through the introduction of cross-bred varieties. But we still questioned whether cross-breeding (to the optimal generation) should be carried out in a controlled environment or an uncontrolled setting (such as Bonpara). The cross-bred varieties were more susceptible to disease and predators (they were bred for laying and not for running). Not all the castrations of local cocks proved complete. We needed to cross-breed to an optimum generation to maximize production and to minimize disease, but cross-breeding raises not simply technical, but also managerial problems.

Cock-exchange, as the Manikganj annual report for 1977 states, "requires the cooperation of and benefits the whole village." With village-wide cooperation in 12 villages, Manikganj staff distributed 500 white leghorn cocks. But, in both Jamalpur and Manikganj, the initial enthusiasm for cock-exchange had led to certain confusion. The first foreign cocks had been distributed free. But now mixed-breed cocks had been born and needed to be sold off or killed. The question was: "To whom did these cocks belong?"

Year III: Technical Staff

1978 was a year for rethinking and redesigning BRAC's poultry program. The major decision taken was to centralize the training and technical support of the program at BRAC's Training and Resource Center (TARC). Two poultry houses were constructed on the TARC campus and stocked with foreign cocks and local hens. Cross-bred chick and egg production was started. Previously, BRAC relied on outside expertise for technical training and assistance. But now BRAC hired its own poultry trainers. These technical trainers were expected to conduct more adequate feasibility studies and trainings and to coordinate supply of inputs.

Previously, BRAC supported poultry-rearing in all village households through cock exchange. This approach was abandoned in favour of supporting poor men and women through:

—centralized breeding and distribution of cross-bred varieties
—coordinated training and extension from TARC
—continued pressure and lobbying to procure government vaccine (until now, very much a process of high-level BRAC pressure on central government departments: ideally, should be procured from local livestock officers by the poor themselves).

Year IV: Extension and Management

In 1979 we introduced another cadre of workers to support the poultry program: the poultry "paravets" who, after training from

TARC, are posted to the field projects to provide on-the-spot supervision, extension, and management with technical back-up from TARC.

BRAC had found there are several critical elements to a successful program: skills training—stock and supplies—extension—management. BRAC has been able to develop a poultry program which includes all these elements:*

—skills training
    by BRAC technical trainers
—parent stock breeding
    by BRAC technical trainers at a centralized breeding farm
—vaccination drives
    by BRAC-trained paravets using government vaccines (obtained by BRAC technical trainers)
—extension
    by BRAC-trained paravets who help to develop systems of distribution and supervision
—management
    by BRAC field staff and the paravets

So far BRAC plays the role of broker between BRAC's poultry program and the government. Ideally at some point, BRAC will no longer play that role and the women will procure and receive what they need directly from local government livestock officers.

4. Fish Culture

Fish culture, like poultry rearing, can both enhance home consumption and generate incomes for poor women. In theory, a one-third acre pond can yield 10,000 taka ($666) worth of fish per annum. In reality, only richer households own ponds and often allow their ponds to erode and dry up. BRAC decided groups of poor villagers could be organized and supported to lease, re-excavate, and stock ponds.

Take the example of Aurangabad village near Manikganj. Four owners had allowed their ponds to fall into disuse. With BRAC support 24 members of a male group and 15 members of a women's group in

---

*As of December 1982, nearly seven hundred women were supported by BRAC in poultry rearing (BRAC also involves men in its poultry program).

Aurangabad leased the pond for 15 years. They re-excavated the pond in early 1978. The group members donated 20% of their labor, BRAC paid for the remaining 80%. The members of the groups started the scheme with capital they raised through individual subscription: each member was asked to put in 2 taka per month to a group fund for roughly a year. They invested the following amounts of taka into the pond scheme:

fish fries (3,000)	469
rice husks (2 maunds*)	125
lime (30 seers*)	60
oil cake (1 maund)	83
chemical fertilizer	20
taka total	757

They also supplied some cow-dung from their own stocks. They realized a profit of roughly 4000 taka from the first year of their scheme: an average investment by each of the 39 members of 19.50 taka for an average return of 103 taka ($1.30 for $6.80).

Most typically, the government and other agencies engage men in fish culture. Men are the fishermen, or so their thinking goes. However, women in fishing communities perform major functions: net-making and fish-processing. And in many communities, young women and girls harvest fish from village ponds. BRAC considered pisciculture a potential scheme for both men and women. BRAC's experience has shown that women can negotiate leases; provide the heavy labor required during excavation; and cultivate and harvest fish. I discussed the potential for women in fish culture with a UNICEF fishery expert and we arranged the first national training for women in fish culture in January 1978. Since then, women have been regularly engaged in fish culture by BRAC, UNICEF, and other agencies.

As with poultry, BRAC soon found the advantage in hiring its own fish culture experts to provide training and technical support from TARC. TARC re-excavated one large and two small ponds at its rural campus in 1978, which it stocked with nilotika and carp. TARC technical trainers give regular training in fish culture and in the design and

---

*One maund equals 82 pounds; one seer equals approximately two pounds.

construction of fish ponds. The management of fish pond schemes are handled by the field projects.

All schemes encounter problems; fish culture is no exception. First, there are the terms and conditions under which the ponds are leased. Some of the early leases negotiated in Jamalpur were not court certified. These contracts eventually fell through and the groups got disheartened and the schemes were discontinued. Now all leases are certified, but the terms differ.* Some leases are negotiated for a share of the profit (shares vary from 20–25% of the profit) and others are negotiated on the basis of cash downpayments. Second, various technical problems arise. There is an optimal depth to which ponds should be excavated to prevent seepage and allow for maximum cultivation. If time and effort are taken, fingerlings can be obtained free of cost from the government. TARC breeds fingerlings as a back-up stock. Each group has to be trained as to how much feed to be given at what intervals. Third, there are the human and organizational problems involved in pooling labor and sharing a profit. Marketing presents few problems. One group decided to let a fisherman community harvest the fish in return for 5,000 taka ($333). Some groups (depending on the size of the pond and the condition of its banks) grow banana, papaya and other fruit trees around the pond to prevent erosion and to bring in an additional income.

5. *Paddy Husking*

The case of paddy husking must be examined at some length because currently:

—about 70% of all paddy produced in Bangladesh is husked by rural women;**
—over 50% of all paid work available to women is from husking paddy,***

---

*By the end of 1980, BRAC-organized groups of men and women had leased, re-excavated, and stocked 16 ponds in Manikganj.

**Harris, Barbara. *Post Harvest Rice Processing System in Rural Bangladesh*, Bangladesh Agriculture Resource Council, Dacca, 1978, p. 1.

***Cain, Mead and S. R. Khanam, S. Nahar, "Class Patriarchy, and the Structure of Women's Work in Rural Bangladesh," *Population and Development Review*. 5(3), 1979, pp. 34–35.

—over 40% of rural households, the poor and marginal households, survive given the value-added of their women's labor in paddy husking.*

Paddy husking provides not simply employment but the critical margin of survival to millions of poor and marginal women and their families. I described in detail women's post-harvest work in chapter three. Let me briefly recapture the critical steps in paddy-processing:

Parboiling is done exclusively by women. Parboiling is a process of boiling paddy in large drums over slow fires. This process is very time-consuming. All paddy for domestic consumption and for sale as rice is parboiled.

Drying of grain is carried out by women. The drying surface must be prepared (plastered with mud), dried, and swept. The grain is set out to dry. It must be turned at regular intervals and protected at all times from poultry and birds. Grain is dried and cleaned several times: post-threshing and pre-storage as paddy; post-parboiling and pre-storage as paddy; pre and post-husking; and, intermittently, during the storage period.

Husking is done by women. This process is very labor-demanding. Most typically paddy is husked first and then polished in a foot-operated hammer-action implement known as the *dekhi*.

Winnowing, like drying and cleaning, is done several times. Post-threshing, post-parboiling, and post-husking. Women manufacture the bamboo winnowers.

Storage of domestic and market stocks of rice, paddy and seed is women's work. Women prepare the storage bins and supervise the storage of the grains. It is women who can judge rice, paddy, and seed for its quality and moisture before and during storage.

What is the value-added from processing raw paddy into rice? The value-added per volume of paddy varies with:

the price of paddy at harvest
the output of rice
the use and cost of fuel
the output and value of by-products
the price of rice at sale.

Who Gets What and Why, BRAC, 1979, pp. 75–77.

One informal survey (conducted by field staff in Sulla over a five month period) showed an average value-added of 18 taka per maund of paddy at an average price of 90 taka per maund of paddy: a value-added of 20%.* The share of labor in this value-added is high. Paddy-husking involves a low fixed capital cost: the *dekhi* costs roughly 125 taka ($8.33).

How much labor must be expended for this amount of value-added? Informal BRAC surveys and observation indicate that women can, on the average, process 1 maund of paddy in 10 hours (parboiling, drying, husking, winnowing). The labor time remains more or less constant but the labor effort is reduced if the women work in teams rather than alone. Moreover, the process is more cost-effective if the women work in pairs or threes, as the cost of fuel and implements (vats and *dekhi*) are roughly the same whether 1 or 4 maunds of paddy are processed at the same time.

What returns to their paddy-husking labor do women receive? First, it must be noted that some women process their own domestic stock of paddy for consumption, some women are hired to process paddy for others, and some women (i.e., those with access to working capital) process paddy as a business. Second, it must be remembered, that none of the women face any opportunity cost to their labor. Paddy-husking is one of the few paid labor options for women. What then are the returns from paddy-husking?

—women who process their domestic paddy stocks into rice contribute a value-added of between 18 to 28 taka ($1.20 to 1.87) per maund of paddy (10 hours work)
—women who process paddy for sale as rice can earn that same amount
—women who process paddy into rice for others earn between five to seven taka (33 to 47 cents) per maund of paddy.

Which women try to maximize on this return to paddy-husking

---

*At least one formal study indicates a higher return. Saleha Begum and Martin Greeley, *Rural Women and the Rural Labour Market in Bangladesh: An Empirical Analysis*, IDS Discussion Paper, 1979, p. 16: "Women processing their own raw paddy into parboiled rice contribute value-added of approximately 28 taka per maund of paddy: wage employment for the same work will give them a cash equivalent of only six to seven taka."

labor? In an indepth study of one village in Manikganj,* we found that the poorer households maximize the value-added in processing paddy into rice. Although we found a marked preference for sale of paddy as rice throughout Dhankura village,

   —in the land poor and landless households 95% of sale was as rice, whereas in households with more than 3½ acres 80% of sale was as rice; moreover,
   —the land poor and landless households use mostly unpaid women from their own households, whereas richer households often hire in women from other households.

The labor of women brings in an income which is often the critical margin of survival for poor households. Indeed, without the share of paddy processing activities in the value-added from sowing to consumption the poorer households would simply not survive.

What can be done to assist these women in paddy-husking? First, BRAC decided to help women who wanted to undertake paddy-husking on a commercial scale. Paddy-husking as a joint economic activity has several advantages. It is based on existing skills, equipment, and markets; brings a quick return (within two days) and carries few risks; and has traditionally been operated as a micro-business by some women. The only constraint is lack of working capital.

This is where BRAC comes in. Groups of women interested to undertake paddy husking take credit through the group, work in pairs or threes and market the rice through members of their individual families. The group is the umbrella for receiving loans and the group members work as mutually guarantors one to another. Initially, BRAC provided enough credit to each woman to purchase 1 maund of paddy. However, once we recognized the cost-effectiveness of processing more volume at one time, we began to provide each woman enough credit to purchase two maunds of paddy: 180 taka or $12. A small amount of credit that goes a long way. With that amount women begin to earn between 36 and 56 taka ($2.40 and 3.73 per week.**

Second, we tried to help the women increase the productivity and

---

*Who Gets What and Why: Resource Allocation in a Bangladesh Village. BRAC, 1979.
**As of December 1982, nearly four thousand women were engaged in commercial paddy husking.

efficiency of their paddy-processing. We experimented on a very limited scale to increase the efficiency of the various steps:

—drying: black polythene sheets were tested as a drying surface but
were found to sweat and, therefore, smell. They were then tested
as a cover against rain and found to be expensive relative to the
benefit;
—husking: a tribal rotary husker was imported, but we were unable
to carry out a proposed "output" study because we could not
maintain and repair the husker;
—storage: BRAC staff conducted an informal study of "loss" during
storage but found existing technologies more appropriate and
efficient than any BRAC could offer;
—parboiling: BRAC proposed to introduce the simple steam parboiling device used in custom mills.

BRAC had no real experts in appropriate technology and did not want
to "tinker" in the area or to take on substantial technological research
and experimentation. Others were better equipped to do such experimentation. We told such experts that BRAC was prepared to assist
in "field" testing once such technologies had been "laboratory" tested
and had the expertise to design delivery, supervision and extension
systems with proven technologies.

Third, we wanted to prevent or reverse the displacement of women
from this critical set of operations. BRAC drafted a policy paper on
appropriate technologies under pressure of displacement which found
that "mechanical and automatic mills, encouraged by cheap capital
provided by the nationalized banks and subsidized electricity, are
gradually taking over the market, increasing unemployment and des-
titution."* The introduction of rice mills threatens to deprive a large
number of women from one of the few traditionally "female" paid labor
options and to deprive poor households from a critical margin of income. The issue is not simply that the machine displaces women's
labor and is controlled by men. The critical issue is that the mills
displace the labor of marginal and poor women and is controlled by
men from rich and middle households. An issue not only of gender but
also of class.

_____

*Appropriate Technologies under Pressure, BRAC, 1980.

Because we could see that the *dekhi* was the key to women's economies we decided to demonstrate that women using the *dekhi* are productive and efficient and could, through *dekhi*-cooperatives, handle a significant volume of paddy. We worked out a proposal with the Ministry of Agriculture and the Department of Food under which BRAC-organized *dekhi*-cooperatives in Jamalpur would process government stocks of paddy. Because we could also see that the *dekhi* in some areas (where subsidized electricity was available) was soon to be displaced no matter how hard we lobbied, we proposed to convert some *dekhi*-cooperatives into cooperatives which owned and managed small-scale custom mills.

Admittedly, we never implemented either of these two proposals. This is not to say that they should not both be implemented, but that BRAC lacked the institutional will and field staff time to do so. But the will and the time must be found by BRAC and others. In those areas where the mill is seemingly inevitable, we cannot let the benefits of technology be at the expense of, rather than in the interest of, the women. If large automatic mills are prohibited, and only small-scale customs mills admitted, women could be organized to own and manage these mills. BRAC and others have considerable experience in organizing women and could provide the managerial back-up to women's custom-mill cooperatives. In those areas where the mill seems less inevitable, we cannot offer employment schemes with our right hand while taking away the single-largest employer of women's labor, manual paddy-husking, with the other. BRAC and others have considerable experience in organizing and providing loans to women's *dekhi* cooperatives. Women should not lose their major traditional source of income as the country adopts capital-intensive techniques of production.*

EMPLOYMENT EXPANSION SCHEMES

Almost all women in rural Bangladesh possess the skills to produce many decorative and utilitarian crafts. Some women in rural Bangla-

---

*In addition to those discussed here, BRAC has undertaken the following schemes to enhance women's traditional production: oil crushing; net-making; basket, mat and fish trap making; jute work; fish-drying and selling.

desh perform paid work within their villages and a few women seek paid work outside their villages. Yet women's skills have generally been disregarded or undervalued and their employment circumscribed. There is limited effective demand for women's goods in the local markets and virtually no demand for women's labor outside the villages. This is so in large part because women have been bound by tradition to certain skills and to certain work. Moreover, women's skills and goods have not been diversified or improved upon over time. In order for women's craft production and paid work to expand these trends need to be reversed.

We have, therefore, undertaken schemes which aim:

—to commercialize traditional skills through new markets
—to revive and adapt traditional skills and designs
—to impart new skills
—to mobilize demand for women's labor.

Commercializing Traditional Skills through New Markets—

Women process certain items for which there has been little or no effective demand in the local markets. These are items which each rural household produces for its own needs and which, until recently, even urban households prided themselves in making. But under the various pressures of urban life, many urban housewives no longer produce these items and turn to urban (and even foreign) markets for these goods. BRAC has tried to capitalize on this latent urban market for these traditional items and to develop new lines of goods based on the traditional skills.

Reviving and Adapting Traditional Skills and Designs—

Women (and men) produce many hand-crafted items for which Bangladesh is reknowned: *kantha* (embroidered quilts); muslin; *jamdani* (figured muslin) saris; and more. In the past, some of these crafts were bought or commissioned; that is, patronized art. Others of these items were produced as gifts, dowry, or for households decoration and utility: that is, unpatronized art. Those items that were previously patronized have now slipped into disuse or poor standards: most rich no longer patronize traditional art forms. Those that were previously unpatronized are no longer being produced, due to pressures on time and resources in most rural homes.

In an effort to find new patrons and markets, BRAC has undertaken a scheme to revive and adapt traditional skills and designs. What BRAC means by adaptation is an effort to adapt traditional skills and designs to new lines of functional, marketable items. What BRAC means by revival is the effort to revive in women (and men) the original skills, imagination, and creativity to produce art in the traditional form.

Imparting New Skills—

However substantial the range of women's skills in Bangladesh, most generate little income and only a few can be upgraded and expanded to command a higher price or to employ significant numbers of women. Given women's need for higher incomes and expanded work opportunities, we turned also to skills not typically "female"; the skills of men in Bangladesh and the skills of both men and women in other countries of the region. We felt the women could and would do any type of work provided they receive the requisite training and are offered the opportunity.

Why did we turn to "male" skills? Women as much as men need access to the major employment sources. In Bangladesh, agricultural field operations are the single largest employer of rural labor. If women could be trained in agricultural field work they would then not only have access to that employment but would also be recognized and counted among the wage labor sector. If not, women's needs for wage work would continue to go unrecognized.

What other skills did we turn to? Silk culture and block-printing. This is not to say these skills were not practiced in Bangladesh but that they were traditionally not skills for which Bangladesh was renowned. To impart and upgrade skills in these areas some degree of expertise was imported.

Mobilizing Demand for Women's Labor—

Current wisdom would have us believe that the constraints to women's employment is on the supply side: that women will not perform certain kinds of labor. But our experience told us that the problem is on the demand side: that employers, all men, do not consider women's labor.

We knew that women need work. But how could we mobilize a demand for women's labor? One way was to impart "male" skills to women. If women were to be seen working in the fields, they might then be hired as agricultural laborers. Another way was to lobby for women's participation in public employment schemes: food-for-work and other construction work. If women would be seen working on the roads or at construction sites, gradually the taboo against women working in "public" places would lift and women might then be hired as construction labor.

1. Food Processing

Traditionally women process many food items. We hoped to market these items that could be preserved and stored for lengths of time. Each rural household produces these food items for its own needs. Until recently, urban households did as well. But many urban households no longer produce these food items and turn to urban (and even foreign) markets for these goods and delicacies. We decided to try to capitalize on this latent urban market. If we could develop a market and adapt the technologies, these processing skills of women could be the base for a rural industry for women.

There were several reasons for our interest in food processing:

—the latent urban market for traditionally home-processed food items
—the seasonal gluts and attendant losses of fruits and vegetables in Bangladesh; if these surpluses could be preserved and then sold and/or consumed both producers and consumers would benefit
—existing skills and technologies; if these can be tapped the capital requirements are low and the labor requirements high

Phase I: Experimentation

We began the food processing project in September 1977. At first, we experimented with the various food items known to one group of women. We visited the project each month to discuss varieties; seasonality of the ingredients; utensils and implements; recipes and processing techniques; costs; quality, etc. Between each visit, the women produced samples of various items. Meanwhile, we researched the potential range of preservable and marketable food stuffs and the local food-processing technologies known to women. Early on, we listed the following as possibilities: pickles and chutneys, preserved mango, ground spices, and certain snack foods. Later, we added: rice crackers, lentil balls, coconut and pumpkin preserves, natural food preservatives.

Phase II: Training and Commercialization

We contracted a woman from Dhaka, who herself knew many types of preservation and had experience in training rural women, to provide a week's training to the group. We asked her to find ways to improve and standardize the products; to improve on the sealing and bottling; to assure hygienic procedures; and to test for quality. Three months later, after the women were in production, the trainer was called back for a one-day refresher course.

As production stepped up, some of us began merchandizing the products. We investigated the range of locally-available bottles; designed and printed labels; took samples to various craft shops and middle-class food outlets; and conducted a very small survey of middle-class food shops and bazaar food stalls in Dhaka to see what items they might carry at what price.

Phase III: Upgrading Production

The products needed to be improved. We contracted another woman who knew a range of "gourmet" recipes for pickles and chutneys. She was asked to retrain the women producers on the recipes and the techniques to be used. She trained the women for one week in Dhaka.

The management of production needed to be improved. This type of food processing, where strict quality and hygiene must be controlled, could not be done in the homes. Raw materials must be purchased in quality and bulk. Standard recipes and techniques and hygienic standards must be rigorously maintained. Although women came from quite a distance to work at a central workshop, production still suffered as we did not provide on-the-spot expertise or supervision.

Phase IV: Pricing and Merchandizing

BRAC priced its items on the basis of: cost of raw materials, cost of labor (calculated on a sliding scale to adjust for increasing productivity of labor), and a percentage for overhead and transportation. But our prices needed to be competitive so we researched the prices of similar items on the market. We realized the need to purchase raw materials in bulk at the best seasonal prices to keep the prices down.

We adopted a brand name for all BRAC products: *Shuruchi* which means literally "good taste" and can be applied to mean either "good flavor" or "refined taste." Separate labels for different lines of products were printed. But we never managed to get the women to code each batch of pickles and chutneys.

Meanwhile, we ran into several technical problems. The shelf-life of the products was not of uniform or adequate length. The moisture content of certain ground and powdered spices had not been controlled. Some batches developed mold, although we had tested the pickles and found the bacterial count to be well within the range of safety. Initially we had arranged to receive free technical assistance from a variety of sources (e.g. a local nutrition institute tested out pickles and a local food science institute advised on techniques), we now needed regular technical assistance.

Phase V: Technical Collaboration

We decided to collaborate with a technical agency, the Mennonite Central Committee (MCC). MCC had a food processing technologist who for two years had been working to adapt solar dryer designs and techniques to Bangladesh. BRAC needed MCC's technical expertise and MCC perceived some advantage in working closely with BRAC on technology-transfer and extension problems.

We hired a paratechnologist to apprentice with the MCC dried food project staff. MCC and BRAC collaborated on a marketing study. We shared ideas on marketing, pricing, and merchandising.

Phase VI: Specialized Staff

After some months, the MCC-trained paratechnician joined the Manikganj field project. BRAC and MCC worked out the following steps for him to take:

—construct and test the new technology (two types of solar dryers)
—demonstrate the technology by applying it to current lines of production spices and pickles

—provide training and extension services to producer groups

—apply technology to new lines of production: dried fruits and vegetables

—assist BRAC's head office marketing unit with marketing promotion

The field staff of the project area worked out a management system to incorporate the new cadre of paratechnicians, like this one. It was decided that the overall management and development of the producer groups rests with the responsible field staff. The technical extension and back-up of various producer groups rests with the paratechnician.

BRAC's food processing scheme has made only minimal progress. Several groups of women are grinding spices and making pickles and chutneys. The paratechnician did not work out as planned and was reposted to the marketing unit at BRAC's head office. Although we have not worked out all the technological and management problems, BRAC sees a potential for growth in this agro-based industry.*

2. Traditional Craft Development Scheme

BRAC has undertaken a series of projects to increase the quality and marketability of Bangladeshi craft. Initially, we encouraged the production of hand-crafted items by a number of women's groups: basket makers, embroiderers, mat makers, lace makers. In 1978, BRAC and MCC opened a rural craft center in Dhaka called Aarong, to promote traditional crafts (through its retail outlet) and to provide support services to disadvantaged artisans (through its design and outreach teams). After working sometime with crafts, we decided that handicrafts would secure a stable market for the producers only if they reflect indigenous design traditions and only if they are diversified over time to appeal to the changing tastes of the customers. Several further steps were needed to ensure these principles were adhered to.

First, we decided to document and catalogue the designs and motifs of indigenous art forms. In so doing, we tried to guard against external influences on these art forms. Our standard for design and form is what

---

*As of December, 1982 the following numbers of women were processing the following types of food:

pickles—9; spices—12; snack foods—9; oil pressing—10.

was done of old in Bangladesh. We visited museums and private collections of traditional art; talked to old masters in various art forms; and researched and catalogued old motifs.

Second, we experimented with adapting the indigenous designs and techniques to new lines of craft. We also experimented with reviving the indigenous forms by ensuring that quality materials, equipment techniques and designs were available and used.

Third, we wanted to strengthen the technologies and productive capacities of disadvantaged artisans. We decided to locate master craftsmen with whom apprentices could be trained. BRAC also started a Textile Design and Service Workshop under the guidance of a foreign industrial designer. The staff of this center were to streamline BRAC's research and documentation of traditional designs and, as importantly, to strengthen the technologies involved in Bangladesh textiles: equipment, weaving, washing and dyeing, stitching, printing, etc. They were to prepare formulas for dyeing, identify wholesale prices of various goods, record all technical and design information. They were to design prototypes of textile goods using traditional motifs and to continue to experiment with the design, lay-outs, color schemes, etc. of textile samples.

Fourth, we needed to stimulate markets for the products based on traditional designs. The primary outlet for the near future would remain Aarong. We decided to hold periodic exhibitions to stimulate public interest. Eventually, we would prepare a catalogue and go into export marketing.

Kantha Revival

Women in Bangladesh have for generations stitched *kantha:* cotton quilts from layers of old pieces of cloth stitched together. *Kanthas* were made in different sizes for different usages: large *kanthas* as bedquilts; smaller *kanthas* to cover or wrap books and valuables. *Kanthas* vary in type according to the particular choice of embroidery stitches and embroidered motifs. The *kantha*-maker draws her motifs from a variety of sources: local fauna and flora; the hearth, the home, and the farm; religion. The beauty of old *kanthas* lies as much in their lay-out and pattern as in their variety of motifs and stitches. Many motifs handed down through generations of women have acquired symbolic meaning.

BRAC decided to revive the rich but dying tradition of *kantha* to the commercial advantage of women in Jamalpur. BRAC began its *kantha* project in mid-1979. Earlier, I had developed a personal interest in the celebrated *nakshi kantha* (embroidered quilts) of Bangladesh and had researched the history and symbolism of the quilts. The areas famous for *kanthas* were not areas BRAC worked in. In early 1979, however, in our search for women's skills we asked a group of women in Jamalpur what their grandmothers and old aunts used to make. They brought *kanthas* to show us. We asked the group of women whether they too stitched *kanthas*. "A little. But not fancy ones," was their answer. Once we knew the women possessed the skill and shared the tradition, we started the *kantha*-revival scheme.

Phase I: Research and Development

We placed our first order in April 1979: for 24 tablemats in imitation of samples we had found in the villages. Meanwhile, we continued my formal research: visiting museum and private collections, reading articles, perusing books for pictures of old quilts, taking photos of various collections. We also initiated an informal research: asking women to bring in *kantha* samples to monthly meetings in Jamalpur. At these meetings, we discussed stitches, motifs, lay-outs shapes and sizes of the *kanthas*. We tried to establish the name, symbolism, and usage of each. We were shown *kanthas* used for purposes we had not previously heard of: for the seat of the wedding palanquin; as runners for an eating place; to cover the Quran; even one to cover a match-box.

The women's excitement and interest grew with each visit. We soon declared Jamalpur a *kantha elaka* ("place of *kanthas*") because so many women were lending and bringing old *kanthas* for us to see and so many women were beginning to produce new *kanthas*. In exchange, we brought photographs or borrowed *kanthas* for them to see.

Several groups of women were engaged in test production. We would choose samples to imitate photographs or village samples. Each month we discussed the quality and cost of materials, the quality of work, the stitching and the motifs of each sample.

Phase II: Production

After testing the market with the samples the women produced, we increased the numbers of women in *kantha*-making. Any group of women who had a majority of members with demonstrated ability and interest in stitching *kanthas* were involved in the program. We continued monthly order-and-deliver sessions in which we exercised quality control and gave new orders. We continued to diversify the range of *kantha* items: with different designs, lay-outs, sizes, and shapes each month.

Once production stepped up, we contracted a woman in Jamalpur to serve as draftswoman and supervisor to *kantha* production. We also hired a part-time draftsman in Dhaka to execute prototype designs from photographs. The major bottleneck to increased production was the transfer of the design from the prototype onto the cloth to be stitched. We experimented with various transfer systems used in embroidery but none were very efficient. We also needed to record and file the designs we had collected in a more systematic way.

Phase III: Exhibition

BRAC had been advised by handicraft experts that it is very important to mobilize the taste and purchasing power of the general public through exhibitions. We decided to hold an exhibition of *kantha* at the Aarong shop in Dhaka. For several months, we gave orders for new lines of *kantha* products (that is, items on which the *kantha* stitch and motifs had been applied); children's clothing, cushion covers; table mats; baby quilts; wall hangings; full-size bedspreads. We prepared special labels for all *kantha* items and a pamphlet describing the *kantha* tradition to be distributed at the exhibition. The exhibition served to stimulate sales and to determine public taste and preference.

Phase IV: Technical Back-up to Production

BRAC contracted a design consultant to develop a Textile Design and Service Workshop. This designer and his staff were able to assist us with various problems faced by the draftsman: enlargement of designs, design transfers onto cloth, recording designs, etc. The part-time draftsman hired earlier was transferred to the workshop to work full-time on recording design originals and transferring designs. The Workshop staff also trained some women to vat dye their embroidery threads in a measure to reduce cost.

There are at present 260 women in Jamalpur stitching *kanthas*.*

---

*As of December 1982.

They are supervised by a specialist staff in Jamalpur. The design and marketing decisions are made in consultation with the women's program staff in Dhaka. The demand for their products is currently higher than their production. The field staff are determined to increase output and efficiency.

Jamdani Revival

The closely woven muslins of Bangladesh are well known in the region. Perhaps the most beautiful muslin are the *jamdani*. The *jamdani* fabrics are distinguishable from other muslin by the figurative geometric patterns which are woven into the fabric during the actual weaving. The history of muslin and *jamdani* weaving goes back to the 5th century A.D. The weaving reached a peak of excellence with the Moghuls. The area around Dhaka was noted for the cultivation of a very fine variety of cotton. Its weavers were highly skilled. The result was an extremely delicate fabric.

But the standard of excellence has dropped over the last several centuries. After the British arrived in the area, cotton cultivation dropped off. More recently, the patronage of high quality *jamdani* has decreased. With this lack of demand for high quality saris, the variety and intricacy of motifs has deteriorated to some extent.

BRAC decided to undertake a scheme to revive the *jamdani*. One step was to recreate a taste and demand for fine quality *jamdani* saris and to lobby that fine threads and good quality dyes be made available. Another step was to research the old designs and to reintroduce them to the weavers. A third step, the one that directly affected the women BRAC has organized, was to use the *jamdani* motifs on new lines of products: block-printed saris and embroidered garments and woolen rugs. This application of *jamdani* motifs would serve to revive a national art form but also to develop another line of craft production for women.

The *jamdani* scheme began in late 1979. Motifs were collected and documented. An old master weaver was commissioned to supervise the weaving of two sample saris; each sari contains different border and body motifs every six inches. The names and descriptions of these motifs have been recorded. A limited amount of fine thread was imported to demonstrate the potential for reviving the finer quality saris. And several women's groups in Manikganj have been engaged in fine quality embroidery of *jamdani* motifs onto cotton and silk garments.

And a set of *jamdani* blocks were made to add to the collection of traditional designs used by BRAC-organized block-printers.

A *jamdani* exhibition was held in early 1981. A wide range of *jamdani*—inspired items were displayed: hand-woven saris (the original form) plus woolen rugs, garments, block-printed saris and linens, stationery and greeting cards, leather goods, jewelry, and fibre-glass products. The exhibition proved very successful and helped generate a demand for handcrafted items with *jamdani* motifs and for high-quality *jamdani* saris.

3. Silk Culture

Since the mid-1970s in Bangladesh, the government's silk board and several voluntary agencies have looked into the potential of different types of silk culture to generate a natural fibre for the nation's handloom sector and to generate an income for village women. Having learned about the feasibility, cost-benefits, and requirements of silk culture from the staff of the government's silk farms and of other voluntary agencies, BRAC embarked on its silk culture program in mid-1977.

Phase I: Research and Training

Initially, BRAC put an emphasis on ericulture; the cultivation of a variety of silk worm which feeds off castor bush leaves and spins a variety of silk known locally as *endi*. *Endi* silk was reputed to be seven times as strong as cotton and less expensive than mulberry silk and to involve a labor intensive technology (hand-spinning) rather than a capital intensive technology (machine-reeling). Ericulture promised to provide a steady income with a limited investment.

—little capital
    $6.33 for a spinning wheel
    $5.00 for racks and other implements
—little training: the skills required in cultivation, rearing, and spinning of *endi* silk transfer more quickly and easily than with mulberry silk

After we had researched and planned the scheme, three women (two from Jamalpur and one from Manikganj) were sent to train as trainers (in silk worm rearing and silk thread spinning) with another voluntary agency.

Phase II: Experimental Production

The three trainers trained five women each. Test production was initiated: the cultivation and rearing of silk was carried out in one village and the spinning in another. Certain problems were encountered early on: the need for steady supplies of castor leaves and *endi* eggs; the diseases of the cocoons; and the low price for spun thread.

In consultation with a dedicated government officer who offered his assistance, we planned our silk culture program. The elements of the program were:

—home-based cultivation, rearing, and spinning of silk
—service centers to supply training, input (eggs, cocoons, seeds) and to purchase finished products
—a weaving factor, to weave, dye and finish (e.g. block-print, embroider, stitch) silk fabrics.

Phase III: Further Training and Production

BRAC arranged trainings at the government's silk farms for three levels of personnel. Successive batches of village women were trained in silk cultivation, rearing, and spinning. The trainers were given further training (in disease control, castor and mulberry cultivation) and were upgraded to work as full-time paratechnicians. The field staff responsible for developing BRAC's silk industry were given a two-week orientation at a government silk farm on the stages of production; technical and support systems; pricing and marketing.

Phase IV: Production, Management and Extension Systems

After our trial phase of silk culture, we developed new systems of production, management, and extension. In so doing, three critical decisions were taken.

First, all stages of production should be undertaken by each woman to ensure her sufficient income and incentive: from cultivation of the plants and rearing of cocoons to spinning of thread. Spinning is relatively simple and the most attractive stage of operation in terms of return to labor. There is very little profit in rearing in and of itself. It would be dangerous to train some women as spinners and others as rearers. The spinners would do well and prove reluctant to rear. The rearers would do poorly and want to give up rearing for spinning.

Second, only worms, not eggs, should be supplied to the women for rearing. Supplying worms reduces the extra care required for young worms, the time necessary for rearing worms, the demand for leaves in the villages, and ensures only quality worms are reared (since diseased or small worms could be weeded out at BRAC's Service Center).

Third, BRAC's Service Centers should supply all worms and seeds/seedlings and serve as collection depots on set days of each week: to purchase spun thread. The BRAC policy is that each woman must deliver her own thread; that a small amount is to be deducted each week from individual incomes to pay for spinning wheels purchased on loan; and that no woman is allowed to sell less than 20 hanks of thread at one time. The district government nursery supplies BRAC the "parent-stock" of eggs, seeds/seedlings; expert back-up; and a market for the silk thread. BRAC purchases damaged thread or low-quality thread at a low price for experimental weaving.

Phase V: Expanded Production and Associated Problems

The number of women involved and their output increased significantly. The village of Chander Char, by way of example, reported the following: seven women started ericulture in November, 1978; within two months, two of these women had purchased spinning wheels and produced 30 hanks each that month; five months later, all seven women were operating their own spinning wheels and produced 100 hanks each that month.

The senior field staff of the Manikganj project describes an unplanned impetus the silk program received:

In April, 1979, a young woman named Jahanara who had been earning 20 taka per month fetching water for rich households, decided to try her hand at silk spinning and rearing. Each week she brought her hanks to be counted for her payment. She knew how to spin. She knew that the thread had to be wrapped around a frame 210 times to make one hank- (there are 210 yards in a hank). But instead of counting the four sides of the frame as one yard, Jahanara counted each side of the frame as one yard. On the day the women deliver their hanks of thread, Jahanara had the most: 110 hanks. She was paid 110 takas for one week's work. Everyone was surprised and her hanks were remeasured. She had actually spun 28 hanks and had to return some of the money. Rather than becoming dismayed, the women took heart. Somehow the impossible seemed possible. The women felt that if they worked harder they could possibly earn 110 taka a week. Somehow Jahanara's mistake launched the program. And Jahanara knew that even 28 taka per week for spinning thread is far better than 20 taka a month for fetching water.

The real bottleneck to production was the volume of leaves available to feed the silk worm. One informal BRAC study showed that the women and the spinning wheels were being used only to 40% capacity. BRAC staff were further trained in tree cultivation, pruning trees, and controlling for pests. BRAC experimented with intercropping and spacing the plants at its own nursery.

And, that same year, an unseasonal drought threatened the silk industry throughout Bangladesh. High temperatures and low humidity killed off most of the worms throughout the country. Fortunately, one or two government farms had reserve supplies of frozen eggs. The various voluntary agencies involved in silk culture scrambled for a small supply of parent stock. The damage was shortlived but taught everyone the value of planning ahead for such eventualities.

Phase VI: Diversification

Given its progress in ericulture, BRAC decided to branch into the cultivation and rearing of mulberry silk. BRAC's Service Center and paratechnicians were now equipped to provide the greater care required by both the mulberry plant and worm. BRAC began to weave silk cloth engaging poor traditional male weavers. The first batch of *endi* silk-and-cotton cloth was woven in June, 1979. The cost needed to be brought down and dyeing, printing, and finishing of the woven fabric needed to be improved but BRAC was hopeful of expanding the market for silk producers through woven fabrics.

Phase VII: Increased Production and Forward Planning

BRAC needs to learn more about weaving. The flat weaving typical of Bangladesh needs to be diversified with varying techniques and effects. Silk weaving could be diversified with varied techniques of twisting the threads and weaving, dyeing, and finishing the fabric. Block-printing and hand-embroidery of the fabric have been introduced.

BRAC has found that castor tree cultivation, *endi* silk rearing and spinning can provide a supplemental income to poor women who engage in silk spinning in and around other activities or a primary income ($6.33 per month) to women who engage in silk spinning for eight hours a day. BRAC believes that ericulture has the potential of large-scale employment for many women. It can provide a year-round income despite the seasonality of the plant and the women. The outstanding problems are: adequate supply of leaves; disease control; and improved weaving techniques.

One further point. It should be noted that the collective aspect of silk culture does not center around production, which is carried out in individual huts, but around training, credit, supply-and-delivery, all of which take place on specified "silk" days at the Service Centers.*

4. *Agriculture*

In Bangladesh, agricultural field operations are the single largest employer of rural labor. Traditionally, only men (not women) engage in and are employed in field operations. BRAC decided to train women in agricultural field work so that the women would not only earn an income but also gain access to the rural labor market. If women were to be seen working in the fields, they might then be hired by others as agricultural laborers. If not, women's need for wage work would continue to go unrecognized.

BRAC decided to support groups of women who wish to lease or sharecrop land to cultivate their own crops. BRAC was prepared to help them plan and manage their cultivation and to provide loans for the inputs required. During some bad years (after a drought or flood) BRAC is also prepared to subsidize (with wheat payments) such agricultural schemes. During those years, group members get a double benefit: wheat as wages during cultivation and income from the crop at harvest.

What are the necessary steps in agricultural schemes? How have the

---

*As of December, 1982, over eight hundred women were rearing and spinning castor silk and another fifty mulberry silk.

women undertaken these steps? How have the women acquired the requisite "male" skills?

- —land leasing or sharecropping. With BRAC loans and advice, women lease or sharecrop land. Initially, the women were not good judges of what quality or quantity of land to negotiate for. Now, the women have gained this expertise.
- —land preparation and ploughing. Women have not undertaken ploughing but contract men (on a daily wage basis) to perform this function.
- —cultivation. Previously, women did not have the skills of trans-planting/planting, weeding, etc. Initially, the women contracted men to work alongside them and to train them in these operations. Within the first season, the women acquire the necessary skills.
- —harvesting: As with cultivation, the women have had to acquire the skills and have been able to do so with relative ease.
- —marketing: The markets remain the one corner of the male domain that women have not yet penetrated. Currently, women market their produce either through male members of their family, BRAC field staff, or a middleman. Some groups have been cheated by the middleman and have had to learn to negotiate adequate terms and prices.

We found that women effectively acquired the requisite skills in a single agricultural season through informal training (that is, hiring male laborers as their trainers).

I described the cases of different groups of women engaged in agriculture in several BRAC newsletters:

Pachbarol Village, Manikganj

The women leased two acres of land, cultivating potatoes on one acre and sugarcane on the other. They paid for the seeds and fertilizer from their savings. In the mornings, they worked as before at odd jobs and rice processing. In the afternoon, the group leader explains, "We worked until dusk in our fields. We built small boundary walls around our fields. We sowed and weeded and harvested. We employed two men to do the plough work." They invested 900 taka ($60) of an additional BRAC loan to purchase 25 *kodals* (spades) for the upcoming food-for-work season. They spent 475 taka ($32) on a calf for their cooperative. The rest they kept as savings.

When the food-for-work season came, they worked at food-for-work in the morning and in their own fields in the afternoon. Saleha adds, "Last year we had to rent *kodals* at 50 paisha per day. This year we own *kodals*. We use 10 *kodals* in our own gang. The other fifteen we rent to other gangs." After the food-for-work season, the Pachbarol women hired themselves out as day laborers to harvest pulses. They also harvested their own potato crop: 8 maunds of potato which sold at 50 taka ($3.33) per maund. Their sugarcane crop will be harvested after the rains.

Kashipur Village, Sulla

Indramati Das, Secretary of the Kashipur Women's Group reports proudly: "Our demonstration plot is a shining example of the fact that women themselves can cultivate high yielding varieties of rice." In 1975, ten members of the group attended BRAC's functional education in their village. During the winter season 1976, they cultivated wheat and sweet potato on half an acre of *khas* (public) land. During the rainy season 1976, BRAC supplied them 25 pounds of nylon-twine at cost price. They made 15 nets which they sold for 600 taka ($40).

Although their profit had been marginal, the group's confidence and cohesiveness had grown. They decided to rent two acres of land during the 1976–77 winter season. They rented land for 1,500 taka ($100) from a private owner. They invested another 50 taka ($33) in seeds and fertilizer. BRAC gave them a loan of 2,000 taka ($133) for the inputs and 500 ($33) for food during the period of cultivation. They planted and cultivated IRRI 8 in the two acres. Despite the early rains, because their land was relatively protected, the women have harvested 100 maunds of paddy. The paddy should sell at 50 taka ($3.33) per maund (perhaps higher this year because of the extensive crop damage). The Society should realise a net profit of 3,500 taka ($233).

Patrail Village, Manikganj

A group of twenty women in Patrail village decided to cultivate paddy on one acre of leased land. As the women had not grown any seedlings, they were forced to purchase seedlings from a village two miles from Patrail. And as they had never done field work before, the women contracted a landless male group from their village to plough the land and to teach them how to transplant the paddy. All went according to plan through the first day of transplanting.

But on the second day, as the women left Patrail to gather more seedlings for transplanting, they were stopped by some elders from a neighboring village who demanded: "Why are you women working in the fields? Don't you know that to do so is against Islam?" The women answered with a simple, compelling logic: "We need to earn money. We have worked before at construction sites cutting earth. You did not object them. What is so different about working in the fields?"

The debate grew stronger. A crowd quickly gathered including a number of landless men from BRAC-organized groups. The elders began to question the type of food-for-work schemes financed by BRAC. Some of the landless men answered back: "Whoever said wheat is for roads and canals? Wheat is for the poor. Roads and canals benefit you, not us." At this point, numbers if not logic prevailed, and the elders quieted down. With this backing by the landless male groups of the area, the women of Patrail completed their transplanting. . . .*

In this chapter I have discussed in some detail selected small-scale industries that we developed to employ large numbers of women and selected measures we took to enhance women's traditional productive work. BRAC's experience has significant implications for those who wish to design programs to increase the incomes of rural women. I discuss these implications in chapter eight.

But before analyzing the lessons from and implications of BRAC's programs for women, I would like to return to the women for whom the program was intended. What has been the impact of BRAC's economic and social programming on the women, on the organized groups to which they now belong? What has begun to happen in their lives and in their villages?

---

*During 1982, nearly two hundred women engaged in agriculture. In addition to those discussed here, BRAC has undertaken the following schemes to expand women's employment: block-printing, cigarette-rolling, weaving, embroidery, crochet and lace.

CHAPTER SIX
What Begins to Happen

"But what," visitors ask BRAC's field staff, "begins to happen to the women? What has changed in the lives of the women?" We had some concrete answers for the visitors to BRAC. We told them many women now earn steady incomes. We described visible changes in the homes and homesteads of women. Some homesteads have been cleared and cultivated. Huts, porches, sheds, tin roofs have been added to many homes. Most women own more hens, goats, or even cows. Many women have lost their veneer of shyness to become assertive and outgoing. In the words of the field staff, some of the women are "sophisticated 100 times."

"How can we predict," BRAC field staff ask themselves, "which groups of women will prove weak and which strong? Why does one group work well together, another fall apart? What are the signs and causes of relative strength and weakness?" We had only tentative answers for ourselves. We recognized certain signs of weakness and strength. Some groups meet less regularly than others. Some groups resolve conflicts more easily than others. In some groups, the women's interest and participation is high. In other groups, the women's interest and participation has slackened off. But we needed to understand impact and change from the perspective of the women themselves.

BRAC's Executive Director and I discussed the possibility of a research-cum-training exercise designed to acquire a fuller and more systematic understanding of the impact of group participation on women. Selected field staff and I would design and conduct the research plus process and analyze our findings.*

Rather than try to measure or to prejudge the impact of BRAC's women's programs, we chose to let the women speak for themselves—to tell us what had begun to happen in their lives. Our first hunch was that the impact the women would describe would not be subject to precise measurement. Our second hunch was that the impact they would describe could not be easily judged or observed by outsiders, even the BRAC field staff. And so we wanted the women to talk freely rather than answer questions. We conducted six sets of open-ended interviews—each set included one group interview and four individual interviews.

The group interviews were conducted where the weekly group meetings were held—on mats in an open courtyard at the end of the day. Our presence at the weekly meeting caused relatively little stir. Each group was asked to narrate the history of the group. We posed an initial set of broad questions: Please tell us about your group. When, how, and by whom was it formed? What activities have you undertaken? What expectations did you have when you joined the group? What are the benefits and the risks in being a member of the group?

The individual interviews were conducted inside a BRAC office building—modest structures to which the women regularly come for trainings and workshops. Tea and biscuits were served. We sat cross-legged on wooden beds. The women knew us. We were all comfortable. We asked each woman to narrate the main events of her life—childhood, marriage, motherhood. We asked each woman to describe her involvement with BRAC's programs and any changes in her life

---

*The following steps were planned and taken:
  preliminary discussion on research design
  preparation by field staff of short case-studies of 12 groups (6 weak and 6 strong)
  workshops with field staff to discuss these preliminary case-studies
  selection of groups for in-depth interviews
    three strong groups
    three weak groups
  selection of four members from each group for in-depth interviews, to include:
    1 leader
    1 "blocker"
    1 "patroness" (more on these personalities below)
    1 general member
  conducting and taping 30 in-depth (2 hours each) interviews
  workshops with field staff to analyze findings

given this involvement. And we posed an initial set of broad questions: Please tell us about your father. What did he do? Did he own land? What was your childhood like? How does your life differ from that of your mother's? When did you get married? At what age? To whom? When did you join the group? What were your expectations? What benefits have you received? What problems have you faced?

After asking the initial questions, we let the women talk. Some—the freer ones, the born story-tellers—needed little prompting. Others— the more hesitant ones or the tricky and clever ones—needed some prompting with additional or more specific questions. The field staff brought to each interview a great deal of prior knowledge and familiarity with the women. They were able to catch omissions and/or distortions. They were able to frame specific questions if necessary: Please tell us about such-and-such incident. But isn't x related to y? But, earlier, you told me. . .

We heard the women's words and listened for patterns. Patterns over time—the process of belonging to and developing a group. Patterns between women—the impact felt by many women in many villages. I will present below an amalgam of individual voices. Included are those voices which to me best reflect the views held by many women, what we heard repeated again and again. In the interest of brevity, I have shortened or combined certain voices. In the interest of understanding the processes involved and the impact experienced, I will present the individual voices within a framework (by headings) and with a commentary (as necessary).

CHANGES IN THE GROUPS

We began each set of interviews with a group interview as we wanted to hear what the women had to say about the various stages of group formation and development. We knew from our experience as organizers that methods-in-practice are often quite different from methods-in-theory. We had developed our own perspective but wanted to hear the women's perspective on BRAC's methods of organizing.*

---

*In chapter four I outlined BRAC's methods of organization. In this chapter I will present these methods in practice from the perspective of women from both strong and weak groups.

Preliminary Discussions

Most groups recalled the preliminary discussion on functional education.

= The first day she came and told us: "You all study. I will supply books. You all will observe many things in the books. At first, she discussed all this. She also told us to gather together and she would come to talk with us. She told us about (functional) education. She also asked: "Whatever I have said, do you all agree to this?" We all agreed to read and see what there is in it.

We asked them what expectations they had about being educated.

—What was desired and what discussions took place?
= We are poor. We have no sound intelligence. If we study, our intelligence will develop. We will be able to read and write. Our income will increase. We will no longer simply render a thumbprint.
—Did you join only for that purpose or to get a loan?
= Both! We are poor.
—What was the main reason you joined?
= I thought, "We have no shelter. During the rainy season, rain falls through our roofs. If we increase our income, we could build a house."
= There are so many ways to increase income.
= If any type of relief comes, we can get that. If we face any trouble, we have no place to appeal for justice. We will get the scope to appeal and get justice.
—Did you understand that you will appeal and get justice before you formed the group?
= It could be.
—Did you think so?
= Yes, certainly.
= Because our teacher teaches us, she may be called by someone for judgement. For this reason we have come to study.
—Why did you study?
= We are poor. Our children can't go to school. If they can go, they wear rags. Then others say: "The children of beggars have come." Then we joined with them in thinking that if we can acquire the knowledge and intelligence and be able to get better food and clothing, the group will give money and increase our income and development. We will get better food and clothing.

Other groups recalled a preliminary discussion on forming a group.

= She came to the village and told us to form a group. She went house to house. She asked us all: "Will you form a group? If you form a group it will be good for you. If you form a group, you will have peace and happiness." Some said they will form a group, some said they will not form a group. Some asked: "What is the benefit of forming a group?" It is human nature to want to understand the situation. She told us that if we formed a group it would be good for us: "You all are passing hard days." In this way she made us understand the benefits of the group. Ten of us women got together and formed the group. After that, the membership has increased. We learned how to read and write and acquired knowledge. We were landless, the ten members. We saved four anna* and eight anna and saw the light of progress. We took a loan, reared poultry, grew vegetables. Before we did not do all these and did not understand profit and loss.

Two members of a weak group—one an earth-digging gang leader, the other an intermediary chosen by BRAC—remembered the beginnings of their group in slightly different ways. Neither recalled any preliminary discussion with general members of the group.

The Gang Leader—He (BRAC staff) told us: "You should take functional education classes and, at the same time, go ahead with your earth-cutting work." He instructed us in this manner. So, at one time, we used to attend education classes and at another time we used to cut earth.

The Intermediary—He (the same BRAC staff) made us understand the importance of education. He told us in this way: "You receive education, form a group, and you will be able to go for development." He told me to select a volunteer teacher for (functional) education.

Functional Education

In most groups, the first activity is functional education. And for most women, the classes are the first time they have sat together to discuss and analyze their environment. They begin to look at themselves, each other, and that environment in a new way. One woman described the impact BRAC's functional education and health education posters had on her.

= We all studied together and learnt as follows: how to rear poultry, how to recognize a T.B. patient. When I looked at that picture I immediately said that he (the T.B. patient) is like Shamsur's father (literally, her son's father; idiomatically, her husband). Others used to laugh, hearing that. I

---

*In the old currency, there were sixteen annas to a rupee. In the current currency, there are 100 poisa to a taka. Many people still think in terms of anna instead of poisa and still divide the rupee/taka into 16 rather than 100 parts.

told them that I spoke correctly. He is a man suffering from cough and my husband is also suffering from cough. Both have the same condition. I also saw the picture of a man who has gone to the market and is standing there with a look of disappointment as the price of commodities is very high. He has got many children and he has not got enough money to buy things. I also told others, showing them this picture, that this man is like Shamsur's father thinking of his children. Others laughed. Looking at a picture of children sitting with empty plates, I used to say that they were like my children. When my children cry saying that their mother should give them food, I think of cutting my flesh and giving it to them to eat. If it was not painful, I would have done so. There is another picture of a pregnant mother who has four children, no rice in the cooking pot, children crying with empty plates in their hand. The mother is also crying because she is not able to give them food to eat. After that, whatever lessons came, we read all those. I used to sit alone and think of those pictures, that all those pictures show our condition. Some of the women said: "What rubbish pictures. Why are you studying in your old age?" After that we have formed the group. To make the group, we had to face a lot of difficulties and bear a lot of ill-talk from others.

The weak group got off to a bad start. The BRAC-chosen intermediary was threatened by the literacy and status of the volunteer teacher. "She did not like me. I have my prestige. She rebuked me. I did not say anything and rushed to my husband and told him about this. I told him: "You go and manage her." Two volunteer teachers were tried but neither proved acceptable to the group. After some time, functional education was dropped but the group was formed nonetheless.

Group Formation

Typically, towards the end of the functional education classes the women discuss the possibility of forming a group. Most women recognize the benefits of interaction and the strength of numbers.

= If a tree is cut down it is difficult for one man to carry. But if ten of us help then it is quicker and less laborious for men to carry. We came to understand all this, the value of joint labor. Then we proposed that we would form a group and would see that work can be completed by two or more persons working together and not by one alone.

= I alone will not be able to do so. There is a proverb: "A group can do easily what an individual finds difficult to do." If all of us agree, we can do it, definitely.

= We discussed how it is difficult to do work alone. They show us how 10 or 12 men get together to do work or build a table. Then the women thought that we should also get together and work. After a few days we came to know that no one can do ten persons' work alone. Then we thought that if we formed a group it could be good.

Typically, the groups start by pooling their savings to develop a group fund and by discussing plans of how to invest the group fund:

= We formed the group two years ago. During those two years, I deposited nearly 60 taka. Then we decided to invest the money in the purchase of cows. We earned a profit from the cow-rearing program.

However, the weak group did not develop a group fund through mutual savings. They had not learned the benefits of interaction during the functional education phase. They took a loan from BRAC which they did not use for a joint purpose but divided into individual loans:

= See, first time we took a loan from BRAC—100 taka per woman. There was a quarrel because everybody did not repay the loan in time. But there was no quarrel with me because I made a business and repaid the loan by giving 2 taka per week.

= We made our group in the month of Badra. We were told about development. And we bought a cow. Right from that time we have been jobless. Nobody tells us anything. Everybody was supposed to give one taka as a monthly subscription. But nobody gives.

Economic Action

Functional education—group formation—savings—group fund—BRAC loan—joint activity—profit—profit sharing: this is the BRAC scheme-in-theory. Very few groups run as smoothly as theory would have it, but most groups follow roughly this scheme.

= We collected 1350 taka. Everyone deposited 25 taka. We bought two calves. At first we lost some taka because we lost one cow. After that, the other calf died. But, after some time, we made some profit. Then, everyone started taking loans. Everyone said: "Previously, we bought a big cow. But now, we will buy a small cow. Then, we took a loan of taka 5000 from the office. With that money, some people took loans to start paddy-processing, saying that paddy-processing would be more profitable. We did not buy a cow. 1800 taka was disbursed for paddy-processing. We also bought four calves with the balance of the taka. We had already bought three calves from the group's taka, we had already distributed those three calves. Afterwards, we distributed another four calves which were purchased out of the office loan. We are fourteen members in the group. Six members took money to start paddy-processing. Those who are not doing paddy-processing, they have not made much profit. We have not sold the cows as yet. Now the price of cows has gone down. We have paid off the loan for paddy. We have paid back 1940 taka to the office. The balance of about 3000 taka is still with us.

The weak group was unable to follow the typical pattern because of its internal conflicts. A very young and poor general member of that group describes the problem.

= See, first time we took a loan from BRAC—100 taka per woman. There was a quarrel because everybody did not repay the loan in time. But there was no quarrel with me because I made a business and repaid the loan by giving taka 2 every week. But I repaid the loan. Then I heard BRAC had some work for us. Work came. We sent our guardians to BRAC to find out. They told us the work had come. We went to Alinagor to cut earth. We started work and used to get wheat after 4 days at work. We used to save half a seer of wheat. Then we were told to sell the wheat. But nobody in our group could pay for the wheat. So we sold the wheat to some other person. And with that money we bought a cow and gave it to a Hindu woman for rearing. Before that there was a lottery as to who would keep the cow. But we had to work at cooking, so we could not attend that meeting. We heard that she (the gang leader) won the cow in the lottery. There was a problem regarding the rearing of cow. Some said they would rear, others said they would. So the lottery was arranged. She said: "I will not give the cow for rearing to Dalu's house." We said "We will not give the cow to you for rearing." Then she said she would take the cow by force. But everybody decided to give it to the Hindu woman. We could buy cocks, ducks, etc., to rear and we could earn a profit for our development. Is it not so? If we could buy one duck, we could earn a handsome amount of money. Now 4 eggs cost 4 taka. In this way we could increase our fund and could buy one more chicken. Now, what kind of earnings do we get? She holds the money.

Finances

The financial aspects of the groups elicited more comments than the leadership issue. Most groups start as a small savings group.

= BRAC staff told the volunteer teacher and she told us to save a handful of rice and at one time we would sell this rice. The value which we would get after selling the rice we would deposit together. With this money we would be able to purchase something—even a cow. We thought in this way: "We will save a handful of rice. It will not be harmful to us." We had no mat for sitting. Each of us prepared a piece of mat.

Almost all the women saw the immediate advantage in having some place to deposit small amounts of saving. At issue was not the security of their savings but the simple fact of removing small amounts from the daily kitty to preclude their being spent: "We were hard up. If we were able to accumulate 5 takas, the next moment we were forced to spend it." The women soon recognized that small amounts of individual savings added together become an investible amount: "If we collect money from every member, then it becomes 1000 taka."

Each group member must purchase a share worth ten taka per year and is encouraged to save a minimum of half a taka per week. The accumulated savings and shares constitute the group fund. BRAC staff assist in the maintenance and recording of these funds, although the actual records are filled out and kept by a member of the group. These funds are used as a rotating fund to finance either: 1) small loans to individual members, who otherwise are forced to take loans from money-lenders at exorbitant rates of interest; or 2) group capital for small-scale joint income-generating activities. BRAC extends loans for larger-scale income-generation activities upon submission and approval of a production plan by the group.

Even a small group fund can be converted into a revolving loan fund for the group members:

=At first, the volunteer teacher brought money and deposited it with me. Then she told me that I should deposit money as well. So I started depositing money. Then every month they brought money and deposited it with me. They deposited. I deposited. Like this, we saved about 700 to 800 taka. Then we began to take this money as a loan according to our need. Some of us borrow money for medical treatment. Some borrow for expenses at home. We each then return this money.

The group funds can also be invested:

=We bought two goats and nine hens with this money. The balance of this money is in the office. We could not buy so many things with one person's money. We were hard up. If we save 5 takas the next day we must spend that. Moreover, we have educated ourselves. We have become wise. Before we could not count if we spent a loan given by others.

Procedures

No set rule for profit-sharing exists. Each group works out its own procedures in this regard. Sometimes the rules are changed midstream which leads to confusion and tension within the group:

> = In our group it was decided that one taka interest will be realized against 100 taka of loan per month. I agreed. Suddenly one cow died. Then, another cow. It had been established we would take half a share of the profit from cow-rearing. I did not agree with this opinion. Some of the group members were of that opinion and they convinced me. Then, I was agreed.
>
> —Why did you not want to give your own opinion?
>
> = At first, it was decided the interest would be realized. Then, the decision was changed. The decision was taken that half of the profit from cow-rearing would be realized. Given this decision, I would incur a loss. That's why I did not agree.
>
> —Why would you incur a loss?
>
> = If interest is collected against the loan each month, then we will get a good profit. But to share half of the profit does not give a good profit. For example, if I take a cow from the group at the rate of 500 taka after a while when I sell this cow for 1000 taka I have to submit 500 taka for the loan and the rest of the selling price will be divided equally. One portion will be deposited in the group fund. And the other portion will be taken by me. If 250 taka is the profit, 125 taka will be deposited in the group fund.
>
> —But the group fund is yours, why do you not want to deposit the money?
>
> = I did not understand. Everybody convinced me and then I agreed.

The method of profit-sharing consented to by this woman seems to work best. Another group discusses the same system:

> = For example, if we buy a cow for 500 taka, after rearing, its selling price will be 1000 taka. Then, the group will get 250 taka and the cow rearer will get 250. If the cow dies, the loss will be borne by the group.
>
> —What if the cow rearer does not take good care of the cow?
>
> = If so, then the cow will be taken back.
>
> —If anyone of your group will not take care of the cow, then will you be able to take it back?
>
> = Of course. Why not?

We discussed this system of profit-sharing with the leader of a strong group.

= We have purchased 14 cows.

—How many members are there in your group?

= We have 30 in the group. We will not distribute cows to everybody. Some have no house. Some have no grass and some have no capacity to rear a cow. We will not distribute a cow to them.

—When you distribute cows, then you call a meeting. At the meeting, do you discuss the cow distribution, who should get or who should not?

= Yes. We discuss it like this in the meeting. Every member can understand who is suitable to rear a cow and who is not. I ask every member whether the person I have chosen is suitable or not. If every member gives her consent, then I do that.

—You discuss the problem with every member, do you not?

= Yes.

—Is there not such a person who is able to rear a cow, but due to shortage of cows, it will not be possible to give her a cow? Then doesn't she mind?

= No. She never minds this. She says, "You rear the cow. When these increase, then we rear it."

—You are 25–30 members in the group. But the number of cows is only 14 and only 14 members rear it. Then every member of the group can imagine that these cows belong to the group. You have part of these although you do not rear it?

= Yes. They can imagine it. They can imagine, but they did not look after the cow. We, or minimum members look after the cows. Somebody rearing cows thinks that without rearing, they are getting a portion of profit. So they benefit.

—If one cow is lost, then all the loss is absorbed by the group, is it not?

= Of course.

—Some take care of cows and some do not. You don't discuss these problems?

= Yes. It takes place in our discussion. One of our members said that she did not know about our cow purchasing. Then I told her: "Your neighbor is rearing a cow, how is it that you don't know?"

When the group decides to pool its labor as well as share the profit, procedures become even more difficult to establish.

= Rehnana's mother does not work equally with us. But she gets an equal share of the profit. We give them equal shares to avoid quarrels and cliques. We have to tolerate them. If we quarrel we will not gain. If we quarrel, still we have to see them.

—Those who do not work equally with you, why do you not expel them from the group?

= If we expel them, they will accuse us of excluding them and then they will quarrel with us.

—You are afraid of expelling those who are not working?

= We do not expel them simply because we want to avoid a quarrel. It does not matter that we work a little more than they do.

—You are afraid?

= Yes, because to do so might create cliques, etc. They might say: "We are expelled, but others are still there."

= Many members don't come on time. One says: "I cannot go in the morning." Another says: "I cannot go." Some come, some may not come. Sometimes all of us come to work.

Another woman in another group is less afraid of a quarrel:

= The volunteer teacher and myself work on the (vegetable) plot. She does not come to join us. Whatever we are going to earn from the plot the two of us will not be sharing only. All of us will be sharing. So, all of us should work.

BRAC field staff are often called in to arbitrate when rules have not been established or conflicts are not resolved. Eventually, the groups should work out such "quarrels."

I would not agree to that because many times she did not work but paid for her share of work. Then, all the members of the group said: "We shall not accept that. You will not work but pay for your share, that is not right. We are 14 members, we could collect 1 taka each and hire labor, but that is not the way to work for the group. You will have to work yourself." This is how we argue among ourselves.

Sometimes one or two members of a group will consistently refuse to work.

= Sometimes, some members go first and others join later. There are a few members who try to avoid work. Like Karimon. When we went to catch fish in the pond, for example, some did not come. I think the likely reason is that they are ashamed of having to work. She comes very seldom. We do not know the reason. When we ask, she says: "I have many things to do at home. You have no work at your home, so you go."

= Most of the days she has some excuse. For example: "Today my son-in-law has come, is it possible for me to leave him home and come to work?" But we told her to come to work and we would release her early. Then her son-in-law said: "Amma, you go to work." Then she came. She always has this kind of difficulty.

We began to call these members the "blockers." We wanted to understand why they consistently refuse to work, why they more than others seemed to be "ashamed of having to work." We interviewed one "blocker" from each group. We tried to find out why they and not others could hold onto notions of dignity and shame. We had to probe with very specific, fairly relentless, questioning. And we found our answers. The "blockers" proved to be either women who in their own childhoods were better off than they are now or women who even now have influential patrons or relatives in their village of residence.

Social Action

Most women described the affection that develops between the members of a group:

= We have good feelings between us. Our love and affection for one another is stronger than our love for our children.

= I love the group members like my own children. I cannot stay alone without seeing them. If I do not find time during the day then I go to see them at night.

Very often, this affection translates into small gestures of helping and sharing between members of the group. Occasionally, this affection translates into significant gestures of helping the poor and needy outside the group:

= In the last storm an old woman lost her house. Then, we all helped her to rebuild her house. She is from our village, but not a member of the group. She is poor and has no ability to work. Nothing to eat. We still have something to eat. She cannot work and has no children. If we do not help her, then who will help her? The rich will not help. The poor can feel for the poor. The rich never help the poor, they do not even talk to the poor.

= It is our hope that we can build houses for those who have no house, we can give food to those who have no food, we can give medicine and treatment to those who suffer from disease. For these types of betterment, we are in the group and we will try to develop our mentality. In the meantime, we have done such work as repairing three houses of outsiders (i.e., outside the group) with 350 taka. Then, they joined the group.

These social actions are motivated by and reinforce a growing identity between poor women. One group classified its members by a very
simple, compelling criterion: those from households which cooked a
meal the previous day and those households which did not. The group
decided that the women from those households which did not cook the
previous day were to be given the first opportunities for paid labor on
that day.

Most women spoke of themselves as the poor:

= I am poor. I will mix with the poor. All my relations are rich but they
do not come to my help. The poor understand my difficulties. All my
sisters are rich and I am poor. I do not go to their house. They tease me
saying that my husband is a laborer—a rickshaw-puller. I feel hurt. I also
said that I will not go to their homes until I become like them. I would
like to make good together with the group members. I do not want to
become rich alone.

—You have two groups now. Will it help you in any way if you make
more groups?
= We are not going to become rich alone. We will take them with us.
—What is their family condition?
= Like us.
—Those who are well off, will you take them in the group?
= No. Have they inquired about us when we were in difficulty? If we
call them, they will not come. We will not take them. The rich do not
mix with the poor. The poor mix with the poor. The two groups have
gained so much strength. Three groups will gain even more strength.
—If there were four groups in this village do you think the rich would be
able to fight with you all?
= We would beat them.
—What have you all gotten out of the group?
= We have gotten wisdom, money, strength. If our children were quar-
reling with the children of the rich, then they said: "Catch and bring
them. Bring them out of their house." Now they would not be able to say
so. All the group girls will go and fight.

Some members of weak groups do not share this identity with other
poor.

= If we help outsiders then we will not be able to live well with our
children. Has anybody helped us?
—Why do you have no unity?
= How can unity be achieved? Everybody is busy with themselves.
Everybody thinks of their own belly.

Group Development

Membership—

Over time both BRAC and the women recognized the problems in "mixed" membership, in mixing women with different obligations and interests in one group. Not only do rich women not mix well with poor women, but women of different "shades" of poverty do not always mix well one with another. BRAC's target group includes the marginal and poor women. Initially, we did not know what they thought of each other or whether they should be joined in one group.

There are the poor women, who dig earth. Women who, in the words of others, "have to work daily. They are earth-digging women. They collect paddy from the field. After returning home, they cook and feed. They cannot come to read." Women who, in their own words, "will not study. There is no need to read. We have to work daily. If we study, how will we survive? We dig earth. When can we read? We are in the group, but it is impossible on our part to study."

And there are the marginal women, who will not dig earth. One of these women, who tries to monopolize her group, when asked why she did not dig earth, replied, "That's not a problem. If I am there, they will get the correct wages. I will always be with them to supervise their work. I will take them to the earth-digging site and supervise them." Another agrees, commenting about the earth-diggers: "They will chalk out their program for their survival. But I will not agree with their program." "That is the problem," replies one of the earth-diggers, "we want women like us. Let like-minded women join with us." BRAC found that in order to develop workable groups it is, as a general rule, better to separate the poor (earth-diggers) from the marginal (non-earth-diggers).

Attendance—

Weaker groups are characterized, if by nothing else, by irregular attendance.

= At Mohammed's house we had our meetings regularly. But those days meetings would be held regularly. The (BRAC staff) used to come to the meeting. But our people did not come to the meetings regularly. Sometimes we used to come but they did not. In this way, everything happened. Nobody came to the meetings. Nobody gave the monthly subscription. They are not concerned with the group.

= Already, when we had reached lesson 20 a few members were absent. I wanted to know the reasons. They told me they were not finding any benefit in it. So the numbers dropped to 8. He (BRAC field staff) said a group cannot run with only 8 members.

And strong groups are characterized, if by nothing else, by regular attendance.

= We like the meetings. I feel badly if the meeting is held only once a month. But if it is held every Sunday then we all feel better because we can discuss and acquire new knowledge. But if the meeting is held only once a month, we forget many things and our knowledge does not increase very much. Even if I say 'no meeting today,' nobody listens. Everybody spends the day at my home and asks me to conduct the meeting.

Even weak groups have some general members who perceive the need to be regular.

= Many things are needed to make the group a good one. First, the weekly meeting of the group is a must. Every Saturday or Sunday, we should have our weekly meeting. A monthly savings of 1 taka is needed. When there is earth-digging work, 2 taka can be given as savings. All these things are needed to make the group a good one. Otherwise, if nobody pays anything, the group will not be a good one.

= We must think of our own eagerness. We should use our own initiative to attend the meetings for our betterment.

And even strong groups have some general members who must be constantly reminded to attend meetings.

= Sometimes members forget the time schedule. Then we have to remind them. . . The day when we call a meeting I inform everybody. Yet most of them do not come to the meeting. At the time of the meeting I have to call them again.

Weekly Meetings—

We asked the women what they discuss in their weekly meetings.

= We discuss how we can increase our income and how we can develop ourselves. Besides this, we listen to valuable talk of the members and

discuss how we can improve our behavior. If anybody's mind is depressed, after participating in the meeting, her mind will be refreshed.
= After coming to the meeting everybody states their plans. Somebody says that she thought about this and someone else says that she thought about that. Their plans are discussed and reviewed during the meeting. We decide what will be good. After a first phase we do other work. For example, somebody suggested that we cultivate ginger. Another said we should first cultivate fish. We have uniformly decided to grow ginger. We will think about fish cultivation after this. Now we do not discuss fish. But we have decided what we will do. We give less importance to what we will not do. What we need to do in preparation to start work we discuss vigorously among ourselves.

We do not talk only about economical matters. We talk about so many things. We talk about family problems. Somebody says that a quarrel took place in her house or that she had a grave quarrel. "Now what should happen, now what is necessary?"

Somebody wants to do something in their own family. Sometimes they ask: "I want to do this. If I do this, how will it be?" Then we think among ourselves. If we think it is good, we advise her to do this. If we think it is bad, we advise her that it is bad, not to do this now but to do another thing.

Leadership—

The women had a great deal to say about leadership—good, bad, indifferent, or conflicting. The women often quoted proverbs about leadership.

= If the guardian is strong, all the workers will be strong.

= In a single forest two tigers cannot survive. Only one tiger can survive in one forest.

The women confirmed our experience that several different types of women tend to emerge as leaders of the groups:

- the *volunteers* contracted by the group and BRAC to conduct functional education classes;
- the leaders, called *sardarni*, of earth-digging work gangs;
- self-appointed *"patronesses"* who do not think of themselves as general members;
- self-imposed *"blockers"* who either obstruct group decisions and/ or vie for leadership;

- BRAC-chosen *intermediaries* whom BRAC field staff choose to help them work in the village;
- general *group members* whose personality or other traits earn them the respect and trust of the group;

The general members of the groups are quick to judge the leaders as to whether they feel on "a par" or "above" the general membership or whether they want to "manipulate" the general members. The general members of one group had this to say about a "blocker" who tried to manipulate her group.

= She does not have any sympathy for the poor. She herself is poor. But she has a little land and she thinks that she is rich. She tries to create problems. Sometimes if all of us agree to do something, she goes against it. She will say different things. Or, maybe she thinks that she is not being given the leadership. Maybe she thinks that the poor are achieving something. Or, maybe she does not think that a poor woman should be given any importance.

The general members of another group had this to say about the *sardarni* who manipulated her group.

= Some *sardarnis* take a commission for providing work. But we will not pay any commission. For that reason, she did not like to take us. There are many dull members in the group, they don't understand the tricks of the *sardarnis*. If the *sardarnis* give them two seers of wheat instead of 2½ seers, they don't understand. They are happy with 2 seers, but we are not like them. We demand 2½ seers. That's why she does not like us . . . If she can eat something (idiomatically, get some interest) from us, then she is OK. But if we maintain correct accounts of money from her then she is not satisfied with us, she thinks we are her enemy. She does not maintain good relations with us because we do not work according to her wishes. That's why we are not united with her.

Often the "patronesses," who perceive a status in working for the poor, told us how they feel about the general members.

= I have joined the group to serve the poor. Moreover, I cannot keep the money in hand so I deposit my money in the group fund like others. So when I need money I take it from the group fund . . . I have benefitted in this way that through me many others who need my help have gotten it. Whatever I told them to do they did it. I can save money through the group fund.

There are, of course, many examples of good leadership. The general members of one group referred to the volunteer teacher who is now their leader as the "soul" of their group. Sometimes the "patronesses" learn to feel on "a par" with the general members.

> =I slowly and gradually learned all this. Others say: "Whatever you teach us, we will follow." I said: "All of us should be developed equally, otherwise it will not be OK." We should not depend only on the volunteer teacher. What the teacher-helper can do we should learn how to do, we should acquire the accounting skills and knowledge quietly. We should not depend on the teacher-helper only, or an Apa (literally "sister;" used to refer to BRAC female staff). Then nothing will happen. Isn't that so? We should ourselves understand our own affairs. Is that not so, Apa?

The interviews confirmed staff misgivings about how leaders actually emerge in the groups. Are leaders tacitly selected by BRAC field staff? Does BRAC rely too heavily on their chosen intermediaries or on the volunteer teachers? Do some leaders emerge from the general membership? Which sorts of women prove to be the best leaders? Soon after the interviews were completed, we organized a planning and evaluating workshop with field staff on these and related issues of group formation and development. More on that workshop below.

Decision Making—

Many of the groups make joint decisions and resolve loss and conflict through group discussions. We asked the members of a strong group how they handle conflicts and make decisions.

> =We discuss in the meeting how to better the group. If we hear that someone wants to give land on share-cropping, we think about taking that land, etc.
> —If many people work together there are quarrels. Don't you quarrel with each other?
> =No. Before we quarreled, but we do not quarrel now.
> —In the meeting, if some women say they will cultivate silk and other women say they will cultivate something else, then what will happen? Is there a quarrel over this? Will you break the group over this?
> =No, why should the group be broken? We will divide [into subgroups] for our work, but we will remain united.
> —If the day comes that all the members work together, then how will you make decisions?

= Whatever decisions need to be taken we will take by a majority vote of the members.
—You all obey your leader. If she makes a wrong decision then what will you do? Will you all agree to her decision?
= If it is a bad decision, then we will not agree. Before we did not think about all this. After working with the group, we discuss and take advice before doing anything.

The process of reaching a consensus is not always smooth. One group met for seven days to decide which rules and procedures to follow. Sometimes consensus is not reached or taken. Weak groups often cannot reach a consensus. In some groups, neither very weak nor very strong, the general members consent to the decision of the leader.

Conflict Resolution—

All groups face internal conflicts. The difference between weak and strong groups is that strong groups are able to resolve the conflicts that arise and move on whereas weak groups are not able to do so. Conflicts within a group test the resilience and viability of a group. If handled well through group processes, internal conflicts can help strengthen a group. A member of a strong group put it simply: "If a dispute arises, we make negotiations with each other to resolve our dispute."

Take the case of the Ramdia Women's Group, a relatively strong group. During our interviewing, we found two problematic members in the group. One member, a "blocker," felt above the general members, would not actively participate in schemes involving manual labor, and was generally obstructive. The other member, a "patroness," felt above the general members but participated actively because she derived a certain status from patronizing the group (from, in her words, "helping the poor"). Despite these two members, the group has been able to resolve a series of conflicts (one for each scheme undertaken) mainly because the general members recognize the importance of group activities to their survival. In the words of one of the general members, "We have no shelter or food. We must work and be united, otherwise we cannot survive."

The Ramdia Women's Group's first activity was cow-rearing. They took a group loan and invested in calves to be reared by individual members. They decided that each rearer will earn half the profit from rearing, but they did not settle who will bear any loss that occurs. As it so happened, one of the calves died despite veterinary attention. Whose responsibility? Whose loss? The "blocker" insisted it was the responsibility of the rearer. The general members did not agree. They met for two days to discuss the matter. Finally, after being asked to consider "what if god had taken her cow," the "blocker" was convinced.

The group's next activity was paddy cultivation. The village was in disbelief. Women cultivate paddy? Women in the fields? The women were ridiculed. Someone in the village composed a song that was sung throughout the village. The lyrics stated that women working in the fields was an unlucky sign and that the drought of that year (1979) was a measure of that bad luck. The general members carried on their cultivation but the "blocker" did not join in.

The group conflict arose at harvest time. A day had been set when the members would collectively harvest the paddy. As usual, the "blocker" did not appear. Two of the general members chastised her, saying, "No one is available when it is time to work, but when it is time to share the profit everyone is on hand." Hearing this criticism, the "blocker" decided to take matters into her own hands.

= We took the decision in a meeting to cut the paddy on a fixed day. On that fixed day I was unable to be present for the work. Then the group members became angry with me. Seeing their attitude, I cut the paddy down the next morning. When I cut the paddy, the others said to me "Why have you cut the paddy? Everyone had decided to cut the paddy collectively." They asked me: "Why didn't you call the group members to come to the field?" I said: "Yesterday I was not able to work. I worked in the morning to make up the lost work." When I was cutting the paddy, the others went to the (BRAC) office. The staff of the office came. They accused me: "Why have you cut down the paddy without the consent of the group members?" I said: "Today is the second day for cutting the paddy. So I am cutting." The women became angry with me. I begged pardon for my action. Then I took the decision not to remain in the group. Later on they convinced me, so I changed my decision.

The group again convinced the "blocker," but the general pattern of her behavior remained clear and predictable.

What is the role of BRAC field staff in such conflicts? Conflicts within the groups not only test the group's strength but also test the skills of the BRAC field staff. The role of the staff is a delicate one. They can help resolve conflict but such interference can cost the group's development. Generally, the field staff prefer to let the groups handle their own internal conflicts.

But in some instances, especially when there are problematic members, BRAC field staff step in to help. BRAC field staff believe that certain obstructive members, those who exercise status considerations or who have patrons in the village elite, should be "eliminated" from the group. BRAC staff see no purpose in trying to continually "convince" such members to accept group decisions. In the words of the senior field staff at one field project: "If we (BRAC) make them united, there will again be a quarrel. There is not unity with a stepmother. No unity of mind. As much as a father tries to unite the stepmother and the stepson, there will never be unity between them. Usually the general members cannot take the social and political risk involved in "eliminating a blocker."

In such instances, BRAC field staff determine the strategies of "elimination." The most common strategy is to encourage the general group members to undertake more and more manual labor schemes. The obstructive members most often do not want to do the hard, and therefore non-statusful, work involved. The "blocker" in the Ramdia group, for instance, refused to participate in paddy husking.

=I am sick. I cannot do this. If rice is needed, paddy must be husked in a mill.
—But some of your group members are living hand-to-mouth. What if they say: "If we take up a paddy husking program cow-rearing scheme, the profit will come only after one year. But if we take up a paddy-husking program we can save rice, we can meet our needs.
=If they can, they should take up this program. They should take the program they like. We should give advice to them. They will chalk out their program for their survival. But I will not agree with their program.

The Ramdia Women's Group was a relatively strong group with two weak links. We puzzled over the attitudes of the two obstructive members, the two weak members. The case of the "patroness" was quite straight-forward. She felt superior to the general members because of her own superior position in the village: her husband had been a military officer and her brother was influential in the village. She played the role of "patroness" because her survival did not depend on the group but on her own "patron" in the village. The case of the "blocker" was far less straight-forward. In fact, during her interview, she was quite evasive to the point where we took a tea break in order to distract her and to reformulate our line of questioning. Finally, after we had settled back into the interview after our tea, the facts spilled out. Her father was very well off. She had been married to a distant poor relation, after her engagement to a rich man had been broken by the groom's family. Her father still sent monthly remittances to her. Despite the appearance of her home and herself, she was better off than we had calculated and, therefore, more concerned about her status than the general members.

By way of contrast, consider the case of the Chandor Women's Group, a weak group. During our interviewing, we found the dynamic of this group quite different from that of the Ramdia group. There was little consensus and little feeling of group cohesion. Everything was discussed in "we-they" or "me-her" terms. It did not take long to identify the main weakness of the group—two women vying for leadership. One woman, the BRAC-chosen intermediary, played the role of "patroness" who derives status from patronizing the group. The other woman, the *sardarni,* tried to manipulate the general members and to cheat them out of correct wages and terms at work sites.

The Chandor group's first activity was collective agriculture with another women's group. Together they leased land on which they cultivated mustard and tobacco. The landlord was to get 50% of the produce and the two women's groups were to share the remaining 50%. The other group collected both shares of the harvest. The Chandor group had not been able to collect their share. "But, why," we asked, "was it not given to you?" The Chandor women, it turns out, had not been regular, either in the field work or in attending meetings. They did not even appear to harvest the crops.

> =This is our fault. We did not attend the meetings regularly. We did not go to the fields at first. The reason is that we don't attend the meetings regularly and we don't give a monthly donation. If we could attend the meeting, we could get the crop, I think.
> —Why didn't you go? Why didn't you attend the meetings? Why don't you have unity?
> = How can unity be achieved? Everybody is busy with themselves. Everybody thinks of their own belly.
> —But can't you attend a meeting once in a month? You are not the only earth-digging group. You are not the only poor. We see other groups. In fact, there are over 200 groups.

=We must think of our own eagerness. We should use our own initiative, to attend the meetings for our betterment. But nobody does.

The Chandor group worked regularly on construction sites at work arranged by the troublesome *sardarni*. They not only worked for a pittance but also had to rent the spades to do the work. There was a conflict with the *sardarni* over the rental fee.

=There was a quarrel over the rental of spades. We were 33 people. She collected one taka from each woman. But we told her: "We will pay the actual rental price. We will not pay one taka in advance. If we pay one taka and if there is a surplus, who will refund the surplus money to the (BRAC) office?" Someone said there would be no surplus, that one taka is needed for the rent. We said: "We will collect half a taka per person and give it to another *sardarni*. And, if there is a shortage of money, we will pay again." But she was not willing to take that amount of money. But the other *sardarni* took that amount of money.

The group's suspicions of the troublesome *sardarni* were well founded. She kept the group's fund, lent it to her son, and refused to let members borrow against it. The women were not even certain how much money there was in the group fund. Some of them recognized that the fund could be well invested or used to finance small individual loans.

=We could buy cocks, ducks, etc., to rear and we could earn a profit for our development. Is it not so? If we could buy one duck, we could earn a handsome amount of money. Now, 4 eggs cost 4 taka. In this way we could increase our fund and could buy one more chicken. Now, what kind of earnings do we get? She holds the money.
=If any of us are in difficulty, we should be able to borrow money from time to time. But she holds the money.

The Chandor group earned some wheat from a BRAC-financed food-for-work scheme. The BRAC terms were that 25% of the wheat must be kept as a group fund. The group sold the wheat and used the cash to buy a cow. But they could not resolve who should keep the cow.

=Some said that they would keep it. Others said that they would. Some said to give it outside the group (for rearing). Others said to give it inside the group. At first, the *sardarni* took the cow. But later, she returned it. She said that people from the intermediary's house would steal the cow from her. What made her think like that? Would we steal the cow? Was it possible to steal a cow which was given by BRAC (on loan)? Actually, she said this to discredit us as thieves. She also said: "I will not give the cow for rearing to the 'intermediary's' house. We said: "We will not give the cow to you for rearing." Then everybody decided to give it to a poor woman in the group, a Hindu woman.

At this point the BRAC-chosen intermediary interjected: "We could have bought a better cow. And then they gave it to another person, a Hindu. But we Muslims should have kept it." Several of the general members answered back: "What does being Muslim have to do with it? She is also our group member. Now the cow is OK. She is taking good care of the cow."

Such difficulties continued to plague the group. A goat was purchased by the group. The goat was stolen. The rival leaders, the *sardarni* and the intermediary, accused each other. We asked the group: "Your group seems to create more problems than work. Why?" One of the general members answered: "Why do we quarrel? If I eat better today she can't tolerate it, and if she eats better I can't tolerate it. It is always the same thing. Whenever I ask for monthly contributions, they say 'no.' But they can give whatever they can afford, but they are not willing to pay anything."

= If we could buy small-sized chickens, we could buy at least 3–4 chicks. And by now we could have sold those chicks for 20 taka each. In this way, we could make 100 taka.
= We hope for many things from the group. If we could get some money from the group, we could buy 4–5 cows. We could take land on sharecropping. And then we could cultivate crops on that land. Thirty or more members of our group could contribute one or two taka per month each and buy some land. In these ways we could progress.

Some of the members of the group have plans. But so long as the two rival leaders remain, the group had little prospect for realizing those plans. We questioned our own decision to work through an intermediary who proved unwilling to identify with the group. We questioned the *sardarni* on her background to try to understand why she did not identify with her earth-digging gang. We discovered she had a history of working in the town and, for a short time, even in the capital city. She had developed very selfish, opportunistic instincts and ties with local government officials during those years. She regularly obtains work for several gangs of women, never works alongside the gangs, and surfaces only at pay time. The BRAC field staff described her as clever and self-centered.

Our interviews with the women stimulated a great deal of informal discussion among BRAC staff. What could we learn from the interviews? Could we better predict which members would prove to be "blockers" or which groups would prove strong, which weak? What led to group weakness or to group strength? Why? What was the role of BRAC field staff in fostering relative weakness and strength?

These informal discussions led to a meeting of BRAC senior administrators and programmers to discuss BRAC's group formation methodology. At that meeting, BRAC decided to conduct a workshop with field staff to analyze and to redesign BRAC's field methodology. During that workshop, the field staff formulated new guidelines for group formation and development. I will present these guidelines in chapter 8. Our research had served its dual purpose: research and training. During the next year, BRAC field staff applied their new guidelines in restructuring and strengthening the Ramdia and Chandor groups.

BRAC field staff recognized that in order to further strengthen the Ramdia Women's Group the "patroness" and the "blocker" should leave. But they were not going to leave on their own accord and the other women were not going to force them out. BRAC would have to apply its own tactics to the situation. BRAC staff knew that neither the "blocker" or the "patroness" favored schemes which entail manual labor and prefer the less-demanding schemes, such as calf-rearing. During the next year, BRAC staff purposefully did not offer to finance calf-rearing. BRAC staff also kept distant and silent about the group. As BRAC's interest in the group seemingly dropped, the interest of the "patroness" and "blocker" dropped. After some time, they gradually withdrew themselves from the group. The general members, all earth-diggers, gained strength. The group is stronger than before.

BRAC field staff recognized that in order to continue the Chandor Women's Group the two rival leaders needed to go. The *sardarni* was impatient and left on her own accord after yet another conflict—this time over the wages for earth-cutting. The intermediary who preferred her statusful work as a family planning worker was deflected by BRAC staff into doing that work on a more full-time basis. The group has been expanded and divided into two earth-digging groups. Interestingly, one woman from the Ramdia group was deserted by her husband and returned to Chandor (the village of her parents). She has joined one of the newly-reconstituted Chandor women's groups.

CHANGES IN THE WOMEN

Before the village elders and union-council members abused and threatened us for joining the group, now they are silent . . . Before we did not understand our wages, now we understand profit and loss . . . Before we did not know our rights to rations or medical services, now we are conscious and exert pressure to receive our due . . . Before we did not go outside our homes, but now we work in the fields and go to the town . . . Before our minds were rusty, now they shine . . .

We asked the women again and again what changes they had experienced in their lives after joining BRAC's program. Most women replied quickly and enthusiastically: "Oh! So many changes!" When we asked them to be specific, they started in with many before-and-now statements. When we asked a group of women in Dapunia village (Jamalpur), for example, each woman wanted to speak.

= Before we were scared to talk to any outsider. Now we talk freely. We can write our names. When we go to town we can read the sign boards. We keep accounts with a pen.

= We have learned how to keep accounts, grow vegetables, rear poultry to better ourselves. We have learned why we should keep our things clean. We can stitch quilts, clean our houses, separate our latrine from our bathing place. I learned all these matters after reading and seeing the pictures (i.e., BRAC education posters).

= I did not know the difference between dirty and clean or how to earn and value. Before we stayed hungry if our husband was not working. Now we do not stay hungry. We earn and eat. My husband has a pain in his leg and is sitting in the house. But I am running the house now.

= If my husband does not work for two–three days I work and meet the household expenses. He is good (to me) because of that. Before we used to respect our husbands. Whatever quantity of food they brought we ate. Now, if he brings one kilo of rice I find that is not sufficient and then I add half a kilo and cook that. For this, my husband is very happy and eats as much as he can.

= Well, we eat thrice a day, wear good clothes, go to the cinema, send our children to the school. We do not eat *jaw* (flour cooked like barley).

Before we were illiterate and could not talk with others. Now we can talk to everyone. We can speak better Bangla now. If we go to other houses they give us a chair to sit on. If there is a wedding, they call us. After forming the group we wear saris worth sixty takas.

So much has happened. So many women contrasted what it was like before and what it is like now. In the interest of understanding the range and degree of change, I will divide the women's comments by those that indicate changes in the *relationships* they maintain and negotiate, the *resources* they have access to or control, the *power* they exercise, and the *attitudes* they hold.*

Changes in Relationships

Women to Women

Before the women had few opportunities to socialize beyond the home and the family. Now BRAC-supported women come together, to meet and to discuss mutual problems. The new experience of sharing develops new loyalties. Many of the women expressed an affection for the other women in their group. This affection very often translates into small gestures of helping and sharing.

= If any member of the group goes hungry we give them rice as a loan to be returned later. Like this, we have gotten opportunities and capacities. No member goes hungry.

= If anyone is staying hungry we inquire after each other. We inquire house to house about the group members.

= When Asia's son was getting married she had no money. I had 54 taka which I gave to her. She took a loan from the group fund. We all helped her and got her son married. This is good.

= This person with four children does not have any place to stay. If we can give her a house or clothes, then it will be good. If we eat three times and they cannot eat then there is no peace in our minds. If all of us can eat then it is a different kind of happiness. Then all of us together

---

*We did not ask how many women experienced what kinds of change. Our purpose was to understand what kinds of change (how, when, and why) are experienced by significant numbers of women. I am not asserting all the women experienced all the kinds of change described below, rather I am asserting that the changes experienced are of the kind I describe. Some women's lives changed a great deal. Some women's lives far less. No woman's life was ever quite the same after joining a group.

made fences for Vimala's house, completed the roofing over that house
for 10 taka, and repaired Mongol's house for 80 taka.

Not all such gestures are of a material nature. Some gestures involve
emotional support from one woman to another.

= If another person does something bad to me, another member of the
group will come forward to protest it . . . I was alone, but now with me
there are ten other members. They give me support.

—If any *matbor* used any bad words against any member of the group,
then what do you do?

= Then that victim cries and goes door to door. Then we call a meeting
and discuss the matter.

The new-found affection also serves to minimize the tensions and
conflicts that existed between members of the groups.

= Before there were quarrels among the villagers.

—What were the causes of the quarrels?

= Over children, poultry, goats and vegetables. But now we keep ourselves busy with work and do not have time for quarrels.

—What do you do if there is a quarrel between the children of two
families?

= Slap them and take them home. Before there was fighting, even with
sticks. But we do not quarrel now.

= Now everybody rears poultry through the group and no one says
anything if poultry stray into each other's houses. Before it was not like
this. There was no unity before the group. There were quarrels every
day with one's neighbors over goats, even poultry, even children. Now
everyone's things are the group's things. If anything is lost, then we feel
for each other.

Women and Their Families

Before women seldom left their homesteads and even more rarely
left their villages. Now these women regularly leave their homesteads
to attend meetings and to participate in joint activities and periodically
leave their villages to attend workshops or trainings. The simple yet
dramatic fact of women's mobility indicates that changes are occurring
within their homes and villages.

Most women face some initial resistance from their families when
they express an interest in joining a BRAC group. Almost all the
women made some mention of this initial resistance.

= Some of the members' husbands stopped them from coming to the group. They did not understand what the group is. What will they do? Who will come? What will happen? And why will it happen? To think all this through has taken time.

—Did your husbands and fathers give their consent before you joined the group?

= In the first stage, most of them were not in favor of our joining the group. At first, I was prevented from talking with BRAC staff. At that time my husband said: "Why are you talking with an outsider?" But, after observing the terms and conditions and advantages, they now give their full consent.

After the initial phase, most families agree that their women can participate in the group. However, the society exerts pressure on some women's families. These women had to explain the purpose and advantages of group participation to their mothers-in-law, sons, or husbands.

= It was tough to minimize the dispute earlier. When we started working in our group, some people used slang language against us. The volunteer teachers told us not to be frustrated. They said: "The people who are making such bad comments towards us, they will be with us in the near future. Let them do this." They told us: "We are also getting bad comments for our work. It is nothing. Don't be nervous. Let the outsiders do their activities." Then we continued our work vigorously. At first, my son was not in favor of this work. Later, he changed his attitude and worked for us. When I was working with the group some people made comments to my son. They said to him: "Your mother is not getting rice from your family. She is not getting shelter in your house, etcetera." But my son changed his attitude. Then he countered and opposed all the comments, saying: "The group will be enlightened. They will get education. This is a good thing. They are working for their good not only for food."

Once they join a group, the women derive moral and emotional support from the other members. With this mutual reinforcement, individual women are able to negotiate more adequate relationships within their own families. Many women testified that their husbands abused them less.

= Now my husband does not beat me. Our friendliness is increasing. My husband is taking lessons from me. Before he did not know how to write his name. Now he can write his name.

= My husband did not say anything to me before. He used to do things according to his own wish. He used to go to the cinema. But now he gives me the money and says: "You run the family as you like."

= My husband never says 'Go to your father's house' if we are in hardship.

= I told my husband: "You work along. I want to work with the women. We will get some extra money. Will you give me permission?" My husband agreed.

During one group interview, the husband of one of the women was present. She spoke freely in his presence about his initial reactions to her attending functional education classes.

= My husband stopped me like this. He said: "You have broken from the religion. What will you do studying in your old age?"

We asked her husband whether what his wife said was correct. He agreed. We asked him why he stopped her. He replied,

"I thought these women do not know how to mix with others. They will not succeed. But with the help of BRAC they have done a lot now . . . At first, men bad-mouthed them a lot. I was also angry with them. They went to Dhaka (to be trained in jute handicrafts). How will they live there? I was worried over that. Will they walk around without religious restriction? Now, I am not worried at all. I also instruct her to continue this work."

Before women had few opportunities to earn a cash income, now women are earning incomes from BRAC-supported economic schemes. The impact of this income, however small, is felt immediately. Their income earns them affection and respect within their families.

= I am earning money. So everybody, like my mother-in-law, sister-in-law, husband, they like me.

When we asked women whether their husbands or fathers perceived a benefit to their participating in a group, many women said their male guardians favored their group activities because of the income they earned.

= They say: "If you are able to get better food and clothes, then the group is not bad and you can remain with it."

The income women earn combined with the strength of belonging to a group has led to one (if no other) significant impact: that women who have become members of BRAC groups have been able to avoid being deserted or divorced. Often when I walked through the villages with BRAC field staff they pointed out women who "would have been divorced" if they were not now spinning silk, embroidering quilts, weaving mats, or raising chickens. The women confirmed this impact.

In some instances, the husbands return to wives they abandoned once the wives start to earn.

> = There is another girl who was abandoned by her husband for three years. We asked him to take his wife back home. This year we asked him: "Tell us whether you are taking your wife back or not." He said: "Well, as you are asking, I will take her." Then he constructed a house and took her back.

We asked whether this occurred because of the group's pressure. They said the group put pressure on the husband and gave the woman a cow to rear.

Another woman was taken back by her husband after her family had been given three cows to rear by the group. The wife in this instance refused to let the fact of owning a cow be the reason for her being taken back.

> = We gave three cows to three families in Habia's home. Habia got remarried. But Habia's father-in-law said: "Why should our daughter-in-law leave her cow at her father's home? She should live with us and she should bring her cow to our home." Her husband took the cow to his home. She said to her husband: "My mother deposited money for me in the group. So why should I take the cow from her to your house? The cow should be kept at my mother's house." Her husband cried: "What can I do?" So we told him: "You should pay back the money deposited in the group by her mother in her name. This is the right thing."

We asked whether he had in fact paid back the money to his wife's mother. "Not yet," they said, "but he said he will do so."

Many women explained that husbands of group members threatened to abandon them or to marry others. We asked them what the group did in such instances.

> = Some of the members' husbands say so, but we tell them: "If you marry, we will not allow you to bring your bride into this house." In any

other villages there is a couple, the woman has not given birth to a child and her husband said: "You are not giving birth to a child, so I will marry again." Then we threatened him. We told him: "You go and marry but we will not allow you to bring your bride into this house. You'd better take your wife to a doctor." After that, he did take her to a doctor and she has given birth to two children.

Women and the Village

Perhaps even more dramatic than the changes taking place within the families are the changes taking place within the villages of these women. Some of these changes take place whether or not a group proves to be strong. More of such changes take place when a group proves its strengths. The women spoke of these changes throughout the group and individual interviews.

When the women spoke of changes in the village, they referred either broadly to the "society" or specifically to three types of rich-and-powerful personalities in that society.

—the *Members* of the Union Council: local elected officials who govern the Union (lowest electoral unit) and, typically, exert control over the public goods and services which are channeled through the Union to the villages;

—the *Matbors:* village elders, recruited variously (often through heredity) who sit on the village councils where they exercise explicit power or officiate village functions and events where they exercise implicit power;

—the *Mullahs:* religious leaders appointed for limited terms of office by a local mosque committee. Although they are invested with the power of that appointment to dictate or endorse religious norms, they remain under the influence of the village elders (who constitute the majority on the mosque committee).

And, lest we forget, the women spoke also of their relationships with the wives of the members, *matbors,* and *mullahs*.

= In Matborpara, the wives of the *matbors* used to say many things against us. "Do not go out. If you go, it will be shameful. It will be sinful." The *matbors* did not say anything. Their wives spoke against us.

Before the women depended on the counsel and advice of the members-*matbors-mullahs* and turned to them when they needed loans, food, work, or security. But now much of that relationship has changed. Initially, the rich-and-powerful try to interfere in the activities of the groups. Gradually, the groups of women begin to resist that interference. In the process, the relationships between the women and the rich-and-powerful of the village change significantly. The women described the interactions between themselves and the rich-and-powerful again and again. We asked them what kinds of interference they faced? How they resisted this interference? What they have gained or lost in the process? Later, we sequenced what the women told into a *pattern of interference* (by the members-*matbors-mullahs*) and the *pattern of resistance* (by the organized groups of women).

Pattern of Interference

Rumors are spread through the village or directed at the households of group members. The rumor-campaigns persist through all phases of group development, but the rumors carry the most weight during the early phases when the confidence of the women (both individually and as a group) has not developed.

Some rumors, perhaps the most persistent, focus on the religious consequences of women participating in group activities. The norms of *purdah* are invoked. The women are accused of being *bepurdah* (literally, without *purdah*). The BRAC staff and workers are implicated in these charges.

= They said that our volunteer teacher does not observe *purdah* and she is not good. "Only Christians walk like that." But we did not listen. They also talked about the BRAC field staff: "She is a Haji's (one who has made the pilgrimage to Mecca) daughter. Her father gives *azan* (call to prayer) in the mosque and looks after the mosque, but his daughter has become *bepurdah* and moves around village to village." They criticized like this. These two women have done a lot for us. Allah give them peace.

= The day I went to the paddy field, they said: "We have lost the respect of our village because of this woman. She goes out without hesitation."

Other rumors, perhaps the most insidious, focus on the morals of the women and of BRAC staff. Under the norms of *purdah*, association with strange ("outside") men is forbidden. Under the BRAC program, association with strange men (most of BRAC's field staff are men) is unavoidable. Both the staff and the women recognize this dilemma. Sometimes the insinuations are quite explicit.

= When we met in my aunt's house rumors spread all over the village: "When conducting the meeting, BRAC staff allowed two people into the house and two were allowed to go out." People asked: "What type of group is this?" At night, four people came to my house and asked why and how we formed a group. I replied: "We formed a group. Why should I explain it to you?"

Still other rumors focus on BRAC's credibility.

= BRAC is a meaningless organization. It has no ability to pay money. Those who are involved in BRAC programs should do government work, then they will get money.

= "Those who entice you to work to form a group, they will occupy our state. Why are you forming a group?" I told them: "If I get rice and shelter, it will be sufficient for us. No matter to me who will take this state or not." They said: "You should leave the group." I told them: "What I have done is good. I should not leave." I did not follow the command or words of any outsiders. We are going ahead.

Another rumor, more easily dismissed, was that the women were to be recruited for work in the Middle East (referred to broadly as "Arab").

= As the rich people said: "You will be taken to the land of the Black Sea. And will never again be in this country. And, you will be taken to the Arab." For that reason, some (women) left the group. But I was never afraid of these remarks. It is better to go to the land of the Black Sea with the BRAC staff than to stay in this country with the rich.

The women are *ridiculed*. People make jokes at them. People whisper remarks as they walk by. The women spoke frequently of the "whispering"—public criticism to shame them out of participating in BRAC activities.

= When we first formed the group, I used to walk to the houses of the group members. Villagers used to insult me by saying: "Who will take care of you? The servant of Arab has come." Things like this. I used to remain silent.

= While I was going to the (BRAC) office, the rich people commented: "Arab employees are going by."

= My mother-in-law stopped me before. Now she does not.

—What did she say?

= "If a woman goes to work outside there is no increase in that income. Man should work outside the house. She walks like a shameless one outside the house. She leaves the children at home and goes out." The *mullahs* (religious leaders) say: "When they will die we shall not bury them." Villagers say "Wherever they want, they go. They do not cover their heads. They talk with men. They will be sinners." I said: "If Allah does not see us when we stay hungry then Allah has sinned." Now I have no fear of such talk. I went to Dhaka to attend the meeting. I do not care about anybody now. Now I understand how I will have to run my family. We will live on whatever we earn with our children. Do you know, Apa, what hard days we passed at first? Men used to laugh at us showing their teeth. Husbands used to beat me. If I was late from the group's discussion, my husband beat me when I returned home. He said: "Go and do that." Yet I did not leave the group.

Fairly serious *threats* are voiced as well. One type of threat is that the woman or women will be "banished from the society." Ostracism of this type is not uncommon and is called either *ek gore* (literally, one house; figuratively, ostracism) or *somaj bandho* (banished from the society).

= Then the *mullah* does not allow us to talk in the road or to go out of the house. A social barricade is created. "You will not be allowed to take water from the tubewell. If you go into the field, your legs will be broken."

We asked the women what else is denied, what else must be endured. Under this temporary banishment all the normal, small village reciprocities—the offer of a cup of tea, the loan of a bowl of rice—are denied. Those who are ostracized are prevented from bathing in the ponds, collecting water from the tube-wells. Other villagers will not issue invitations to households that are ostracized, nor will they attend the ceremonies in those households. Marriage proposals from such households are not considered.

Another type of threat is that the woman will be "banished from the religion." Again, we asked what this type of banishment means. The women explained that the *mullahs* will not participate in any of the women's social or religious functions. The *mullahs*, typically, officiate at birth, marriage, and death ceremonies. "They will not pray for our souls," the women explain.

The third type of threat was that the village judicial council, the *shalish*, would be convened to "judge" the actions or behavior of the women. These *shalish* are traditionally convened and controlled by the *matbors* and members. Under this threat, the charge (or pretext for the *shalish*) is often simply that the women have been "bad" or held a meeting with men.

Some small, but significant, *incidents* have taken place. *Shalish* have been convened to "judge" the actions and behavior of the women. Some women have been denied a loan of rice, a day's work, the use of a tube well. Thieves (known to the women) have stolen the group's funds in one or two villages. Thieves have stolen the women's goods in several other villages. Fortunately, to date, no major incident has occurred.

Pattern of Resistance

The women help each other resist the interference by the rich-and-powerful: to resist the rumors-ridicule-threats-incidents. As the women develop a mutual identity, they pay less heed to what the rich-and-powerful say against them.

= If we want to go anywhere, we can't do that alone. Men criticize us, hate us, whisper about us. But if we are together, we can do it easily. People can't criticize us, hate us, whisper about us. So for our betterment, we became united within the group. If anybody comments on any member of our group, we will not tolerate it.

= The rich do not respect us or obey us. If we die for lack of food they do not help us. If we go out for food they criticize us. When they see us they say: "Look, she is coming to beg for something." If we go to their house while they are eating, they say: "Look, she is staring at our food."

= Everybody used to bad-mouth against me. I did not listen to them. They are the rich. Why should we listen to the rich? They walked on our bodies. We should not listen to them. They should listen to us. I was very poor. I could not eat properly and buy any clothing. We started studying in the (functional) education classes. We discussed our problems, etc. . . . Now, everything seems good to me.

= Yes, they say many things. They say that what we do is shameful, carries no dignity, no respect or honor, and, above all, it is not good to talk and work with men. I say: "What is wrong in working with men, in talking with men? We also have brothers, we treat them as our brothers and fathers." What is the shame? We went to them. They gave us 1500

taka. We bought cows and we made profit. Those who say all these
things, do they give us any money? If we die of starvation they will not
give us anything. Would it be good to sit without work and food abiding
by what they say?

And they begin to look at the rich in a different way.

= We do not listen to the *mullahs* anymore. They did not give us even a
quarter kilo of rice.

= The rich stopped me. The rich criticized us. They said: "Give them
the path they are going to college." But we did not listen to them. Now
they want to send their wives and children to the group.

= We said to the *matbors*: "If we do not cultivate land, then how can we
maintain our lives? You may say whatever you like, but we will not listen
to you. We are in the group and we will cultivate land."

= They said we will become Christian and English people will take us
away. We are ruining the prestige of the village and breaking *purdah*. If
we can get food, we will become Christian. If there is no food in our
stomach, *purdah* does not feed us. If there is no food, then no one looks
after us. Before people used to inquire about caste before marriage. Now
people inquire whether or not the man will be able to support the girl.
Whoever has rice and clothing he has got caste. We do not listen to the
mullahs any more. They also did not give us even a quarter kilo of rice
(on loan). Now we get ten maunds of rice (i.e., because the women are
earning incomes). Now, people help us.

As the women obtain training, credit, and work through the groups,
their dependence on the rich-and-powerful for advice, loans, and work
is reduced. We asked women who they now turn to for advice. Most
consult each other. One woman said she still goes to the *matbor*. We
asked her whether she now finds his advice helpful. She answered:

= I will think myself whether he gives me good suggestions or bad ones.
If he gives me a good suggestion, I will try to understand how far it is
good for me. Or whether it is a bad suggestion.

As the women's perceptions change and as the groups progress they
begin to earn the respect, however begrudging, of the rich-and-
powerful. We asked the women about the changing attitudes of the
rich-and-powerful.

= They say: "She has done a good thing. She is working while sitting in
the house." They also say: "You have done good. People come to you,

give you work, and show you how to do new work. We (the rich) have passed our metric, but these people do not come to us."

—You have earned some money from your group activities. What else have you achieved? Have you earned any respect?

= Now people respect us and value us. I now have a cow. People say: "They have done an intelligent thing to have formed a group." They listen to us. Now people invite us and talk with us, entertain us with betel leaves, etc., but previously they did not talk to us. Now if we go through the village, women call us to ask about family planning pills. They have more confidence in us now. But previously they never talked to us, listened to us, and never gave us any respect. But now they respect us. We are more accepted now than before. Because of the group we are more respected now. Previously if we went to people's homes, they assumed we came to ask for something. So they used to act very indifferently to us. But now they show us respect and we are very friendly.

We asked whether anyone opposes them now.

= Now nobody talks ill of us. They say: "They have formed a group and now they earn money. It is good." Now nobody speaks ill of us. Many say: "You have formed a group. Please allow us to join you."

= There are other changes. If we walk through the streets now, the *matbors* do not say anything. Now there is no problem.

We interrupted to ask whether the *matbors* behaved well with them now.

= Yes, because they now know that if they do anything bad with us they will face a problem. The members also do not say anything against us now. They support us. Yesterday a member said: "Why have you brought BRAC staff so late in the day? You should bring them to our homes. We can then talk to them." I said: "Why should I bring them to you? You are our enemies. They come to see our condition. If you want, you can invite them, then you can talk to them. They do not come to see you." The things you BRAC staff discuss with us, if the *matbors* would have discussed these with us, then we would have no problems.

We asked them whether they will be able to resist future interferences by the rich-and-powerful.

= If we stay united then the rich will not be able to do anything. We will not go to work in the houses of the rich.

—Then how will the rich get women to work in their houses?

= They will hire women from other villages to work in their houses. But

those women also do not want to work. The rich behave very badly with
the workers.
—But the rich will get angry with you saying: "Because of you we are not
getting women to work in our houses."
= No. If they say anything, we will not leave them alone.
—What do the rich say to you? Do you go to their houses?
= Yes. If we go to their houses they offer us a place to sit and they
behave nicely with us.

Not all women are able to resist the interference of the rich-and-
powerful. Many of the women are fearful and hesitant at first. Some
women are more confident or, simply, more needy. If the hesitant
women receive no family support they are unlikely to join the BRAC
activities. If the hesitant women receive some family backing they
follow more confident women. The more confident or needy will join
the group even if they get no family support. If they get the backing of
their family they may strike out as leaders. In each village, there are
usually one or two women who with or without the backing of their
families will lead the others.

hesitant without family support—drop-outs
hesitant with family support—follower
confident without family support—follower
confident with family support—leader
independent with or without family support—leader

So long as one or two women have the initial strength to resist the
interference, others will follow, and the interference will persist but
will lose its impact. The stronger groups usually have at least one
woman with an independent nature.

Changes in Resources

Income

Before women had little access to or control over cash incomes. Now
these women are earning small (but significant in their terms and lives)
income. BRAC's aim is to engage as many women as possible in
schemes which will earn them between 150 to 200 taka a month ($10 to
13). In the early phase of a scheme, some women earn very little—
maybe 25 to 50 taka a month. In the Bangladesh rural economy, the

simple fact of women earning is significant and even those amounts are
not insignificant.

> = Because of this women can have some freedom in life. If we can work
> for 15 taka a month, it helps to do something.

Some women have earned 200 taka a month for several months or
years. Some women have earned a total of several hundred taka. What
the women value over the exact amount of income is the steadiness
(i.e., security) of earning season after season. What they have suffered
under is the chronic unemployment of the male earners in their
families and the uncertainties of their own paid work.

We asked the women again and again how they use the money they
earn? Do they educate their children? Do they buy clothes or jewelry
or land? We listened for patterns in their answers—patterns of investment.

Most of the women spend their first earnings on the immediate
needs of their families. Food comes first. In the past, many have had to
make a small quantity of rice last their family for several days.

> = I have passed many hard days. I ate half a seer of flour between my
> children and myself. Two or three days I have remained hungry. Those
> who have lost husbands and cried sitting with their children. Now Allah
> has been kind to us.

From our discussions with many poor women, we calculated the
minimum standard of living to which they aspire. The standard is
indeed minimal:

1 or 2 meals a day
shelter (a hut made from jute straw and thatch)
clothing:
   2 saris—for women
   1 pant and 1 shirt—for children
   1 *lungi* (sarong) and 1 *genji* (undershirt) and 1 *gumcha* (scarf)—for
   men

The men need the scarf to wrap and protect their heads when they
work in the sun or carry heavy loads. The women need two saris
because they bathe fully dressed. They need a dry sari to change into,
but often they make do with only one sari.

If they are able to provide this minimum standard to their families, the women will then take several steps to ensure the security of the family: repay debts, redeem mortgaged goods, or repair their homes. Before many women mortgaged jewelry or brass utensils in order to feed their families. Now women are able to redeem those goods and even buy new ones.

> = Before I sold my nose ring and spent the money for food. I mortgaged groceries, sold old saris, and suffered hardship. We ate a *khitchuri* (gruel) made by mixing potato and flour. But we do not eat that now. I sold my nose ring for seven takas and now I purchased one for eighteen takas . . . We earned this money. Now I do not go to mortgage things.

Before the women and their families were often locked into the dreaded cycle of indebtedness that led only to mortgage and to loss of their land. Now some women are able to repay outstanding debts although only one or two have been able to redeem their land. Before few women could save, but now many women are saving their earnings as a hedge against the uncertain future.

> = I do not go to work in other people's houses and I do not sit in my house either. Whatever income I get from the group activities I enjoy that. Before we did not know what earnings were and we were not intelligent. If we husk one maund of paddy, we get 20–25 takas. Sometimes I earn 10 takas. Whatever my husband earns we eat off that. And whatever I earn, I keep that aside. Isn't that a benefit?

> = Now we understand profit and loss and rear poultry and grow vegetables. We collect a handful of rice every day (a traditional form of saving called *mushti tuli*) which I did not do before. We can sell as well as eat eggs and vegetables.

Before few women could obtain loans in their own right and those they could obtain carried a very high rate of interest—an average of 10% interest per month or 120% interest per year. As one woman said: "If we want loans, no one gives us loans. If anybody agrees, they want interest." But now the women are able to take personal loans against the group fund and group loans for joint activities from BRAC.

> = By trying I have found relief and hope to get more relief. We help the new groups from our savings. We are seventeen members and we help each other in case of need. We do not work on others' houses anymore and do not go then to the rich (for loans). For my son's wedding I took a loan of 200 takas from the group without interest.

Once they have repaid their debts or redeemed mortgaged goods or saved a little, the women will invest their earnings in certain assets: poultry-goat-cow (in that order) or a tin roof or an addition to their huts or an agricultural implement (day laborers earn a higher daily wage if they come equipped with a plough). And, very occasionally, some women are able to spare a little income for themselves.

   = Now I buy my own needs with my own income. I buy a sari, blouse, sandals, and bangles. I could not buy so many things out of my husband's income. Somehow I was able to buy a sari for daily use out of my husband's income. Now everyone has some money in hand after depositing some in the group fund.

We heard many women. We talked about what we heard among ourselves and agreed there was a pattern to how the women use and invest their personal earnings. The pattern is shown on the next page.

Employment

Before women had few options for work other than those prescribed to them—subsistence tasks in their own homes and subsistence tasks (for minimal pay) in the homes of the rich. Now groups of women are working in the fields or on the roads. Because of impoverishment and the need to earn a wage women have sought work at food-for-work sites. With BRAC support some women now cultivate fields, lease land, and grow their own crops. The women face resistance to their search for employment options.

   = Before we did not go out. After forming the group, we go. I know now that if we go out we will not become bad. By sitting in the house, we can become bad.
   —Is it good to cover your head?
   = Women are supposed to cover their head. But if I want to become bad, seven *topis* (caps) will not be able to prevent me.
   —You go out and work, doesn't anyone say anything?
   = People used to criticize us. Still some criticize us.
   —Why do they still criticize you? You say that you have got courage now?
   = They say we will sit for our metric examination. We will become Christian. English people will take us away.
   = They think we are bad because we move on the road. But the wives of the rich do not cover their heads when they walk in the city. They use the fields as a latrine. And if they talk to their laborers, then they do not lose their sense of shame. Only we lose our sense of shame.

INVESTMENT SEQUENCE

food	
	immediate needs
shelter	
	minimum needs
clothing	
debts repayment	
goods redemption	
	security
savings	
house repairs	
poultry	
goats	
cow	
	assets
tin roof	
addition to hut	
personal items	
children's education	future benefits
land	ultimate security

Women cultivating wheat, paddy, or jute. Women hired as agricultural laborers in the fields. This may seem typical, but in Bangladesh this work is still considered "male" work. Our first line of attack, together with the women, has been to demand "male" work for women. Our second line of attack, only after the first has been secured, has been to help the women address the terms and conditions of this work.

Before the women who did secure some "male" work knew little about the wages. Together we discussed their wages.

= We have dug earth for only 1 taka (7 cents) a day.

= We have received 1 or 2 taka per day. We worked for eight days and got 16 taka.

= I have received only 14 taka for eight days of work.

= We do maximum work but get minimum wages.

Now some groups have begun to demand better, the bare minimum, wages. Individual groups of earth-digging women have begun to contact each other to form an informal union. Otherwise if one group refuses to work for less than the minimum wage then other groups will agree to.

Before women had little or no control over the means of production. Women had access to their own small vegetable and fruit plots but exercised little control over their produce. Now women negotiate to lease land and cultivate their own crops. As the secretary of one women's group reported proudly: "Our demonstration plot is a shining example of the fact that women themselves can cultivate high yielding varieties of rice." Now women negotiate to lease ponds to cultivate fish.

One group of women played off two rival groups of landlords in an effort to gain access to some *khas* (public) land. Earlier all public land had been promised to the "landless" by the government. One group of landlords had illegally occupied that land for 15 years. The rival group of landlords told the group of women they would pay them wages to harvest the paddy of the other group and afterwards the women could claim the land. Actually, the rival group wanted to claim the land (also illegally). But the women took the matter into their own hands. They harvested the paddy early—while the paddy was still chest-deep in water. They kept the paddy and occupied the land (their legal right). Both groups of landlords are now not only scared of each other but also of the women.

Changes in Power

Before men "represented" women in the local judicials. Before few women voted and fewer still ran in the local elections. Before the poor, much less poor women, seldom received or demanded their rights from the local government. Now some of this is changing.

Women and the Local Judicial Councils

Before women were seldom regarded as able to be wronged by the society. If they were so regarded or if they were accused of doing wrong, women were "represented" by their male guardians in the local judicials or in court. But gradually women are beginning to represent themselves in legal matters. The local judicial councils, known as the *shalish*, are convened when an aggrieved party can command enough backers to sit on the council. Typically, the *matbors-mullahs* are considered to have the skills and powers to judge on the *shalish*.

One of the threats against women who join in BRAC's programs is that so-and-so will call a *shalish* to punish such-and-such action. Gradually the women have begun either to resist the verdict of a *shalish* initiated against them or to convene their own *shalish*.

When we asked one group of women what they might do if the husband of any member wanted to marry for a second time,

> = We will not allow that. Already he has got a wife, so why should he marry again? The way we will punish him, he will give up notions of marrying again. We will also call a *shalish*.
> —But aren't *shalish* convened by the men?
> = A women's *shalish* will be convened by women. And from now on, we will hold our own *shalish*.
> —What happens if there is a fight in the village and the *matbors* come to the *shalish*, do they call you to attend that *shalish*?
> = If the *shalish* is connected with our group, then they call us.
> —Suppose there is a *shalish* about your group and the *matbors* conduct the *shalish* and blame your group's members, then what will you do?
> = If the *matbors'* judgment is not correct, then we will not accept it. We will call the *shalish* again.

From representation by men to self-representation to initiating legal proceedings to calling for a retrial. A great deal is changing in the villages of these women.

Women and the Local Elections

Before few women voted and fewer still were elected to public office. Typically, the candidates (backed by certain factions) promise nigh everything prior to the election but deliver precious little after the elections. And the poor are locked into factions from which they hope to derive certain benefits in return for their vote.

Most women organized by BRAC are no longer gullible to campaign promises.

=In the past we lived under the control of the chairman and the *matbors*. Now we would like to be self-reliant. At the time of the election, *matbors* and the chairman begged for election votes from door to door. But after the vote, we cannot see them. They said that they would give us sugar at the rate of 62 poisa, but after the election they did not even come to us.

=I do not cast my vote. Why should I cast my vote? I understand everyone has the right to cast a vote. Before the election they call us Mia-bhai (affectionate title). After the election they forget us. They come and say: "We will give you rice and wheat. They offer us beetle-nuts. After they win the election and we say: "Mia-bhai, please give us a ration slip so we can buy cloth." They say "Not now, come later on" or "I do not have time now, come at night." We go at night for the slip. "I work the whole day and at night. And, you all come for a slip." This is how they win the election and how they behave. That is why I do not cast my vote for him. We will select a poor person and vote for him.

We asked about the reaction of those who lose their votes.

=They are not losing my vote. Someone becomes my husband's wife and casts a vote. What is there to do? All the rich are bad.

We asked what the women will do in the next election.

=None of us will cast our vote. No poor will cast their vote. Rafique is rich, but we do not like him. We are poor. We like the poor.

We asked how they have learned to talk in this way. We are told very simply and vividly: "Words come from the stomach." We asked whether they talked like this before.

=No. I did not think before. I did not talk to anyone. Like a dog, I used to work in the houses of the rich. After they had eaten, whatever remained in the pot, we ate. They used to give us rice for daytime work. No food for the nighttime work.

Given that the women are no longer gullible and given the strength in numbers of their groups, the rich-and-powerful recognize that these women need special handling and cannot be overlooked. During a recent election, one group of women who had won a case in the local judicial, were approached for their votes. The women answered back.

= Why should we cast our vote for you if you don't give us work? We cast our vote according to our own choice. We will not vote for anyone now, we will select someone from our group and vote for her. We will make someone (from our group) president.

Although no woman has been elected president, at least one BRAC-supported woman has addressed the president of Bangladesh.

Imagine a lean woman in her mid-forties. She is speaking to the local village council. As it so happens that day, the president of the country is visiting her village and listens to her speech. She says that she was once shy like other village women and constrained by the customs of her society. She tells how she overcame her shyness and began to organize other women. "It started two years ago. We came to know that women of other villages were earning and supporting their families by working in food-for-work programs. But there was no move to start similar programs in our village. One day we, the suffering women, approached the Chairman (of the Union Council). But he disagreed with our request and refused to change his point of view. We realized that no one will understand our problems and that we will have to stand on our own feet!" She and the other women stood firm, a food-for-work program was started, and they were employed.

But that was not all that happened to this woman. She and the other poor in her village ran for election as members of the local village council. They won a majority of seats and she was elected the "headman" of the council! And that is why it happened that Ojudnessa addressed the president.

But Ojudnessa is not content. She does not feel that the strength of poor in one village is enough. "Our opponents have more ways and means and scope to play dirty with us. Winning in only one village is no solution to this national problem. Other adjacent villages also need to be organized in a similar way. We will have to maintain unity at all levels. We will have to defend each and every heinous move of the rich . . . This is our turn to win."

Women and Public Goods and Services

Before the poor, much less poor women, seldom received their due share of goods and services from the government. In an in-depth study of Dhankura village, we found that public rations are distributed by the union-council politicians on the following basis:

—ration dealerships go to the wealthy supporters of the union-council members and chairman

—90% of luxury rations goods are distributed among the rich of the village (70% of these to factional supporters, and 30% to keep other rich happy and pacified)

—the remaining 10% of luxury ration goods and the non-luxury goods are distributed to the factional supporters of the union-council politicians

We wanted to establish whether this was the common pattern and what the women thought about their rights to public goods and services. When the women first get together in BRAC-organized classes or group meetings, they do not necessarily understand their rights. But as they meet and discuss together their awareness grows.

= The poor do not understand that the poor should get all the things. The rich say: "Cloth came but ran short." In fact, they sell the cloth.

= This year we have gotten ration cards. The ration dealer gives us half the allotment of rice, flour, and salt. If we say anything the ration dealer says: "I only have this much. Wheat is coming." Before we could not even ask about the wheat. If all the group members go to the local government officer and complain to him about the (ration) dealer, then what will happen to him?

Some women have begun to make just such complaints and to demand their rights. When one member of the women's group in Pathalia village (Jamalpur) was denied medical attention at the local government clinic, ten women from Pathalia village marched to the clinic, announced their right to free medical care, and demanded the woman receive treatment. She did. Now other women, all claiming to be from Pathalia village, also receive the medical care they were previously denied. To this day the women claim: "Mention Pathalia and the doctor gets scared." Another group declared they now have the strength to take similar action.

= They do not supply medicine and talk rubbish. All this time, we have been weak. Now we are 60 members and we have got strength. We will go now. They will have to supply medicine.
—For whom is the hospital established and run?
= For the poor. No, not only for the poor. It is for all. But they should take more care for the poor because the rich can spend money and go to

a private doctor. If a child of the rich falls ill, they will take out a thousand taka and will bring the doctor by motorcycle.

We asked another group what services they might demand from the government.

= We need a tube-well and a bridge. If we go to the dealer's house to bring water sometimes they refuse to give us water. My son went to fetch water and while he was near the tube-well he drank water from the tube-well using his hand. Then they came and caught my son by the neck and forced him to drink water again as he had done. They also poured water on his head. We will apply to the authority. Tomorrow we may go to the authorized office for the tube-well. In our village there is no tube-well. The south and north villages (i.e., neighborhoods) have got tube-wells. Only this middle village has not gotten a tube-well.

Many groups of women have demanded and receive certain public goods and services: tube-wells, food-for-work schemes, and rations.

Changes in Attitudes

Before they never had opportunities to meet outside their homes, now they meet regularly in classes or group meetings. Before they worked only at prescribed tasks within their homes or villages, now some of these women work outside their villages in the fields and on the roads. Before most women earned no personal income, now many of them earn their own cash incomes. Their views of the world and of their village life are no longer quite the same. How do they express the changes in their attitudes?

Knowledge. Wisdom. Confidence. Initiative. Self-reliance. These are the words the women used to describe the changes in their attitudes.

Knowledge

The women spoke gratefully of their new ability to read and write. Before they could not read a letter or do their accounts. Before they could not read the sign boards in the town. Before they could not help their children with their school work. After the functional education classes, they can.

= At first, I did not know anything. I did not even know how to read and write.

= I was not literate. Shanti told us that she would teach us literacy. I told her that I would be a student. Why? Because I was illiterate. An illiterate person is like a blind person. So, I wanted to know something. When I first started I could not read anything. Now I can read. I can recognize numbers and some words. I can sign my name.

BRAC's functional education provides them more than a small degree of literacy and numeracy, it provides them different types of knowledge.

= After I joined the group I acquired knowledge gradually. How to bring up my son in a decent way. How I can bring about changes. How I can live better. If I did not acquire knowledge, how could I say all these things? If there had been no change then how could I have learned and understood all this? Even my mother said yesterday: "You did not use to visit others' homes, did not speak to others. How have you learned to speak so many things?" I said: "Ma, how I have learnt I cannot say. Whenever I am alone I sit with the books (BRAC functional education manuals)." My mother asked: "What do you see in the books?" I said: "Ma, what valuable things there are in the books you will not understand because you cannot read and write." If somebody behaves badly with me, I go home and sit with the books. When I sit with the books my mind becomes better. We also like the meetings. I feel badly if the meeting is held only once a month. But if it is held every Sunday then we all feel better because we can discuss and acquire new knowledge. But if the meeting is held only once a month, we forget many things and our knowledge does not increase very much . . . Even if I say 'No meeting today,' nobody listens. Everybody spends the day at my home and asks me to conduct the meeting . . . Everybody says: "She did not know how to talk before. But now, she keeps all the accounts and account books so nicely. She must know many things."

Wisdom

Before the women had been kept from understanding their relation to the world and from realizing their own capacities. They had been conditioned to depend on men in general and on the rich-and-powerful men in particular for what they call "wisdom." Before the women did not perceive their innate wisdom. Now, after attending classes, meetings, and workshops, their innate wisdom has begun to surface.

Most of the women spoke of this newly-discovered wisdom. The typical expressions were

= our eyes have opened

= my mind was rusted and now it shines

= we have become wise

= we were blind, although we had eyes

"But were you not wise before?" we challenged them. "Yes," they answered, "but we did not apply our wisdom."

We asked the women to describe this wisdom. Some referred to a new-found confidence in their own minds. Some described this wisdom as comprehension.

= My mind is changed. What was bad in my mind is changed. My bad behavior has changed. Also, I have no good knowledge and understanding. As my knowledge and understanding is good now, I will be able to do many things gradually. During the first year of the group, I did not understand anything. BRAC staff used to talk often to us, but I could not catch what they were saying. Whatever they said entered one ear and went out the other. I could not internalize anything. Now, slowly but slowly, I have understood everything.

Many women described this wisdom through citing examples. The woman whose mind "now shines" explained that before she would defer to the wisdom ("verdicts") of the *matbors*, but now she thinks for three or four days before answering a *matbor's* question or judgment. The field staff added that women like her are now "sophisticated 1000 times" and can discern lies told to them.

Other women described this wisdom in very practical terms.

= Before we were blind, although we had eyes. We used to work in other people's houses, but we did not get the correct wages. Now we rear poultry, plant trees and cultivate other people's land on a share-cropping basis. We grow paddy, jute, wheat, onions and potatoes. We make a profit from this cultivation. We do not go to work in other people's houses anymore. Whatever we know how to do, we do that sitting in our own houses.

= Now I know how to take care of my children. Also, I did not know how to manage the household affairs. Now I have learned that also. I took loan from BRAC and purchased a cow. I have repaid the loan and now I have a cow worth 1000 taka. I did not know all these things. That is why I have come here. I have also taken a loan for paddy husking. If I had not come, I would not have known all these matters. How to improve our conditions. And would not have gotten anything. Now I take clients to the Manikganj family planning operation center. I also know how the operation is done. I also know how oral pills are to be taken. I did not know anything about this before.

What has all this new-found knowledge and wisdom meant to the women? We see and they feel a marked shift from passivity to creativity, from hesitancy to confidence. They explain how they have been transformed by the experience of participating in a group into thinking, confident, and dynamic women.

Confidence

The women begin to look at themselves in new ways.

=I had no such courage before joining the group. I know what is right and wrong now. Now, if anyone says anything wrong I answer back, before I used to keep quiet. Where did I get my courage? From my self-confidence and wisdom. If there is a quarrel with the men in our village and we, the members of the group, go there, they will not be able to face us. We are 90 members strong and we have a strength.

=We are benefitted in this way, that before we were afraid of people and could not talk to other people. But, now, we can talk to people and understand what they say. After joining the group, we are able to see many places and have come to know so many people which we could not do before.

What they describe is confidence. Confidence as a group and in themselves. The confidence to take decisions and to follow them with action.

Initiative

Before these women had few options other than those prescribed to them—the subsistence tasks in their own homes and subsistence tasks (for minimal pay) in the homes of the rich. Before these women had no time, no training, no resources, and no capacity to think or to plan ahead. Now the women have begun to plan and to think beyond the day-to-day round of survival.

A few women had developed a knack for enterprise on their own. But their circumstances had permitted them, they were not completely tied down to finding the next meal and someone had lent them some money. But most of the women had never developed a knack for enterprise. They did as best as they could at day-to-day subsistence and survival rounds but nothing in their circumstances (they had no reserve, no resources, no credit) or in their conditioning (they had been trained to minimize risk, maximize security, and struggle day-to-day) had prepared them to think and to plan ahead.

Much of this changed when they joined the BRAC group. The women acquired a knack for enterprise—for saving, investing, and planning their resources.

=Now I can write my name. Also, I learned that if my children and I, myself, work then our income will increase and there will be peace in the family. I did not know this before. I did not care about anything before. What should be done to get nutritious food, etcetera.

=Changes like—how we can raise our income, how we can effectively use the money we borrow from the office (BRAC) and how we can ourselves make money by raising cattle, etcetera. . . Then everybody will say: "They went to the office and through the new knowledge they have wisdom." If we cannot do it then others, even the office brothers (BRAC staff) will say; "We loaned them money but they could not do anything using their own brains." This sister (BRAC staff) now loves us. If we do not do good things then she will also say: "Oh, they know but they do not do anything." She will not then love us. I myself work, then there will be change, otherwise not. I will have to apply my knowledge for change. Nobody will work for me.

Independence

Before these women had been conditioned to be dependent on the men of their households in their subsistence rounds and on the men of the village for wisdom and advice. Now these women have begun to declare their self-reliance, their lack of dependence.

=If we do not follow our own wisdom, and if we follow your (BRAC staff) advice we will be dependent on you. We cannot keep the gun on your shoulder and solve our problems. We must expect to carry the gun on our own shoulders to solve the problems in our lives.

=The brothers of BRAC gave us taka for purchasing cows and goats. They will give us taka for one or two or three years. But after that they will not give. After that they will say that we helped you three times. Now what have you done? So we have to work and proceed in such a way that by investing their taka we will be able to do something. By investing our taka, we must be able to increase our income and purchase cows. And we will not be able to decrease our wants. We must not depend on others' help.

=We must realize that we are working with others' taka. We have to increase our own taka and work with that.

=Still we are begging. We attended the convention in Manikganj by begging taka. In the next convention we will attend by not begging taka.

= All the members of the group contributed taka for attending the convention. So why should we call it begging?

= Because we take the help of the office (BRAC), so it is begging.

= We have to try to be self-sufficient so that we do not have to go to the office for help. And for that we have to increase our group membership.

= We had no knowledge. BRAC gave us knowledge. We had no work. BRAC gave us work by investing taka. They helped us with taka and in support of our living. Now we are rearing cows. Now by following such ways we should not have to take BRAC's help. And we have to try to be united forever. If I take care of myself only, then I alone will have sufficient food and clothing. But within a group, we all have to sacrifice for others.

The women told us of so many changes. In the interest of indicating the types of change evaluators might look for, I will in chapter eight distill a framework for evaluating the impact of any given project on women from the changes described above. But before doing so, I would like to present in their own words the case-histories of three women. You have heard the collective voice of many women, listen now to the individual voices of three women.

CHAPTER SEVEN

Three Women Speak

What follows are the stories of three women told to me and other BRAC staff. Each story was recorded and transcribed and translated verbatim. I have tried to stay as close as possible to the women's words. In the interest of brevity, I have omitted those parts where the woman tells the story of her group and included only those portions where she tells her individual story. And, in the interest of the privacy of the women, I have changed their names and edited parts of their stories. But otherwise, these stories are told exactly as they were remembered. In presenting these three women and their stories, I do not suggest that Rohima, Kamala or Mallika are "typical" of all village women in Bangladesh but I do suggest that each can be seen as to some degree "typical" of the poor village women with whom BRAC works.

ROHIMA OF WEST SHANBANDHA

Baliartek is a market town on the banks of a river which runs broad and slow at this point in its journey to the sea. Recessed steps in the crumbling mud banks lead down to small planks of wood which serve as crude piers to boats of all sizes and shapes. There are large transport boats, small dug-outs to shuttle passengers back and forth, and low, covered "house" boats.

I reach Baliartek by car (forty early-morning miles along a main road) and by motorcycle (along wide mud embankments, across narrow mud dikes between fields, and through villages) and finally by dug-out (across the river). Baliartek is home to one of BRAC's camps: simple office-cum-dormitory buildings for field staff. I plan to visit West Shan-bandha village that afternoon, spend the night at Baliartek camp to debrief staff, and interview the women of West Shanbandha the next morning.

We walk north from Baliartek market across a channel of water on a plank bridge. We pass fields of wild mustard and lentils and wheat. On the outskirts of West Shanbandha, we stop at a dilapidated hut. A woman with a goiter and swollen eyes is cooking on an outdoor stove. She has no homestead land, no family plot for vegetables and fruit. Her hut is, literally, strewn together on the side of the road. She is, I am told, the poorest member of the West Shanbandha Women's Group.

We walk on along a path lined with date-palms. Men shinny up the trees to retrieve the pots, now filled with bubbly juice, they had strapped to the trees in the morning. Most of the huts back onto or face open courtyards. Some courtyards are fenced off with jute straw and others by a hedge. Some homes are more prosperous, others less so.

Rohima's home appears prosperous. There are several huts backing onto a courtyard. Some of the huts are roofed with tin. There are two cows, a few chickens, a date-palm and several fruit trees. But Rohima, I am told, does not share in this prosperity. The household belongs to her brother. Her mother lives and eats with the brother. Rohima lives with her brother but eats alone. . .

The next morning Rohima tells her story. Rohima's face is broad and flat. She wears a red and green sari with a thin, white shawl over her shoulders. Her wavy hair is parted down the middle and knotted into a bun at the back. Some of her teeth are missing and those that remain are heavily outlined with betel juice. She has bright, energetic eyes. She emphasizes her speech with jerks of her head and punctuates her narrative with rhetorical questions: isn't that so? no? She speaks freely and at length. We listen. . .

"My brothers had a small piece of land—only 2 *pakhis* (⅔ acre). My father arranged marriages for all of us brothers and sisters. After 21 years of marriage, my father died.

"After his death I started going to my husband's house. I got married when I was only 7 years old. My father did not send me to my hus-band's house because I was very young. Then after my father's death, I started staying at my husband's house, initially 2–3 days at a time.

Three of my children died: two daughters and one son. Then I had one son and one daughter. This son is seven years old and the daughter is three years old. After my father's death, my brothers got separated and started their own families. Only my youngest brother is living with my mother.

"My husband asked me to bring 1000 taka from my parents' house. I did not know that my husband had been asked to bring 1000 by people where he works; if he failed to do so, he would not be given any work. He agreed. My husband did not mention it to me. He only said: "Bring 1000 taka for me, otherwise I will not provide you food." I asked: "How can I manage this amount of money? My father is dead. We are five brothers and four sisters. With great difficulty and hardship my father looked after us. So, how can I bring money? Now, my father is also dead. How can I ask my brothers for this money? During my marriage there was no condition of money. Now, why does this question of money arise?" My husband said very suddenly, "I know nothing. If you want to eat in my house, you will have to bring 1000 taka." Then, in the month of Bhadro, I fell ill. He said: "Go to your parents' house, try to recover from the illness and then come back." He left me and my children at my parents' house.

"We came to my parents' house in the month of Bhadro. My husband came on the last day of Aswin month to take his son. My brothers were not at home. I was ill and lying on a bed in the house.

"He came and took my son and daughter with him. He told me: "For one month you are here. We have not yet eaten *peetha* (rice cakes), etc. So I am taking my son and daughter." I was weeping. I told my son not to go. My son refused to go. But my husband took him forcibly. My son was crying. When my brothers returned from market, they scolded me asking why I had allowed my husband to take my children with him. After that I went to the *matbor* of the village. He said: "Your husband has taken his own children, what is that to you? You cannot do anything."

"Next day my brother, together with the father and uncle of Sobhan, went to my husband's house to fetch my children. Upon seeing them, my mother-in-law locked the house and went away with my children. My brother said: "Well, if we cannot take them, we can at least see them." He said, "They are not your relations. If they were your relations, they would go to your house and you could then see them." After that my younger brother somehow managed 300 taka for my treatment. I recovered from the illness. After my recovery, I went to my husband's house with my brothers, Sobhan's father and the members of the locality. There was a *darbar* (meeting). My husband said: "I will not listen to anything. She can come and stay if she can bring 1000 taka, otherwise not." My brother said: "How can I manage this 1000 taka? I do not have land. Should I sell my father's land? It is not possible."

"However, after a long discussion he took me back to his home and I was there for about a year. Then one day he forced me out of the house and forced me to render my thumbprint on a paper. When he took my thumbprint, my mother and brothers were not at home. My husband gave a 500 taka bribe to the *matbors* and also gave them 100 taka worth of *rasgulla* (sweets). Then he took my thumbprint. Everybody told me: "Go to your home." My brother said: "It is not dignified to run after a dog. God's justice will come one day." One (union council) member said: "Aunty, do not create any disturbance over this, do not cry. You wait, there will be no problem for your food and clothing."

"After a year, and one day, I heard that some people have made a camp along the riverside. Why and for what purpose they had come, nobody knew. One day my mother told me: "Some people are there in the camp. Let us go one day to see them." We went and, at first, observed them from far away. My cousin-brothers were working there. They asked us why we had come. After two days, BRAC field staff visited us. They said: "We came to your area, but you do not talk to us." He talked to my brother about functional education. My brother said: "OK, let me first talk with the local members and *matbors* because I need their understanding." After 10–12 days, my brother permitted me to attend functional education class. Initially, I did not go. Afterward, however, I went.

"First, my mother bought me a goat for 10 taka, ten to fifteen years ago. Then I sold that goat for 25 taka, and, finally, I made 500 taka. I made this five hundred just two years ago. I came to my father's home, that means six years ago. I gave my son some of his money for buying his shirt, English pants, etc., because he is studying in a school and sometimes he comes to me for money. Just the other day I bought him a pen for 14 taka. I advise him to study seriously. My son says: "Ma, Father has left you, but I will not leave you. Let me earn, then I will look after you." He visits me occasionally, but I do not see him at his father's house. I see him in another house where he comes to see me. Because I do not have the right to see him in his father's house.

"It is good now. Many changes. My mind is changed. What was bad in my mind is changed. My bad behavior is changed. Also, I have now good knowledge and understanding. As my knowledge and understanding is good now, I will be able to do many things gradually. During the first year the group was formed, I did not understand anything. BRAC field staff used to talk more often to us, but I could not catch what they were saying. Whatever they said entered one ear and went out the other. I could not internalize anything. Now, slowly but slowly, I have understood everything.

"Everybody used to talk ill against me. I did not listen to them. They are the rich. Why should we listen to the rich? They walked on our bodies. We should not listen to them. They should listen to us. I was very poor. I could not eat properly and buy my clothing. We started studying in the functional education class. We discussed our problems, etc. Now, everything seems good to me.

"When we first formed the *somity*,* I used to walk to the houses of group members. Villagers used to insult me by saying: "Who will take care of you? The servant of Arab has come," things like this. I used to remain silent. Then the *matbors* started putting pressure on us. We had a meeting at my aunt's house. The *matbors* pressured my aunt that she should not hold the meeting. My aunt came to us and said: "Today you cannot hold the meeting because the *matbors* do not want us to attend the meeting." BRAC field staff came and discussed the matter with us. The *matbors* (village leaders) said: "You have brought women out of their houses." What have we gained from the somity? We raised poultry. We also started goat-rearing. Fourteen goats died. We had a loss of 900 taka. However, we earned some income. Now, we have started cow rearing. We hope we will make a profit.

"There are other changes. If we walk through the streets now, the *matbors* do not say anything. Now, no problem. Because they now know that if they do anything bad with us they will face a problem. The (union council) members also do not say anything against us now. They support us. Yesterday one of the members said: "Why have you brought the BRAC staff so late in the day? You should bring them to our homes. We can then talk to them." I said: "Why should I bring BRAC staff to you? You are our enemies. BRAC staff come to see our condition. They also say you are our enemy. If you want, you can invite

Somity means "society" in Bengali and is the word used by BRAC staff and the women to refer to the BRAC-organized groups.

them, then you can talk to them. They do not come to see you. The things BRAC staff discuss with us, if the *matbors* would have discussed these with us, then we would have no problems."

"The *matbors* used to blame my brothers. My brothers asked: "What are you doing in the group? You are going to bring dishonour upon us." I said: "How have I brought dishonour?" Then one day I requested BRAC field staff visit our home and talk with my brothers. BRAC field staff came one day. I called my second brother and one *matbor* to talk with them. My second brother said: "If the group brings dishonour, I will see to it." My younger brother also came. My second brother said: "As everybody opposes you, you should not go to the (BRAC) office." I said: "No, I cannot do that. If we can change our condition then why should we not? You are our group. We are in one group." Then they asked the BRAC field staff: "What is our sister saying? What is happening?" The BRAC field staff said: "What Bubu has in mind is different from what you have in your mind. So how can you understand Bubu?" I said: "No. I must go in the future. When they start going, I must go. If the *matbors* can, let them prevent me." Then my brothers said: "OK! You go." From then on, I started visiting the office. Now the *matbors* do not say anything.

"Now I have knowledge and understanding. If we can make the group function, we will be able to live comfortably, and we will make progress through our efforts. All the members listen to me. We, the poor, are united because they listen to me. At first, I could not understand. Then after coming to the meetings, I started understanding. Then BRAC field staff, one day, told me how to sit and how to conduct the meeting. Now if any members try to sit I show them how to sit. I tell them: "You should not feel shy and cover your face with your sari. You should feel free to talk. If you come to me, you should act like me."

"First I had a few hens which I used to rear. My mother gave them to me. I used to earn money by selling the chicks. I used to eat the chicks from time to time, and also used to save some for money. I did not eat everything. So I could save some. For three years after returning from husband's house, I got my food from my brothers. Then others began to say: "Your brother also bears the burden of his own children. How long can he support you? For three years he has supported you. So, what about that?" Then I gave 1500 taka to my brother for that.

"Some changes will occur. Now, my brothers behave nicely with me. Definitely, there will be some changes in behaviour. We are not in such a bad state since we have joined the group.

"My sister-in-law said: "Whenever she likes she can take her son. You have thrown her out and you should not say anything." My son said to me: "Ma, you are living in my uncle's house, stay there. I will give you something. You are my mother and I will never leave you so long as you have affection for me." Whenever my son asks for something I try to give it.

"My father-in-law said to my son: "I will give you two *pakhis* (⅔ acre) of land and you can stay with your mother and you can manage together with her income." But my mother-in-law is preventing the registration of these two *pakhis* of land. My mother-in-law said to my father-in-law: "If you give Nurul Islam (the son) two *pakhis* of land, he will bring his mother home. But if you do not give him this land, he will not be able to bring his mother." Then my father-in-law said to me: "If your son wants to bring you, will you come to stay with your son?" I said: "Yes, if my son wants to take care of me, I must comply with and I must take care of him." The other day my son said to me: "Ma, if you give me half of my food support and my father the rest, then I can study one year in the school. My father said he will not pay for my education after one year." I said: "Son, you continue your study. If your father does not pay for your education, I will then pay." If his father does not pay for his study, I have it in my mind to manage the expenses of his study. I have already thought about his study. If my son wants to continue his study, I will of course manage to support his study.

"When I was knowledgeless, I used to become gloomy after hearing what people say. I did not visit anyone else's house. I also did not try to talk to anybody. I used to stay at my mother's house. My mother said to me: "You do not go anywhere and do not talk to anybody. If you do this, then people will say, you are out of your mind." I explained to my mother: "Ma, I will not be out of my mind. Whatever people say is not all OK. I am a human being. Why should I be out of my mind?" Then my mother said: "You should not go to anybody's house." I said: "I will visit everybody's house and talk to everybody." If I start crying, then people can say that she has started crying because she was left by her husband and by her children. Some will say good, some will say bad. Whatever is to happen to me, I must keep in mind. I am thinking how I can bring up my son and educate him, how he can mix with everyone.

I have anxieties for him. That is why my health is not good. If my son would have stayed with me, then I would have good health. Four of my children—two sons and two daughters—have died and now only one son and one daughter are alive. How can I live without them? If my son would have stayed with me, then I would be happy even if I could only eat one time a day.

"After I joined the group, I acquired knowledge gradually: how I can bring up my son in a decent way; how I can bring changes; and how I can live better. If I did not acquire knowledge, how could I say all these? If there had been no change, then how could I have learned and understood all this? Even my mother said yesterday: "You did not use to visit others' homes, did not speak to others. How have you learnt to speak so many things?" I said: "Ma, how I have learnt I cannot say. Whenever I am alone I sit with the books." Mother asked: "What do you see in the books?"* I said: "Ma, what valuable things there are in the books you will not understand because you cannot read and write." If somebody behaves badly with me, I go home and sit with the books. When I sit with the books my mind becomes better.

"We also like the meetings. I feel badly if the meeting is held only once a month. But if it is held every Sunday then we all feel better because we can discuss and acquire new knowledge. But if the meeting is held only once a month, we forget many things and our knowledge does not increase very much. Everybody says: "She did not know how to talk before, but now, she keeps all the account books and accounts so nicely. She must know many things." Even if I say "No meeting today" nobody listens. Everybody spends the day at my home and asks me to conduct the meeting. If I ask them to sleep at my home the whole day they will do so. Everybody loves me. That is why some other people say to my group members, "Why do you listen to her?"

"There will be changes, of course. We have formed this group for change. If no change then why should we go for the group? Changes like: how can we raise our income, how can we effectively use the money we borrow from the office, and how can we ourselves make money by raising cattle, etc. Then everybody will say: "They went to the office and through the new knowledge they have wisdom." If we cannot do it then others, even the office brothers, will say: "We gave them money but they could not do anything using their own brains."

---

*BRAC's functional education materials.

This Apa* now loves us. If we do not do good things then she will also say: "Oh, they know but they do not do anything." She will not then love us. If I myself work, then there will be changes, otherwise not. I will have to apply my knowledge for change. Nobody will work for me.

"Hearing from the women I held two meetings. I said to them: "If I put money in the somity, then I have 500 taka. This person with four children does not have any place to stay. If we can give her a house or clothes, then it will be good. If we eat three times and they cannot eat then there is no peace in our minds. If all of us can eat then it is a different kind of happiness. But if some can eat and some cannot eat, then there is no happiness. Then all of us together made fences for Vimola's house, completed the roofing over that house for 10 taka, and repaired Mongol's house for 80 taka. We talked to Sunil-da [BRAC staff]. Sunil-da said: "I cannot say anything. If you have courage, you can do something." I said, "OK, money is not important."

"People said: "We have never before seen women go out of the house, buy bamboos and repair other people's houses. Why do women repair each other's houses?" I said: "The women will repair houses, they will even work in the fields, they will do all kinds of work. We have no prestige so what is the problem in working? So, we will work in the field, we will repair other people's houses, we will raise poultry. We see no problem in supporting ourselves through work. If we see that our poor brothers and sisters have no fences around their houses, we will help make fences for their houses. Whatever the *matbors* say, we will not heed."

"If we do not follow our own wisdom, and if we follow your (BRAC) advice we will be dependent on you. We cannot keep the gun on your shoulder and solve our own problems. We must expect to carry the gun on our shoulders to solve the problems in our lives. If we see bad things in the village we come to you, talk to you, and then feel better. We came and we will come. People go to *pir's* (religious leader's) houses to learn things. We come to you to learn good things. Is it not good? Whether you talk or not, we will come. If we visit your office, our minds get better.

"Yesterday, when the member's wife said: "I have never seen such a group," I said to her: "Ten percent are rich, ten percent are middle and 80 percent poor. We, the 80 percent, will go to the member's house. If

*Apa means "older sister" in Bengali and is the term used by the women to refer to female BRAC staff.

he takes care of us and give us food, clothing, etc., okay, we will not
then go for a group. If the member does this for us we will stop the
group today. We will throw the BRAC office out. I will do this myself."
The member scolded his wife and said to her: "What do you understand? You eat well and you have enough clothes, so you do not understand what the group is." Then the member's wife went inside the
house. I said to her: "If you do not behave nicely with us, we will not
let you go unquestioned. You may be the wife of the member but we
do not care. I say this in front of the member, so what?"

"There are some changes. In the beginning my mother said: "You
will be mad. People will say she has become mad by forming the
group." I said, "I will not be mad. Don't listen to what people say.
These people will one day come to me." Some people say: "You are
worse than the prostitute, prostitutes observe *purdah*, but you don't."
I said: "OK, BRAC female staff are also prostitutes, that is why they
have printed books for us poor people. They became prostitutes first,
then we. If they did not come to us, would it be possible for us to meet
all these brothers, from different districts, whose parents we don't
know? Could there be a hope like this that we would be together?"

"We used to walk through the streets after sunset. If we walked in
the daytime, our mothers used to object. Even when we formed the
group, people went against us. Even the member's wife teased us,
saying: "I will ask the member to sleep at my side. You ask your BRAC
people to sleep at your side." I said: "I will sleep wherever I like."
Before, if we walked through the streets in front of two or three people, they used to caution us. All women were to remain covered, to
keep their face under a cloth, otherwise the elders used to scold them.
When we walked through the streets, they said; "Why should women
walk through the streets?" If the women of a rich community walks in a
male gathering, then there is no problem. Nobody says anything to
them.

"No problem now. Nobody says anything. We, poor women, if we
walk through the streets, rich people do not say anything. In the
morning I went to fetch water. The *matbor* who was against me said:
"Where are you going?" I said: "I am going to fetch water, then I will go
to the BRAC office." He said: "Not water. You have something else." I
said: "Palm juice. Now you talk to me, before you did not talk to me.
You made me stand on the street." Rich women say: "You women, you
have more power." I said: "We are poor. We have no power." We have
nothing to say to the rich women. We do not like to talk with people

other than our group members. Many people ask us many things—about what we do, etc. I do not reply. I say: "We are poor people. Sometimes we eat, sometimes we do not eat. We discuss that."

"If I could live with my son and daughter then my son would be happy and I would also be happy. My only sadness is that they are not with me. My husband has left me—no problem, but if they could be with me I would have happiness and peace. At the age of seven I got married and since the last four years I have been divorced. So you can understand how many days I was there. I was very young when I got married. I used to stay at my husband's house half the days and then at my father's home and again half the days at a time. Then I started staying at my husband's house. I fell ill and my husband asked for money.

"My husband had 15 *pakhi* (5 acres) land. He used to cultivate mustard, paddy, pulses, etc. I used to assist in processing the harvest at home. Throughout the year I used to husk paddy at home. All paddy was husked at home by me using a *dekhi*. Every day he brought paddy. Both of us used to process this paddy into rice. We did a business of buying paddy and selling finished rice. He used to sell it in the *hat* [market]. Then he fell in love with that girl. She said to him: "You take me I will give you 1000 taka." Then he left me. When he left me, my father-in-law and brothers-in-law tried to prevent him but he wouldn't listen. Then, after two years, I started staying at my husband's house. After ten years, I had one daughter.

"I slowly and gradually learned all this. Others say: "Whatever you teach us, we will follow." I said: "All of us should be developed equally, otherwise it will not be OK." We should not depend only on the volunteer teacher. What the teacher can do we should acquire, we should acquire the accounting and knowledge quietly. We should not depend on the teacher only or on BRAC. Then nothing will happen. Isn't that so? We should ourselves understand our own matters. Is that not so?"

KAMALA OF RAMDIA

Betila is a union council headquarters built on an area of high ground. There is enough high land for a soccer field, several long-low school buildings, one or two brick office buildings. Betila was the seat of a local *zamindar* (landlord) in times past. There are still several large cement houses from that time. BRAC has rented one of these, a two-storied building to house its staff and offices. In front of the house on either side BRAC has constructed two bamboo and thatch buildings: one as a training center and the other as a silk-weaving workshop. I come to Betila regularly on program work. This time I have come to interview the women's groups at nearby Mithura and Ramdia villages.

In Ramdia village, we sit in the courtyard of a large homestead under the long shadows of a late winter afternoon. Eleven members of the women's group sit with us to discuss the history of the group—we form the inner circle. Children wander in-and-out of this circle. Infants nestle in the laps or suckle at the breasts of some women. Other women stoke fires as they prepare the evening meal and eavesdrop on our discussion. The men of the homestead stand silent—like sentinels—at a distance. They form an outer circle. The men cannot hear what we discuss but they watch what we do. A reversal of the typical pattern of men participating in public debates as women lurk in the shadows. All the women in the group come from this neighborhood. They are accustomed to meeting together in this particular courtyard and feel free to talk with us. One of these women is Kamala.

The following afternoon Kamala tells her story to us at the BRAC camp in Betila. She has a young pretty face framed by curly hair and big round eyes framed by bushy brows. She wears a green sari with a maroon border and a maroon blouse to match. She wears a thin choker of black thread, a nose-stud, and three brass bangles. Her children come with her. A young son, barely two, runs around naked. Her daughter, age five, wears draw-string shorts. Kamala is alert and thoughtful. She is reserved and must be coaxed, by our questions, to share her thoughts. Her reserve is not one of shyness, apathy or hostility but the natural caution of one who knows she must conserve her energies and protect her emotions to survive each day . . .

"My father was a laborer. My grandfather had no land. Sometimes my father worked as a boatman, sometimes he worked in the brickfield. He used to give us four annas in the morning. We had some fruit trees at our home. We used to sell some fruit, eat some fruits and thereby pass our days, rather than depend upon my father. We were four sisters and two brothers. One sister died later. We are three sisters now. Both the brothers died together at the same time. Now we are three sisters only. Our eldest sister is married in Dhankura. Somehow she is better off. Our second sister's husband is a rickshaw puller. He also sweeps at the hospital, for that he gets 50 taka. With this income they somehow pass their days. Then, my father worked as a boatman. My mother also worked. With their joint income they bought 1⅛ *pakhis* (⅓ acre) of land. We had a cow. We used to sell half of the milk and drink the other half.

"I was married at the age of 8. I have been married for 15 years. After our marriage, the price of rice was one taka per kilo. My husband had two brothers, whatever they had they divided, and each one took his own share. My father-in-law had some of his own land, that was also divided among his three sons. But none of them were able to increase their landholdings. My husband's older brother did not do anything. He just sat at home. Sometimes he used to dig earth, and from whatever he earned he managed one meal a day. Otherwise they stayed hungry. If his wife questioned him, he replied: "I cannot work. I have no strength. I am ill." They had no money for good food. Whatever cheap food was available, he used to eat that. Instead of one kilo of rice, he would buy 2½ kilos of sweet potato and eat that. The second brother's father-in-law is better off. Recently he came and gave them 900 taka. Occasionally they go and stay with the in-laws for a month or two.

"In the month of Aswin my husband regularly falls ill. During the other months he can work a little. But during the rainy season he does not work. He stays hungry and through hunger falls ill, but he will not go to work. If I say: "The children and we are staying hungry," he will reply: "What can I do?" I work in others' homes. Sometimes I do cane work, stitch *kantha* (quilts) and whatever I earn from this work I spend for the children's food.

"I joined the group with the aim of education—that there is voluntary teacher. I thought that if I can educate myself a little then I shall be able to guide my children. Again I thought that the person who would teach would be paid staff. That person has brothers and sisters. She said: "If you educate yourself, it will be good for you and your children. If you know how to read and write then you will be able to help your children in their education. It will also help you in your work." Then I started thinking: "We are poor. I have no education. If I start reading, would it be good for me? It might be good." Then I started.

"My hope is that if I educate myself then I will be able to give good guidance to my children. My children will know, "Our mother is educated, that is why she is educating us." My father knows a little, but my mother does not know anything at all. Then, when I started going to study, I learnt how to write my name. That was good for me. I advised Nurjahan and Hafeza. I told them: "Let us study. If we all study together, we shall study better." I told them: "If we learn reading and writing it will be good for us. And if we learn counting that will help us more." Like this. We discussed how it is difficult to do work alone. They showed us how ten or twelve men get together to do work or build a table. Then the women thought that we should also get together and work. After a few days we came to know that no one can do ten persons' work alone. Then we thought that if we formed a group it would be good.

"Then we thought, if we make a group and collect money from these 100–160 persons that will be good. If someone faces any difficulty we shall through the group's fund be able to help her. Some women are at home, some of them got married, some of them do not come because their parents do not allow them to come to the group or to study. But when I came to study, my father said: "Good. Try and learn how to write your name, that will help you." My father also said: "Those parents who do not know how to read and write they will not allow their daughter to study. You go and study."

"People bad-mouthed the group. They did not like the group, people bad-mouthed it. And, some said: "I am not used to talking with outside men." With this kind of excuse, they have left the group. Many of them deposited money at first, but later withdrew it. Some of them heard that after completing the lessons money would not be returned. But my father said: "Whether they return the money or not, you go and study in the group." The problem arises within the society. High society people say: "What is a group? Can a group be run by woman?" Those who are the *matbors* of the village say all this.

"The day I went to the paddy field one woman said: "We have lost the respect of our village because of this woman. She goes out without hesitation." If I stay hungry, no one will feed me or my children. Hence, I do not work because anyone forces me to. I work because of my own zeal. I do not take anyone's advice. I cannot make the decision to undertake any new work alone. I must discuss the matter with the group. All the members must decide what will be good and what will be bad. Only after such a discussion can we do anything. We could take land (on a sharecropping basis) and cultivate paddy or a seasonal crop.

"The *jantak* (dowry) system must be lifted from us. We must take *khas* (public) land. Those who are poor like us, they will be persuaded to join the group. This will be of benefit to us because our strength in numbers will increase. In this year we held a convention, from next year the number of people gathered will increase—our strength will increase. We will be able to fulfill our demands from government by this unity. If we place our demands to government in a united way, government will be bound to hear us. For example, we do not get the ration goods at the current rates. When they give us ½ to 1 seer, if we claim more, then they will not give us anything. If we become united, then this problem can be solved.

"In the village there is no set rate for daily labor. Our husbands are getting only 5 taka. From this amount of money what will he take and how will the children live? How will he maintain them? We are not able to give them clothes and also to feed them. For this reason there are so many problems for us. If all of us become united, then the wage rates will increase. If we do not perform any work for less than the minimum rate and if we can remain united, then the wage rate must increase. We must try hard to increase the wage rate. How can a person survive off 4 taka? If we want to buy one seer or rice, and with this we need spices. How will we build up our children to be perfect persons? My husband is sick. He is immobile. He cannot work.

"Only for profit's sake a group cannot run. We must be able to place our demands to government. But we will not be united if one person will not agree to. But if we become united then we will not do any work for less than 5 taka. Then the landlord will be bound to hire us [at a higher wage].

"All must be united. If anyone feels a pinch, everyone should feel the pain. If one member of the group must sell her land and homestead for a dowry, we all must feel for her. If she sells now, how will she survive afterwards? For this reason we must increase our party's strength and we can increase our numbers. Will it lift automatically? Will it lift then and there? There are so many men who divorce their wives with a single word. They must not be able to divorce, they must have to think about it. If she is good, only then will he stay with her, but even if she is bad, he must have to stay with her.

"Before this, I had been beaten very often when I used to go to school. Now they say: "Study more, if possible." Then they used to say: "What is the benefit if you study? Will you get a job?" But they understand now.

"We did not sit together in this way before. We have been able to

learn a lot of things as a result of sitting together. How to chop vegetables? What is to be eaten? Whether vegetables should be washed or
not before chopping, etc. We did not know these things. Now we have
learned these only as a result of sitting together. Now we do not strain
rice starch. Because to do so takes away all the vitamins from the rice.
But energy is within the starch of rice, too. Now we have learned this.

"After forming the group we have turned to somewhat better posi-
tions. As for example, Hazera's husband became cured after taking
medicine on loan from the group. My husband also became cured. We
have done household works. Have made mats from date-palm leaf,
have sewed quilts. We have to work for our development. If we do not
work, where will we find development? Unity strengthens power. All
of us must help each other during bad times."

MALLIKA OF DAPUNIA

Jamalpur town is the district headquarters of Jamalpur district. It
shares with other district towns a characteristic size and congestion and
an essential greyness. Jamalpur is four and one-half hours of steady
driving but only 120 miles north of Dhaka city. I have driven the road
at least once a month for five years and have grown fond of the two-way
(and sometimes three- and four-way) stream of animals, poultry, and
people that accompany and obstruct the drive. In several stretches, the
road is "main street" to villages. Children and chickens dart back and
forth. In other stretches on designated days, the road becomes "main
street" to a local market. Buyers and sellers, all men, mill around the
stalls that line the road. In many stretches during certain seasons, the
road serves as a drying surface for grain and straw.

The road to Jamalpur is for me a passage through alternating stark
and lush canvasses of rural life. Lush: the shimmer of dripping fish nets
in evening light; the golds of harvested paddy strewn alongside the
road and of jute fibre set out on the railings of small bridges to dry; the
patchwork of green paddy fields interspersed with yellow mustard
fields; the colors of a rainbow breaking through a sun-lit shaft in the
dark, heavy mantle of monsoon clouds; and the layer of smoke and haze
that lifts slowly off the earth on a wintry afternoon. Stark: the dilapidated hut and hunger-bloated children of a poor family; the sweat-
streaked backs of laborers working under the enervating heat of the

noonday sun; the scramble of chickens, dogs, and children for a dropped morsel of food at a local bus stand.

My drive this time is in the month of Chaitra (April). Most of the winter paddy has been harvested. The harvested fields are dotted by dark piles of manure and ash soon to be turned under. Even in this dry, dusty month some shades of green: young lime-green leaves and lighter green blossoms of the sal trees and the verdant green paddy in a few irrigated fields. It is a month of digging mud and felling bamboo to repair houses before the monsoon rains.

I have come to Jamalpur this time to interview women in Dapunia and Nayapara villages. We drive south of Jamalpur to Dapunia village. We are told 100 families live in Dapunia of which four families are rich, five are reasonably well-off, and the rest are poor. Women from the ninety poor households have been organized into four groups. We sit with the members of the original group to hear the history of their activities. Mallika is the most articulate member. We ask her if she would tell us her personal history the next day and she agrees.

Mallika is a well-groomed and remarkably energetic woman. Her wavy hair is oiled and knotted in a bun at the nape of her neck. She wears a colorful sari. She introduces me to a colloquial (and symbolic) use of a common word: *kaz*. Literally, *kaz* means "work" but idiomatically, as used by Mallika and (I learn) many others, *kaz* means "marriage." Mallika speaks with great intensity of her marriage and of her widowhood. We listen . . .

"We were twelve brothers and sisters. All died except one brother and myself. I was married in the *char* (sandy area). I always cried. Then my husband told my father-in-law: "Mallika did not live in a village and she does not like village life." Then my father-in-law said: "Whether she likes it or not, she has to live here." Then my husband said: "You cannot keep a person by force. She has not eaten for the last few days." Then my father-in-law said: "All right, you leave the house with your wife and I will not give you your share of the property." My husband said: "Father, I married according to my wish and would like to take responsibility for my wife."

"After that we came to the town and rented a house in Ghose-para. After one year we incurred a loss, because whatever my husband earned as a tailor was not enough for the house rent and our living costs. Then I told my husband: "My father's house is in town and we could stay there." After that, we stayed there. Whatever my husband earned we spent; we saved very little from that despite thinking about the future. Like this, twelve years passed and I became the mother of two sons and one daughter.

"Then suddenly my husband fell ill (scirrhosis of the liver), his belly swelled up. Then I informed my father-in-law. He did not come. Moreover, he said: "You all have gone to town and now I should come for his treatment? You go and do his treatment." Then, what to do? At first I gave him Ayurvedic (Hindu medical system) medicine but he was not cured by that. After that I took him to an allopathic doctor but that also did not help. I asked my husband to be admitted to a hospital. He agreed with me. I got him admitted in the Mymensingh Medical College Hospital. But he was not given good medicine there. After 27 days I brought him home and continued his treatment. Nothing helped him and his condition deteriorated day by day. Then, I got him admitted in the Jamalpur hospital. After 26 days, they discharged him.

"That was in the year of 1974. The price of rice was ten taka and flour was seven taka. Four children, my husband and myself I had to feed that patient (husband) and ourselves. Whatever savings we had that was spent. We had some utensils which I sold. I sold everything except the sewing machine thinking that if my husband recovers he will be able to work and somehow we will live off that income. But, Allah's wish, at last I sold the sewing machine! When the taka was finished I lost my husband!

"Then I faced a very bad hardship and thought 'If I remain idle like this my children will die.' My father was not well off. My father was old and my brothers were small. It was very difficult for him to manage the family expenses. Yet, I told my father: "Father, my husband died now, what can I do with my children?" My father said: "Ma! Somehow I can feed you, but what about your children? I cannot feed them." Then I asked my father whether I could send my children to their grand-father's house. I went and told my father-in-law that I cannot look after the children. "You take the responsibility of your grandchildren." My father-in-law said: "You went to town according to your own wish and now you come to give the children to me. I will not take them." Then I cried and returned. It was the month of Ramzan (month of fasting). I was fasting and in the evening eating only *roti* (unleavened bread). I kept thinking where to go with my children when neither my father nor my father-in-law accepted my children.

"Then I started to work in other people's houses. I was fasting yet processing paddy for them the whole day. They did not give me food. In the evening they used to give me ¼ kilo of *khud* (broken rice). I used to cook that with plenty of water (i.e., like a gruel) and sometimes cooked it like rice and fed my children. Sometimes the children ate it, sometimes they refused. How long could they eat such food? Like this, many months passed. It was the month of Aswin, the same month in which my husband died. My children were disgusted. My eldest son Anwar used to tell me: "Ma! I do not like to eat this kind of food anymore. I feel like vomiting. My stomach pains." Then I said: "Baba, what can I do! Be patient. When you all grow big then you will earn and eat good food. Now, from where will I get good food? Like this Aswin and Kartik passed (October and November). After the month of Aghrahayan, I started taking paddy on loan. I used to process it for sale. From that rice, I used to take ¼ kilo of rice to feed my children.

"In the meantime, I came to know that an orphanage was being opened in Jamalpur and that they took orphans. I went there and asked them to take one of my children. One of them refused. After that somebody from their committee said; "She is very sad. Take one of her sons." They said: "We will take one of your sons." Then they gave me a form. I brought that form at home and had it filled out by someone from the village. My eldest son was admitted in the orphanage. The other son and daughter were left with me. I was working very hard and looking after my children. Like this, with great difficulty, another year passed.

"After that year I went to Apa. Apa said: "You all form a group." At that time I did not know how to read and write, I could only read the Quran. I did not know what a group is. Then Apa called me and explained what a group is. Then I understood something. But sometimes I forgot. Apa said: "You all deposit 25 poisha and like this, begin a group." When I came back home I thought 'Why should I deposit 25 poisha to Apa? I can keep this at home.' Then I kept 25 poisha aside one day, but the next day I spent it. Like this, two weeks passed. The next week I thought there must be some good reason behind it, as Apa said. Then I started depositing 25 poisha with Apa although it was difficult for me. I started depositing 25 poisha, but sometimes only 10 poisha. After 3–4 weeks she said: "You have deposited one taka so far." After another few weeks she informed there were two takas in my account. Then I thought Apa gave very good advice. I could not keep a poisha at home but I could keep it with Apa and it was increasing. "All right, I will not keep any more poisha at home and will deposit them in my account." Like this, my taka increased in the account.

"In the month of Chaitra (April) Apa gave me some books to read. Then I thought 'If I can read Bengali it will help me.' I started reading. Then I could read well and remember. I used to finish my housework quickly, cooked and fed my children, then went to study. When I came back home the children started crying. I told them not to cry, if I could read and write that would be good for them as I would be able to teach them. This is how I did my housework and studied. After one year I could read and write very well.

"Then I took some taka from my account and started paddy processing. I was making a profit. Then Apa helped me by loaning me 100 takas once and, then, 200 takas. Then we started paddy processing on behalf of the group with 300 takas capital. We made very good profit. Those for whom I used to process paddy before, they came and asked me to process their paddy. But I told them "No". Then they said: "You processed paddy for us before." I said: "Yes, I did. But I cannot now because, by the grace of Allah, we have begun a group and it is more profitable for me to work for the group." They used to criticize us by saying we have become rich. We replied "Pray to Allah," like that. We studied and did business with 300 takas capital. In the meantime our group settled down. Before, there was no system, some were always absent. Now, we have a group of members and everyone knows the rules and regulations.

"We are 17 members in the group and we all work together. We hold meetings day and night. Wherever we go, we all go together. When we get orders for paddy processing, four of the group members go to the work. Whenever we get work orders, we take that and do that work happily and do not feel physical tiredness. Now my son is reading in class five. My daughter is also studying. By the grace of Allah, I am living happily. Before I did not know how to grow trees. After reading these books, now I know how to grow trees and to benefit from them. I grow trees now. For lack of taka, I could not rear poultry before. I have bought poultry now and am rearing poultry. I have made some profit. Now my children and myself can eat eggs as well as sell some. Each egg brings 75 poisha, sometimes one taka. Before I sold my sari to feed my children and myself, because I had no other source. I do not need to sell my sari, but can sell hens, chickens and eggs. I can sell one hen for 15–20 takas. Now Allah is helping and my hardship has reduced gradually. I grew a palm tree and there were about 100 dates. We all ate, sold and gave to the neighbors. I have grown bananas. I sell the banana, give to group members, and also to my neighbours. I say to them: "Before I used to take from you all, now you can take from me. Do not hate me, take my things."

"I knew what cleanliness was before. Because I lived in the town and my husband and I used to keep our things very clean. When I saw other houses dirty, I used to ask them: "How can you live so dirty? You should all live cleanly. How can you eat in a dirty place?" They replied: "We do not get the time to clean as well as to cook and to look after our children." I told them: "I have children but I live cleanly. Your eldest child is sitting. She can clean. She can sweep and clean. You should build a latrine instead of dirtying my place. And how can you pass your bowels in an open place which others can see? It is a sin too." They replied that their husbands do not build a latrine. But I told them: "Why should your husbands do it? You all can do it, if you want. You can cut banana leaves and cover the place and build a latrine. If you build like this then others will learn from you and they will build in their houses." Before the rich from the village laughed at us and did not talk to us. If we went to their houses they did not offer us a place to sit. They used to hate us. But now we 17 members of the group work together and we are very close to each other. And now the rich in the village do not laugh at us. In fact, they call us and talk to us. They are afraid of us now.

"The ration dealer used to criticize us, saying: "You all have become rich now. What have you done with your group? Have you eaten up whatever you earned from the group?" I said: "Our group is still running and it is running very well. For this group we have worked very hard and learned a lot." Before we did not know how to keep relationships with each other, how to grow trees, how to rear poultry, how to look after our children, and how to increase money. All this we have learned from this group. Before if anyone was working that did not interest me and I thought, 'Let her do that. Why should I learn that?' Now, whatever work I see interests me and I try to learn that work as soon as possible. If I see anyone working alone and I am sitting idle, I immediately go to help her. Whenever we dig earth we all go together to finish the work quickly and come back soon. Like this, we hold meetings also. Before we did not know agriculture. Now we know it and, in this very way, we cultivated wheat. We put manure in the field, cleaned, weeded and when the wheat ripened we did not hire labor. We, the members of the group, harvested it at night. In the morning we husked it and put it in the sun.

"The group helped us and taught us many things. I have learned how to live unitedly. Before if any rich person abused or criticized, we could not reply. But now if anybody says anything bad, we the 17 members of the group, go together and ask that person why he or she passed this comment. This is another kind of help we have gotten. Before we did not know how to get together and help each other, which we have learned now. Before we did not hold meetings. Each one was busy with their own worries and sorrows, always thinking about food for their children and themselves. Now we, the 17 members of the group, have become very close to each other. If I get any new ideas I discuss them with the others and, after that, we 17 members get together and do that work. Before we did not think whether others had eaten or not. But now we immediately inquire whether anyone from the group stayed hungry and we give them food.

"After I was widowed, many people proposed to me. But I told them: "Never talk about marriage." After that no one has proposed. My father used to say: "Ma, you are young and I do not want to keep you like this. I would like to get you married again." I asked my father whether he was facing any difficulty in keeping me like this because I had no problem. After that my father did not say anything. Sometimes my father-in-law proposed for his other son. But I refused. I said: "When I was helpless you did not come to help your grandchildren. What makes you propose now?" I live in my father's house and will get my share of property from my father. And they live in that *char* (sandy area). If they can take me again they could come to town and share that property. That is their greed.

"At first, when we began the group, the rich used to say: "What will you gain through this group? It will put you into difficulty. You all will ruin everything by listening to that person." But we said: "If anything goes wrong that will be our fault. Now, you will not get the chance to cheat us anymore. We worked for whole days at your house but did not get our actual wages. We will not work anymore for the rich." Some of them advised us that instead of depositing 25 poisha in the group we should keep this poisha at home in a slit in the bamboo pillar of our houses. We said: "No, we cannot keep money at home because we are poor. When we feel hungry we buy food and spend it. But when we deposit with Apa, we cannot ask for it always and this helps us to increase our money." They frightened us saying: "When your money will increase to a bigger amount then they will refuse to give it to you." But we replied: "Let them take it. We are poor and it is the money of the poor. They are rich, if they want to take the money of the poor, let them do so."

"Besides this, one man, who is dead now, said: "If you go to the group, I will not allow you all to use the path which is near my house." We said, "All right, we will use the other road, then you will not be able to say anything." Since then we did not pass by his house. After a few days they proposed a *shalish* (village judicial) and he said: "Would you be able to help arbitrate for me?" We said: "Why did you come to us now? You stopped us from using the path. Now you go and do your own *shalish!* We will not go. We do not do *shalish* for the rich. You all are proud of your money, so do your own *shalish* with that money. We are poor and we help each other. If there is any quarrel among us we settle that ourselves."

"Before the *mullahs* used to say: "That woman is talking loudly, she is bad. She has gone out. She is shameless. This woman must be divorced." Since we have begun this group we go wherever we want to go. We go to the office (BRAC). Sometimes we go to other villages to see other group members and inquire about their welfare. In this sometimes we take newly-married women with us. But those *mullahs* do not say anything nowadays. Even my father-in-law allows me to go out. My mother-in-law says: "You go, I will do the housework." In fact, they encourage us to do the group's work. Before newly-married women were not allowed to talk to others. If anyone talked with the newly-married women, the mother-in-law would come and say: "Why are you sitting with our bride? You will spoil her, go away from here. Do not talk loudly here where our bride can hear." But nowadays, fathers-in-law and mothers-in-law and husbands allow newly-married women to go out.

"Junglepara is beginning a group. But Junglepara is a very bad village. The *matbors* in that village do not listen to others. Now Junglepara has been divided into two parts. One part has begun a group. So the people of the other part are feeling left behind and they are also trying to organize a group. They also see our activities and the outlook of our village, how it was before and how it looks now. They also say, "Do not talk ill of women." They are doing good work and living well through the group.

"We are advising Aliapur village people because they were poor like us. They had no food to eat. Then we said: "We were poor like you. But after forming the group we are living better now. We have educated ourselves, we have learned how to save money and how to look after our children also." Then they said: "You all learned and benefitted in all these ways after forming a group. Now, teach us how to form a group." After that we advised them how to make a group.

"Now we will not cast our vote according to the choice of others. We are 80 women in the four groups and we will cast our vote for a poor man because the poor will understand our difficulties. Then, when he will rule he will think of us that poor people cast votes for me and I am elected. If I rule I will be robbing their share. So let me share it with them. But the rich will not think like that. The rich will say: "I am not elected by your votes only. Other people voted for me as well." Moreover, they are courageous to rule and sell ration commodities. They will think, 'Why should we give all this to the poor? We should sell it and take money to buy land or a house and a car.' The poor feel for each other, but the rich do not. The poor do not take bribes, but the rich do.

"When we hold meetings, we ask about each other's joys and sorrows. Some will say: "I was passing very hard times. But after joining the group I am better now." We will have to inform the women in other groups that on such and such a date we will hold a meeting and we request you all to attend that meeting. When we all get together we will talk about each other's problems. Besides this, we will be able to inform each other that this year we cultivated wheat which they do not know and they stiched *kantha* that we did not see before. Other people will not dare to say anything for they will think: "The poor are getting together and we should not say anything against them."

CHAPTER EIGHT

From Experience to Policy

This book describes the efforts of one agency in Bangladesh to reach poor village women with projects designed to increase their material and social resources. My primary purpose in writing this book was to give the reader an insider's view of what it takes to develop such a program and what it means to participate in that program. My secondary purpose was, through the detailed analysis of that program, to convey to the reader something about rural women, rural poverty, and rural development as a whole. I would argue that because BRAC's program was based on a realistic understanding of poverty, because its staff responded to the realities in flexible and creative ways and analyzed and communicated what they experienced, because the program has had a relatively long history (10 years of accumulated experience) and affected a large number of women (over 6000 directly) in a number of different ways, the BRAC experience offers a range of critical information and insights to the larger world of women, poverty, and development.

I would like, therefore, to share some of the general concepts and specific guidelines that proved significant in our work and should be of some significance to policy-makers, program planners, and project personnel concerned with the participation of women in rural development.

THROUGH LEARNING TO CONCEPTS

Although nearly all village women everywhere work long and strenuous days, until recently this simple fact had not been fully comprehended. Why has women's work been overlooked? In considering this question, we came to recognize several reasons. First, under most censuses only what is directly paid is regarded as work. Second, to many outsiders much of women's work remains "invisible" because not all of women's work is carried out in a visible work-place. Moreover, women's "productive" work is often done in and around their so-called "domestic" work so much so that the productive work of women appears as a "natural" manifestation of their domestic roles. Third, women often produce as much to conserve as to generate income. Fourth, women's and men's economic roles are often so complementary that women's contribution is subsumed under men's work. Fifth, not all women's production is marketed and not all women are in trade.

The result is that myths and stereotypes about women persist. Policy-makers—mostly men and urban men at that—make plans based on stereotyped notions of the nature and value of women's work. So long as this is so, so long as policy makers make the artificial distinction between the farm and the household, between paid work and unpaid work, between productive and domestic work, women will continue to be overlooked. The result is that women who raise and tend the domestic animals; thresh, parboil, dry, store and husk the grain; grow fruits and vegetables; clean and maintain the huts and homesteads; give birth and raise children; produce crafts; and more, are listed as "housewives" even though their tasks are as critical to the wellbeing of their families and to national production as are the men's.

Although poverty is well recognized and the growing number of poor and landless households are calculated, few people discuss poverty in terms of its particular set of consequences on women. What did we learn about poverty from the women? First, poverty is not static. The reality is not simply that some are rich and some are poor in the village. The reality is that poverty has a dynamic in which the poor and rich interact. Most often this dynamic leads only to increased poverty for the poor. Second, poverty forces women to perform non-status work, to seek whatever work they can find in an effort to help eke out an existence for their families. Third, poverty erodes the traditional kinship and family support systems. The first victim is the ties of the extended family and the kin. The next victim is the ties and support of the immediate family.

This process of impoverishment has particular and dire consequences for women because in most economies, although men's and women's work is interdependent, women are conditioned to be dependent on men for their livelihood. This is so because although most women in most villages throughout the world work long hours each day, they seldom own land or assets in their own right, have access to credit in their own right, or receive extension services or training.

However, if one adds the growing numbers of women who head households *de jure* (widowed, divorced or deserted women) to the growing numbers of women who head households *de facto* (women whose male guardians are absent or infirm or otherwise not bringing in an income) in any poor country, one finds a significant number of women managing the day-to-day needs of their families from this position of great disadvantage. Some estimate that one-third of households around the world are headed and managed by women. These women require equal access as men to extension services, credit, skills training, technologies, and rural labor markets.

"But why," some of you may still ask, "shouldn't women be seen and studied as part of the family unit? Shouldn't women's work be seen and studied as part of a family farming enterprise?" I would answer, "Not necessarily in some situations and not entirely in any situation." If women are to be supported in their numerous roles, women must be understood from a number of perspectives. After all, men are part of that same family enterprise and men are thought of in their productive roles. Men receive credit, inputs, training, technical assistance, and extension services. Why shouldn't women? Shouldn't both men's and women's production be recognized and supported? Morever, what if the man should take ill or die? What if the man should abandon or divorce his wife? What are her options if her work has never been valued or supported? What if she has never in her own right exercised access and control over land, credit, or productive assets? Given the numbers of poor women who head or manage families, the "why women?" argument no longer holds.

Although most women everywhere work at a disadvantage, the particular situation of women differs between classes, villages, and countries. I would argue strongly for a situation-by-situation analysis of women's roles and constraints before programs are designed or plans formulated. I would suggest that the following variables be assessed in each particular situation:

—is the hierarchy by sex or by class more predominant
—is the economy labor-surplus or labor-scarce
—is the economy land-surplus or land-scarce

—what is the dynamic of household size and composition over time
—what are the traditional tasks and skills of women
—which tasks of women are essentially income-conserving
—which tasks of women are potentially income-producing
—which tasks of women carry high status
—which tasks of women carry low or negative status
—how many women are managing the day-to-day need of their households
—how much access do women have to rural labor markets, credit, inputs, training, technical assistance, and extension services?

Why do I argue that one needs to understand the specific mix of these variables in each situation? Consider the following policy implications from such an analysis:

—in societies where the class hierarchy is not pronounced, the constraints and needs of women may not differ significantly by class and gender issues may assume priority over class issues
—in societies where the class hierarchy is pronounced, the constraints and needs of women will most likely differ by class and class issues may take priority over gender issues
—in economies where labor is scarce, the introduction of labor-saving devices may make sense
—for tasks which women perform primarily to conserve income and which are routinely burdensome and time-consuming, the introduction of labor-saving devices may make sense (particularly if women's labor and time can be released to some productive end)
—in economies where there is a surplus of labor, the introduction of capital-intensive devices may have very negative effects (particularly on women who perform the "invisible" labor most often displaced)
—for tasks which women can potentially perform for an income (that is, potentially commercial activities), the introduction of labor-saving devices may have very negative effects (because too often these devices are coopted by men of rich households thereby displacing the labor of women from poor households.)
—for tasks which women can potentially perform for an income, what is required are the range of services extended for men
—in economies where large numbers of women manage the day-to-

day requirements of their families, women's entry into the wage labor market is critical. One must counter the "queue" argument which dictates that in situations of widespread unemployment women should wait in line behind men (who are assumed to be the primary "bread earners")

—in economies where women earn less than men, it is important to lobby for and to organize women to demand equal pay for comparable work

—in societies where class hierarchy is pronounced, it is important to recognize the differences between women of different classes

—in societies where all women do not necessarily face the same degree or type of problems, it is important to decide which women one wants to benefit in what ways

—in situations where the differences between women are pronounced, it is better to organize women into economically homogeneous cooperative groups (to forestall latent conflicts)

—in situations of pronounced or increasing poverty, it is important to estimate the impact of impoverishment on the dynamics of household size and composition and on women in particular

—in situations of significant change (either planned or unplanned), it is important to monitor the impact of change on women's traditional work, on women's access to wage labor, and on women's access to public goods and services.

FROM ACTION TO STRATEGIES

The model and methods for working with women described in this book were designed to increase women's access to resources, power and autonomy through a dual program of rural institutions and rural employment for women. By focusing on rural institutions and rural employment for women, we began to witness a tremendous potential for change in women's lives, what I have called the *quiet revolution*. Our experience shows that as women's productivity is raised or their employment expanded (that is, as women begin to earn higher incomes) they also begin to exercise greater power and autonomy within their own households and their villages. Our experience also shows that if women participate in joint economic or social activities, the process of getting together and managing their own affairs soon translates into more active social roles for women not only in their families but also in their villages. In chapters 4, 5, and 6, I discussed at length BRAC's experience in developing rural employment and rural institutions for poor women, but I would like at this time to summarize the specific guidelines and central issues suggested by BRAC's experience.

Guidelines for Economic Programs for Women

In summarizing BRAC's experience with economic programs for women, I will present schematically the critical steps we went through in developing individual schemes, outline the organizational model that evolved as we developed these schemes, and in so doing, state the working principles we adopted. These working principles are not intended as hard-and-fast rules but as guidelines for what should be taken into consideration when one plans or undertakes economic programs with women.

Key Steps in Economic Programming

1. Identification of Women
   - target group criteria: in BRAC's case, marginal and poor women
   - assessment of circumstances and work schedule of women
   - assessment of skills, priority needs, and problems of women
2. Search for Possibilities
   - research into existing skills, raw materials and markets
   - consultation with the women, other action agencies, and technical/resource institutions
3. Feasibility Study: consideration of
   - overall economic situation
   - women's traditional skills and tasks
   - available resources and raw materials
   - existing and/or potential markets
     rural—what is in demand or imported from urban centers
     urban—what is in demand or imported from outside the country
     foreign—what is indigenous to a country by way of designs, products, or raw materials for which there is an existing or potential demand outside the country

latent—what potential customers (from different sectors of the population) need or demand

4. Planning and Development
   - collaboration with outside technical and resource institutions: For example, in the initial phase of any scheme, BRAC sought for and contracted in appropriate technical assistance.

5. Training
   - skill training: Initially, BRAC relied on outside agencies to provide technical training. Once a scheme proved viable, BRAC began to build its own capacities for technical training and support.
   - technology transfer: Initially, BRAC sought appropriate technological assistance as needed. BRAC believes that, for the most part, technologies exist and need only be identified (not invented). Once a scheme proved viable, BRAC began to build its own technical capacities.
   - refresher training and follow-up: BRAC considers preliminary training a necessary precondition but a minor element in the success of a program. Far more critical to the success of a program is follow-up supervision and on-going training.

6. Financing
   - group savings and fund: BRAC encourages each group to mobilize its own resources and to build a group fund. But BRAC recognizes that groups of poor women will not be able to mobilize enough resources to finance any but the smallest economic schemes.
   - subsidy: BRAC has found it is important to subsidize the experimental first phase of many schemes, the phase that includes preliminary training and test production. If one wants to benefit the poorest women, they are precisely the ones who cannot afford the opportunity cost (i.e., their daily wages) to attend a training or to engage in experimental production.
   - credit: BRAC found that small amounts of working capital (an average of $20) taken on loan (with formal terms of interest and repayment) can launch many economic schemes. Other schemes require larger loans for fixed capital expenses and recurring costs. But the amount required is seldom very large: BRAC-financed joint production schemes averaged $200 each. Lack of working capital is typically the major constraint

to production in rural areas. Initially, the loans can be funded through project funds but ideally, over time, the women should be linked up to formal credit institutions.

- mutual guarantors: BRAC does not disburse loans to individuals. BRAC loans are provided to the group, even if the production is carried out individually. The group serves as the umbrella for BRAC support and the group members guarantee each other's loans. If one woman defaults then the whole group suffers.

- cash-on-delivery: BRAC found that producers must be paid cash on delivery of their (quality) goods. If producers are forced to wait for delayed payments, their production will also be delayed for lack of working capital.

7. Experimental Production

- test production: BRAC found that for most schemes (other than those based on existing skills, technologies, and markets) a period of trial-and-error was necessary to work out the problems of production. BRAC decided to subsidize this experimental phase of production (a period which can last anywhere from one month to six months or a year depending on the scheme).

- test marketing: During the experimental period and before expanding into larger-scale production, BRAC staff test the markets with samples produced. BRAC found that prior to test production, without a product to show, only preliminary market surveys were possible.

8. Expanded Production

- centralized or decentralized: Different products require different systems of production. Some activities are carried out at a central worksite. Others are carried out in individual huts in and around other activities. Whatever system of production is adopted by the women, BRAC believes it is critically important to make sure that at least one step in the production sequence be undertaken collectively (whether it is the actual manufacturing or quality control) and that each producer be required to report to a central site on a regular basis. For example, under BRAC's silk culture scheme, rearing and spinning is done in the home. To build up the collective ethic and to stimulate social interaction, BRAC designated a certain day in each week as "silk" day. On that day, the producers deliver their thread and pick up supplies from a central service center. On that day, the producers are also gathered together to discuss production problems and larger village problems.

- day-to-day functioning: BRAC found that the technical and financing aspects of the schemes are not as difficult as the day-to-day management problems that arise. BRAC field staff engage the women as a group in all management decisions. Decisions are reached by consensus. If not, BRAC has found that the strength and unity of the group will not develop.
- payment systems: After experimenting with profit-sharing, BRAC and the women decided that payment should reflect work. When an individual's production can be measured, women are paid on a piece rate. When an individual's production cannot be so easily measured (e.g. in collective agriculture), the profit is shared but many conflicts arise (e.g. women are accused of being lazy). BRAC also found that during test production unless the women are paid a small amount their interest will slacken off. And, BRAC adopted a sliding scale when costing labor into the price of a product: that is, in the early stages of production, when efficiency is generally low, the women are paid slightly more for their labor (as an incentive to production) than they will receive once their efficiency is up. While subsidizing test production and adjusting the returns to women's labor, BRAC staff educate the women on economic realities and explain that wages are tied not only to output but to competition in the open market.
- raw materials: During test production, raw materials are not usually bought at the optimal time or in optimal quantities. Once production is underway, in order for products to stay competitive, great care and effort must be given to purchase raw materials in bulk and at the lowest possible wholesale prices.

9. Development of Support System
   - extension systems: to provide
     on-the-spot technical supervision
     on-the-spot supply and back-up services
   - management services: to provide
     production supervision
     production planning

cost-accounting
financial management

10. Production Planning
    • design research and documentation
    • market research and testing
    • product diversification to adjust to:
      changing consumer taste and demand
      expanding collections of designs, motifs, and techniques

11. Marketing
    • capturing market: by exploring existing markets and con-
      sumer demands
    • expanding markets: by mobilizing consumer taste through ex-
      hibitions, etc.
    • creating markets: by producing new lines of products and
      stimulating a demand through exhibitions, etc.
    • reserving markets: by lobbying for protective legislation (e.g.
      against capital-intensive investments and in favor of quotas for
      government procurement from women producers)

Initially, BRAC undertakes only informal market surveys. Before
new products and skills have been developed or old products and skills
revived (that is, before there is a product to show), comprehensive
market surveys only tend to discourage investments. However, after
test production and before production is expanded on a large-scale,
BRAC undertakes more comprehensive market surveys. BRAC conducts three types of market surveys:
    • preliminary, informal surveys: prior to test production to de-
      termine the fit between existing and/or potential markets and
      existing and/or potential skills
    • comprehensive, formal surveys: prior to production on a
      large-scale with samples from test production
    • on-going surveys: during expanded production as products
      and skills are diversified.

12. Parallel Action
BRAC also found that economic programming requires action at
three levels: with the producers; with the consumers/public: and with
resource, technical, and policy institu'ions.
    • collaboration with technical and resource institutions: Initially

for each new scheme, BRAC relies on outside agencies for technical training and expertise. Gradually, if a scheme promises to be viable, BRAC builds its own technical capacity with assistance from these agencies.

- advocacy and lobbying: BRAC continually advocates and lobbies for women's access to credit, technical and support services, protective legislation, adequate wages, raw materials, etc.

BRAC evolved a particular organizational structure in response to the needs of its economic program for women. At various points in this book I have discussed the key personnel in this structure: the women themselves, the paratechnicians, the field staff, the trainers, and the administrators. Other cadre have been added more recently: marketing and design staff. Other components and personnel may be added over time. At this point, I would like to show the current organizational structure by way of a model:

ORGANIZATIONAL STRUCTURE FOR ECONOMIC PROGRAMMING

VILLAGE PRODUCTION CENTERS
    Personnel: the general members of the producer groups
                 the specialized members of the producer groups:
                      supervisor
                      treasurer
                      quality controller
    Functions: production planning
                 test production
                 expanded production
                 day-to-day management
                 accounting
                 marketing

REGIONAL SERVICE CENTERS
    Personnel: paratechnicians
                 field staff
    Functions: supply-and-delivery
                 extension and management
                 financing
                 market assistance
                 technical training
                 technical and supply back-up

CENTRAL TECHNICAL TRAINING CENTER
Personnel: technical trainers
Functions: feasibility studies
technical training
technical back-up
supply back-up: e.g. parent stock
liaison with outside agencies

CENTRAL DESIGN AND SERVICE CENTER
Personnel: designer
technical assistants
draftsman
Functions: technical trouble-shooting
technical training
testing and devising technologies
designing prototypes
technical training and services

CENTRAL MARKETING OUTLET
Personnel: shop manager
saleswomen
designers
extension agents
stockkeeper
Functions: retailing handicrafts
servicing producers:
placing orders
providing designs and lay-outs
cash-on-delivery
trouble-shooting problems
researching

APEX RESEARCH, PLANNING, AND MARKETING CENTER
Personnel: administrators
women's program staff
Functions: research and development
feasibility studies
collaboration and linkage: to arrange
initial training
initial technical assistance
regular support services
overall production planning
on-going market and product survey
diversification of products, skills, and techniques
overall financial projections and allocations advocacy
lobbying for protective legislation, wholesale prices, reserved
markets
market expansion

On the basis of our experience in economic programming for women summarized above, a few key issues emerge. First, there is the issue of recruitment. Who does one chose to work with in what activities? I would argue for a policy of class homogeneity. Under such a policy, the benefits of a program can be directed towards and availed of by the appropriate target group (preferably the poorest and most disadvantaged women). Otherwise, if women are organized cross-class, the program may not reflect the priority needs or reach the poorest women. Under such a policy, viable rural institutions can be built on common needs and problems to ensure the target group develops adequate participation and a strong-enough voice. If one fully intends to reach the most disadvantaged women in any situation a very useful "screening device" is to choose those women who perform or are willing to perform the work that is considered of lowest status in that particular situation.

Second, there is the issue of credit. If one wants to provide credit to low income women several measures suggest themselves. There is the matter of credit-worthiness. Our experience suggests that the worthiness of the borrower should be determined by her peers—other women in the same group who will share with her the responsibility for repayment. Also our experience suggests that the borrower's worthiness should be measured by her productive capacity rather than by collateral requirements (it is because she lacked collateral traditionally that she couldn't avail of credit in the past). Then there is the matter of the size of loans. Our experience suggests that the amount required is small (BRAC's individual loans per capita ranged between $10–20 with 12% interest) and should fit the seasonality of women's work. That is, in many situations more frequent small loans may "fit" women's needs more adequately than less-frequent larger loans. And, it should be noted that some provision should be made for women to avail of consumption as well as production loans if they are not repeatedly to fall into the indebtedness spiral. That is, when there is illness or a ceremony or a death the women need access to consumption loans. Our experience shows that cooperative groups of women can build up a sufficient mutual loan fund (to cover consumption loan needs of the members) through joint savings and shares. Our experience also shows that repayment rates are high with poor women especially if the loans are disbursed through a cooperative group where the group assumes mutual responsibility for the repayment by each member. One final note on credit. In addition to the actual provision of credit, the formalities of credit institutions should be reduced and simplified and the women should be trained in cost-accounting.

Third, those women not traditionally in commerce or trade require training in management as much or more than they require skills training. If their production is to increase, women must have skills in production techniques, cost-accounting, management, and marketing. Too often economic schemes fail because the women are provided the initial skills training but no follow-up training in these other areas. We also found that not only the women who participate in the schemes but also the staff who implement these schemes require this range of financial and management skills.

Fourth, we found in working at the village level that it was important to also work at other levels. We needed to draw upon and link our activities to outside support services, both those of private agencies and those of the government. It is critical that the cooperative groups of women be linked (without any long-term dependence) to support services beyond those offered by any specific project. Even if government services are weak or have not served women in the past, they are in the long-run the permanent services and should be made more accountable and adequate to the needs of the women. In the final analysis, women alongside men must be seen as participants not only in rural employment or production schemes and rural institutions but also in all sectors of national plans.

Guidelines for Organizing Women

In chapters 4 and 6 I discussed at length methods (in theory and in practice) of building rural institutions for women, but I would like to summarize here several of the critical components in that process and certain specific guidelines for organizing women. First, our experience indicates a great potential for organizing village women and that women can and should articulate their needs, help direct the formulation of the solutions, and participate directly in such organization. Second, priority should be given to organizing women from poor, landless and marginal households which, in many countries, constitute half of rural households. Third, poor women should be organized, at least initially, around their immediate and priority needs. In the case of poor rural women in Bangladesh, we found that when poor women are organized around economic needs they soon begin to translate their newly-found strength (from the income they earned and from being a member of a group) into social resources both within their homes and their villages. Fourth, the individual associations or groups of women, especially if they are to undertake collective economic action, should be kept small in size (15–30 members each) and the leadership of the groups must be adequately screened, developed, and trained in group management. And the individual cooperative groups should be linked with other groups to share experience and insights. Fifth, poor women need not be organized in isolation from poor men but need, in the early stages of organization, separate associations wherein they can articulate their specific needs as women. In the final analysis, women through the strength gained in belonging to women's associations should participate equally alongside men in all rural institutions, whether newly-created or traditional.

The Do's and Don't's of Group Organization*

Entering the village

- Investigate the dynamics of resource and power distribution in each village (the dynamic will differ village to village).
- Develop the "habit of inquiry:" that is, the habit of looking into how each person, each event, each action fits into the larger socio-economic pattern of the village as a whole.
- Remember that you should learn from the village and from the women.

Establishing Personal Contact

- Avoid establishing personal contact with only one or two members of a village. Establish contact with as many people as possible in order to begin to understand the dynamics of the village.
- Analyze your contacts and relationships in the village. Why do people relate to you? What does your contact with them imply?
- Be sure to establish direct personal contact with the target group women. If you maintain only an indirect contact (i.e., through

---

*These guidelines, formulated for BRAC field staff as a result of our interviews and experience with women, should be of interest to readers interested in how to go about developing village-level associations for poor women.

others) with the poorest women, you will not understand their problems.

- Develop and maintain close contact with the poorest women.

Preliminary Discussions

- Formulate critical questions in light of what you have learned about the village.
- Listen for what the poorest women say about their critical problems.
- Facilitate open dialogue. Encourage everyone to speak up.
- Listen carefully.

Functional Education

- Organize the women initially into functional education classes. Without the time spent in the classes, the women will not perceive the advantage in mutual problem-solving and in joint action. Without the time spent observing the classes, you will not be able to judge the commitment of the individual women and the viability of the women as a group.
- Avoid identifying a volunteer teacher and then enlisting learners. Start with interested learners and let them help you identify a volunteer teacher.
- Observe the classes on a regular basis to ensure that the women develop the skills of problem-solving dialogue, consensus-reaching, and the critical consciousness to analyze their environment.

Group Formation

- Each group should have a minimum of 15 and maximum of 30 members. If more women from the target group wish to join, form additional groups.
- Each group should be composed only of women from the target group. Apply all, not just one, criteria for the target group: that is, the target group should include only women from households who sell their manual labor to others for survival irrespective of occupation; provided, they do not have political patrons among the non-target people; and provided, they cannot still exercise status considerations.
- Avoid arbitrary cut-offs on membership (e.g., a subscription fee)

to maintain a ceiling on group membership. Start more groups if necessary.

- Analyze expectations and motivations of each woman in order to discover if any of the women have their own "hidden agenda."
- Investigate the background and relationships of members one to another and to the rich-and-powerful of the village. If you are not careful unwanted women may join the group or the rich-and-powerful may influence the group.
- Attend all meetings during the critical first steps of group formation.
- Help facilitate these initial meetings in order to understand any hidden unrest or hidden agendas in the group; to ensure the leadership of the group is not concentrated in the wrong hands; and to ensure the dynamics of the group does not move in the wrong direction.

Economic Action

- Conduct a feasibility study and prepare a production plan for each economic scheme.
- Raise critical questions to ensure realistic planning.
- Provide technical information and cost-analysis during the feasibility study.
- Avoid being too soft (e.g., do not offer that 'the project will do such-and-such for you') or too hard (e.g., do not demand repayment of loans during lean or difficult months).

Social Action

- Develop the awareness and identity of the women as members of the poor.
- Encourage analysis by the women of the relationship of the poor-and-powerless to the rich-and-powerful in the village.
- Encourage analysis of the problems of the women as women and as poor.
- Encourage the women to pursue the mutual goal of increasing their resources and their power.
- Avoid considering economic achievement as the only indicator of the group's success.

Group Development

- Encourage the majority of the members to be called into all decision making. If not, unrest within the group, external influences from outside the group, and mistrust of the leaders might grow.

- Don't allow any decisions to be taken outside the general meetings.
- Encourage constructive differences of opinions. Conflicts are desirable in participatory decision making so long as they can be resolved through general consensus. Absence of conflict is not necessarily a sign of strength. Where there is no conflict, there is often no leadership.
- Develop the group's discipline: attendance, participation, pooling of resources and labor, etc.
- Develop strategies for "weeding out" unwanted members. For example, do not approve or finance the economic schemes preferred by the unwanted members but only the schemes preferred by the majority.

Leadership Development

- Take care to ensure leadership develops from the target group in order to prevent the rich-and-powerful from gaining control of the group.
- Investigate how each aspiring leader fits into the larger socioeconomic patterns of the village in order to spot those leaders whose interests may prove irreconcilable to the interests of the group as a whole.
- Encourage joint leadership (two or more women) in order to avoid concentration of power in one woman. But avoid factional alignment behind each of the joint leaders.
- Discourage the "blind faith" or dependence of general members on their leaders or on BRAC.

INDICATORS OF CHANGE

In Chapters 6 and 7, I presented case-history material of women involved in BRAC's women's program, which we had gathered in an effort to measure the impact of BRAC's program and to identify relevant and appropriate indicators of change in general programming for women. The women told us of a wide variety of ways, many of them unanticipated, in which they benefited from and used the opportunities provided by the program. In the interest of indicating the types of change evaluators might look for, I have summarized the changes the women described into the following framework.

A Yardstick for Evaluators

The questions to be asked throughout are either: "Has there been a marked increase or decrease in. . .?" or "Has there been a marked improvement or deterioration in. . .?"

I. Relationships
   A. Individual: especially, women to women
- socializing opportunity
- mutual affection
- quarrels, tensions, conflicts
- mutual aid (material and emotional)

   B. Domestic: including parental, conjugal, in-law
- abuse (physical or emotional) from husbands or in-laws
- affection and respect from husbands and in-laws
- incidence of divorce or desertion or polygamy
- relative ease of divorce or desertion or polygamy
- incidence and terms of dowry
- kinship support systems
- households support systems

   C. Public: especially with the rich-and-powerful
- dependence of women on rich-and-powerful for:
credit (loans and mortgages)
security (aid-in-need and labor opportunities)
- disdain or respect from rich-and-powerful
- influence and constraints from rich-and-powerful on role changes by women
- resistance from rich-and-powerful to women's participation in village-level institutions
- women's relationships at following levels:
neighborhood
village
electoral unit
administrative unit
"beyond"

II. Resources
    A. Income
- cash or kind
- amount and/or steadiness
- control over

    B. Credit
- access to (in women's own right) institutional or informal sources
- terms and conditions (e.g. interest rates and/or "fit" between women's seasonal, production, and consumption needs, and volume and timing of credit)

    C. Labor
- domestic or social labor
- use or exchange production
- productivity of labor
- access to rural labor markets (relative to men)
- terms and conditions (relative to men)
- reversal in status associations with women's labor (that is, a reversal in the usual association of high status with no labor and low status with wage labor)

    D. Training and Technical Assistance
- skills training
- access to improved or appropriate technologies/techniques

    E. Means of Production: especially, land and water
- use rights or ownership rights
- land rights in women's own name
- access to public land and water resources

    F. Position on the Investment Continuum (relative to individual women's starting point)
- immediate needs: food
- minimum needs: food, clothing shelter
- security: debt repayment, goods redemption, repairs, savings
- assets (relative to particular situation and economy)
- future benefits (relative to particular situation and economy)
- ultimate security (in many but not all situations, land)

III. Power
    A. Extra-domestic
- officiating at extradomestic disputes

- attending or officiating at extradomestic events or ceremonies
B. Legal
  - self-representation at legal proceedings (both customary
    and formal courts)
  - awareness of women's legal rights
  - legal reforms to strengthen women's rights
C. Political
  - participation in local elections: as voters, campaigners, can-
    didates, or elected officials
D. Public Goods and Services
  - access in women's own right to:
    agricultural extension services
    agricultural inputs
    public employment schemes
    rations
    health and family planning services

What I have outlined above is a framework of realistic indicators of change but not a specific research design. Any adequate evaluation design must address the problems of baseline data, control data, measurement of causality, and the specific conditions under which the program was undertaken and in which the participants live. I would like to share a few additional thoughts on the time-frame of evaluation and on the value of qualitative data.

Not all of these indicators I have suggested should be measured at one and the same time. The types of change indicated can occur within any of several time frames: short-term (2 to 3 years); or medium-term (3 to 5 years); or long-term (5-10 years). Our experience indicates that one can begin to measure participation rates and obtain corrective feedback (e.g., to isolate factors contributing to relative success or failure) within the first year or two of a new development project for women and that one can evaluate the same project in terms of certain concrete, economic indicators (e.g., income, access to credit) within three to five years. Surprisingly, we found that one can also evaluate a project for some less-concrete, social indicators (e.g., more adequate relationships, more participation in public institutions) within three to five years. However, most social indicators (demographic behavior, inheritance practices, conditions of marriage, size and composition of

households, education of children, etc.) can and should only be measured after the long term (5 to 10 years).

Generally, economic indicators are easier to quantify. At the incep-
tion of a project, one can measure how many and what kind of resources have been earmarked for women. In the short term, one can
measure how many resources are actually being delivered. By the
middle term, one can measure how many women have availed of these
resources. However, only in the long term can one estimate whether
women can exercise equal access and control over these resources
relative to men from their own households and to men and women
from other classes of households.

Generally, social indicators are not only more difficult to quantify
but also take longer to be felt. I have argued that many social changes
will occur as an indirect result of economic change. So much so that
economic change must be experienced before many social changes can
be felt. What surprised us was the relative speed with which certain
unplanned and unanticipated social changes followed upon planned
economic change: for example, women's participation in the local judicial councils, women's demand for public goods and services, women's
negotiation of more adequate terms of marriage, and the decreased
incidence of divorce and desertion. However, it must also be remembered that the first woman to run and win in a local election did so only
after BRAC had been working in the area for eight years and did so
only in the newly-constituted (and short-lived) village councils, and not
in the traditional seat of local power, the intra-village union councils.

Finally, I would argue that quantitative evaluation must be built on a
solid qualitative base in order to understand what indicators are to be
used (those based on actual changes that occur rather than those based
on the program targets and objectives or on the women's expectations)
and to understand which indicators of actual change can be easily
judged or observed by outsiders. I would also assert that quantitative
evaluation should be built on solid qualitative understanding of the
base from which the women who were to experience change started.
And, finally, I would assert that some indicators of actual change may
never be subject to precise measurement and will only be subject to
qualitative measurement.

PROSPECTS FOR THE QUIET REVOLUTION

I have argued throughout this volume for development programs and policies that would increase women's access to economic and social resources. I have also argued that a dual strategy of rural employment and rural institutions for women has a tremendous potential for change in women's lives and the well-being of their families. The particular model developed by BRAC succeeded because it focused on women's work and on organizing women. The story of the BRAC women's program is the story of a quiet revolution that began in the lives of several thousand women as a result of that dual strategy.

I would like to close this story with a testable hypothesis suggested by our experience. The hypothesis goes like this. We have heard a great deal about the fact that despite the various development plans and programs developed and implemented during the 60s and 70s more people go hungry each day. What was wrong with development efforts during the past two decades? Or, perhaps the question should be, what was overlooked in the development efforts of the past two decades? My hypothesis is that women were overlooked and that if women's work had been valued and supported the tragic dilemma of increasing poverty despite mounting development efforts might not have been as great. At issue is not only the impact of development on women but also the potential impact of women on development. Women can make a tremendous contribution not only to family well-being but also to national production and development. Therefore, the quiet revolution should spread not only to rural women everywhere but also in the thinking of all development planners and practitioners.

Glossary

ANNA—unit of old currency; 16 annas to 1 rupee

AM SUTTO—mango cheese; a preparation from dried mangoes

APA—literally, older sister; term used by village women to refer to female BRAC staff

BATASHA—molasses candy

BEPURDAH—literally, without-purdah; term used to refer to what is considered outside the norms of *purdah*

BHAI—literally, brother; term used by village women to refer to male BRAC staff

BIDI—hand-rolled cigarettes

BIGHA—a measure of land equal to ⅓-acre

BOLA-BULI—straw scarecrows on long handles burnt at dusk and thrown into the rivers by Hindus to forestall illness

BORI—lentil balls

CHEERA—pounded, flattened rice

CHANACHUR—snack food prepared from lentils, nuts, and spices

CHAR—sandy soil deposits built up alongside rivers or in the bays

DARBAR—meeting

DEKHI—a hammer-action, foot-operated wooden instrument used to husk rice

EK GORE—literally, one house; idiomatically, a system of ostracism wherein one household is banned temporarily from normal relationships and reciprocities with other households in the village

ELAKA—place or region

ENDI—a variety of silk spun from the cocoon of a worm which feeds off the castor bush

GENJI—undershirt worn by men

GHERAO—surround or blockage; a form of protest

GHEE—clarified butter

GUMCHA—scarf worn by men

HALWA—a sweet dish prepared from fruits, eggs, or vegetables

HARPATA—rake-like instrument used to turn and gather grain during drying

HAT—local market

JAMDANI—figured muslin weaving for which Bangladesh is renowned

JANTAK—dowry

KANTHA—cotton quilt; village women in Bangladesh stitch a variety of *kanthas*

KASUNDI—mustard seed dressing

KAZ—literally, work; a word used by some village women to refer to marriage

KIRTAN—devotional song

KHAS JAMI—public land owned by government but available to private individuals on lease

KHITCHURI—gruel; typically made from rice and lentils

KHUD—broken pieces of rice

KODAL—spade

KULA—flat, horseshoe-shaped basket used to winnow rice

LUNGI—sarong worn by men

MADRASSA—Islamic school

MAHR—dower; a sum of money or property the groom promises to pay the bride in the event he divorces his wife or dies

MASHIMA—aunt; an affectionate term for older woman

MATBOR—village elder

MAUND—a measure of weight equal to 82 pounds

MULLAH—religious leader

MURABBA—a sweet dish prepared by crystallizing fruits or vegetables in sugar

MURI—puffed rice

MUSHTI TULI—a traditional habit of saving whereby a woman puts aside and stores (often secretly) a handful of rice daily or weekly from the domestic stock

NAKSHI KANTHA—the celebrated embroidered quilt of Bangladesh

NAYOR—a woman's return-visit to her parental home after marriage; usually an annual visit

PAKHI—a measure of land equal to ⅓-acre

PAPAD—a crisp, flat bread prepared from lentils

PAPRI PITAH—a crisp snack-food prepared from rice flour

PEETHA—rice-cake

PIR—spiritual leader

POISA—a unit of currency; 100 poisa to 1 taka

PUJA—Hindu festival or worship

PURDAH—literally, curtain; figuratively, seclusion of women

RAMZAN—Muslim month of fasting

RASGULLA—sweet dish made from milk solids and sugar syrup

ROTI—unleavened bread

RUPEE—a unit of the old currency; equal to the present-day taka

SADARNI—female gang leader of construction workers

SAGAR—ocean; term used by local residents to refer to a large area of impounded water in North-east Bangladesh

SANDESH—a sweet dish prepared from milk solids and sugar

SEER—a measure of weight equal approximately to two pounds

SHALISH—local judicial council or moot

SHUTKI—dried fish

SOMAJ BANDHO—literally, banned from society; idiomatically, a system of ostracism whereby one person or one household is temporarily denied participation in village ceremonies or religious rites

SOMITY—organized society; term used by BRAC and village women to refer to BRAC-organized groups

TAKA—a unit of currency; 15 taka to 1 U.S. dollar (1975–80)

TOPI—cap

ZAMINDAR—landlord

BRAC Programs

This appendix lists BRAC's major programs to provide a sense of the scope and scale of its operations.

The *SULLA PROJECT* (Sylhet District,* 1972) is the original field project where BRAC began. BRAC's field staff initially extended services to some 200 villages but now concentrate their efforts in 100 villages.

The *MANIKGANJ PROJECT* (Dhaka District, 1976) is the second major field project in which staff focus on the poorest third of 180 villages of Manikganj Thana.* All activities are planned and implemented by the members of BRAC-organized groups of poor. BRAC supports these group activities with training, credit, marketing, and other services.

The JAMALPUR WOMEN'S PROGRAM (Jamalpur District, 1976) is a field project run predominantly by women staff for the poor women of 30 villages around Jamalpur town. The method of operation is similar to that of the Manikganj Project with an emphasis on income-generating schemes for the organized groups of women.

The *TRAINING AND RESOURCE CENTRE*, TARC (Dhaka District, 1976) trains several thousand trainees each year in specialized productive skills (agriculture, poultry, and fishery) and broader de-

---

*There are 19 Districts in Bangladesh, each divided into Subdivisions which are, in turn, sub-divided into *thanas*. The *thana* is the lowest, and the key, administrative unit of the country. Each *thana* covers an average of 170 villages (or 170,000 people). The Union is the lowest electoral unit of the country.

velopment skills (communication, leadership, group dynamics). The trainees include BRAC's own staff, members of BRAC-organized groups, and the staff from other voluntary and government agencies. Under its *OUTREACH* program, certain TARC staff provide support and training to groups of poor from rural areas not under BRAC's field projects.

BRAC has opened fourteen branch banks of its *RURAL CREDIT AND TRAINING PROJECT*, RCTP (Dhaka and Tangail Districts, 1979). Each branch is staffed by a branch manager and five field officers, all with prior experience in BRAC field projects. The basic objective of the scheme is to extend credit to the rural poor through field officers well-trained in rural development problems and rural production planning and management.

BRAC runs a rural craft centre called *AARONG* ("market place") in Dhaka city. Craft sponsored by BRAC and other voluntary agencies and/or produced by poor traditional artisans are sold at Aarong's retail outlet. BRAC also sponsors a *TEXTILE DESIGN AND SERVICE WORKSHOP* to strengthen the design, technology, and production capacity of poor artisans in selected textile handicrafts. BRAC has undertaken a *TRADITIONAL CRAFT DEVELOPMENT* scheme to revive and adapt the traditional craft designs and techniques of Bangladesh.

BRAC initiated its *ORAL THERAPY EXTENSION PROGRAM* (OTEP) in 1980. The purpose of the program is to extend the knowledge of a simple mixture [called oral therapy] of salt, water, and dry molasses for treatment of the diarrhoeal diseases to every household. Usage as well as effects on rates of morbidity and mortality are monitored by a specialized unit of BRAC researchers. This program will run for an initial phase of three years during which BRAC plans to cover all villages of five districts.

The staff at BRAC's *HEAD OFFICE* in Dhaka provide the planning, administration, and logistical support required by the field operations. Moreover, certain substantive programs operate out of BRAC's Head Office:

The editor and journalist of BRAC's monthly development journal, *GONOKENDRA* (1974), are based in the Head Office. The journal, which features development articles as well as current news and literary sections, is circulated to some 65,000 rural readers including all primary school teachers. The *Gonokendra* also features a 4-page supplement in bold type for new literates, including graduates of BRAC's functional education course.

The *MATERIALS DEVELOPMENT UNIT* (1974), four writers and their supervisor, have completed the design and three revisions of BRAC's functional education and preventive health materials. The Unit is currently developing an innovative primary school curriculum.

In order to evaluate its program effectiveness and to understand the underlying, systemic constraints to program implementation, BRAC has developed a *RESEARCH AND EVALUATION DIVISION* (1975). Ten full-time researchers and two supervisors staff the Division. A consultant anthropologist has helped develop this Division. The Evaluation Unit uses quantitative methods (baseline and sectoral surveys) to measure BRAC program impact. The Research Unit uses qualitative methods (in-depth interviews and observation techniques) to investigate the dynamics of poverty and development activities within the rural power structure.

The costs of BRAC's expanding program and projects have so far been met by external grants. But BRAC firmly believes that its dependence on foreign funds should be reduced. In an effort to create a stable domestic funding base, BRAC has decided to set up a number of commercial enterprises consistent with its over-all development objectives. To generate recurring income for its operations: *BRAC PRINTERS*, a modern printing press, is in operation in a suburb of Dhaka. The press was set up to handle the printing needs of both BRAC and commercial clients. The multi-storied building above the printing plant, constructed by BRAC with a foreign grant, houses BRAC's Head Office staff and activities. BRAC's concern for development in the agricultural sector and for improving the incomes of landless and marginal farmers let to the choice of the second commercial project, a *COLD-STORAGE WAREHOUSE*, with a potato storage capacity of 4,000 tons in Comilla District.

The Staff Structure of BRAC

This appendix was written in some detail in order to describe the various categories of BRAC staff and how they are recruited, trained, and deployed.

The Field Staff

BRAC engages three levels of field staff: unpaid helpers, paid para-professionals, and paid professionals.

The Helpers—

> There are 65,000 villages in Bangladesh. BRAC has only so many staff and so much money. Volunteer self-help is the answer to covering as many villages as possible.
>
> BRAC Field Staff

From its beginning, BRAC has relied on unpaid, part-time village workers to assist in the delivery of certain services. BRAC recruited and trained this cadre to help ensure continuous contact and greater accessibility of these services to the villages. BRAC refers to this cadre as "helpers" (literal translation of Bengali original). Who then are these unpaid village helpers? What services do they provide?

Early on (1974) BRAC recruited a cadre of volunteer teachers for its functional education program. Young men and women with some post-primary education were chosen from the same villages in which they were to serve. These teacher-helpers receive an initial five-day train-ing in BRAC's functional education curriculum and methodology.

During that same year, BRAC also recruited a cadre of female family planning helpers. These family planning helpers served as recruiters of family planning acceptors and distributors of contraceptives under the guidance and supervision of a BRAC paramedic. Each helper was to serve, on the average, 100 families in her own village. Later (1976), BRAC added a cadre of female health-helpers to establish, under the supervision of the paramedics, a continuous presence of the BRAC health program in each village. Each health-helper was trained (by a paramedic) to treat in her own village the most prevalent diseases. She was also to refer cases to the paramedic on his weekly village visit and to follow-up cases treated by the paramedic.

The criteria for recruitment as either family planning- or health-helper was that the women be a member of the community, preferably over twenty years of age, acceptable to the community, enthusiastic about her new responsibilities and willing to move freely about the village. She could be illiterate if she met the other criteria. With the introduction of the health-helper in each village, it made sense to merge the inter-related and overlapping functions of the family planning- and health-helpers. In some villages, the family planning-helper was promoted to perform both functions. In most villages, the newly-recruited health-helpers performed both tasks.

Over time, one basic problem was never resolved—the pay or compensation for these helpers. Initially, the family planning- and health-helpers were to be compensated, however minimally, by those who received their services. However, BRAC was not able to develop a self-financing health system. The teacher-helpers were never compensated. Many helpers expected to be promoted to a salaried position or to receive some form of BRAC patronage. As one of BRAC's paid field staff put it: "Those who joined had definite expectations of raising their material welfare."

This is not to say there was no true volunteerism in the villages. BRAC's functional eduction program ran on volunteerism for nine years, albeit with a great number of dropouts and a recurring need to recruit and train new teacher-helpers. True volunteerism did blossom, but BRAC found it could not bank on volunteerism. How then did BRAC deal with this problem of compensation?

After 1977, BRAC began to reduce the coverage of its services to reach only the poorest third of each village. About the same time,

BRAC began to organize the poorest third into small groups, averaging 15–20 men or women each. Given this focus on the poor, BRAC decided selected members of each organized group of poor would be recruited and trained as the helpers for their respective groups. These helpers would be compensated for any loss of their productive time by their respective group funds. In this way, the groups of poor would be served and the capacities of the groups would be raised.

A new problem surfaced. Not all organized groups of poor have an educated or even partly-educated member to be trained as teacher-helper. This is particularly the case with the women's groups given the high rate of female illiteracy, a rate which is higher still in poor households. An interim solution adopted by BRAC field staff was to organize those female teacher-helpers recruited from outside the groups into their own group. These teacher-helpers undertake productive activities (as a BRAC-supported group) during those days they do not teach.

One further note. The teacher-helpers have always been both men and women. Initially, however, the health- and family planning-helpers were only women. Now, as both male and female groups select a member to be trained as the health-helper for their respective groups, a cadre of male health-helpers has been developed.

The Paraprofessionals—

> If professionals are used they get siphoned off or are not willing to serve. The trick then is to train villagers to the point where they are willing to serve but do not share the class characteristics of doctors and other professionals who seek advancement.

> The classic role of the physician as that of a healer is being redefined in BRAC. We view him first and foremost as a teacher, then a planner, and lastly as one directly involved in curing.
>
> BRAC's Executive Director

From its beginning, BRAC has recruited paraprofessionals to help expand the coverage and reduce cost in the delivery of certain services. Initially (1973), BRAC recruited a cadre of paramedics to deliver health and family planning services. Later (1978), BRAC added a cadre of paratechnicians to deliver various technical services.

The paramedic is the key figure in BRAC's health and family planning program. Each paramedic is responsible for five to eight villages.

They must visit each village at least once a week. They help train and supervise the health helpers. They discuss sanitation, nutrition, and preventive health measures and treat the health problems brought to their attention by the health-helpers.

The training of the paramedics is conducted by the BRAC physicians in the BRAC project areas. The paramedics receive an intensive pre-service training (two months of classroom theory and four months of supervised practices). A training manual for the paramedics has been prepared. Moreover, they receive regular in-service supervision and refresher training.

The paramedics are generally recruited from the region, but not the villages, in which they serve. They generally have some secondary education. All BRAC paramedics are male. At one time (1976) BRAC recruited a team of 12 female paramedics. BRAC wanted to reach women and their children with female personnel. Within a year, the female paramedics had all dropped out of the program: to deliver babies, to be married or to pacify the worries of their families about their work (which required moving from village to village). BRAC never adequately resolved the issue that all BRAC medical personnel, above the level of village helpers, are male. To foster female staff required political will and resolve and a flexible and supportive management. In the delivery of health services particularly, such resolve and flexibility is to be recommended.

The BRAC doctors provide the training, technical back-stopping, and supervision of the paramedics. They do not deal directly with patients except in emergencies. The doctors are based at modest clinics where simple surgical procedures, common pathological tests, and family planning clinical services (IUD insertion, tubal ligation, and vasectomy) can be performed.

Over time, the demand for technical skills from BRAC programs has increased dramatically. In response, BRAC's technical capacity has increased steadily but less dramatically. Meeting the demand has been done in several stages. When a new technical program is undertaken, BRAC turns to outside agencies for technical advice and training. Once BRAC judges the feasibility of a particular technology, BRAC begins to develop its own capacities in that area. At first, BRAC developed a team of technical trainers to operate out of BRAC's training center. Few of these technical trainers came to the job with ready-made skills.

Most were sent for skill training or apprenticeship with outside institutions. BRAC soon discovered that a centralized technical support system is not adequate. After the initial skill training, trainees require a continuous technical back-stopping, and not simply periodic follow-up visits or refresher trainings.

This need for continuous technical support gave rise to the *paratechnicians*. BRAC decided to recruit and train young staff in key technical areas: there are few ready-made specialists for those areas BRAC wanted to expand and develop. These paratechnicians are posted to the relevant field projects. They report to the respective professional field staff on management questions and to the training center staff on technical questions. To date, BRAC has recruited and trained paratechnicians in the following areas: agriculture, fish-culture, poultry, sericulture, block-printing, weaving, and food-processing.

The Professionals—

> The main workhorse for BRAC's field activities with direct and multiple responsibilities for identifying and assessing opportunities and needs for field activities and initiating, guiding, and supporting them is the professional field staff.
>
> Manzoor Ahmed on BRAC*

BRAC's professional field staff are multi-purpose generalists. They carry the responsibility for initiating and supervising all BRAC's village-level activities: the functional education, health and family planning programs; the technical programs; group formation and development; group activities and schemes. Each professional field staff is responsible, on the average, for 6 villages.

Consider these figures for one moment. Each village in Bangladesh averages 1000 residents. BRAC aims to reach and benefit the poorest third of each village. Each household in Bangladesh averages 6 members.

$$6 \text{ villages} \times 1000 = 6,000 \text{ people}$$
$$6000 \div 3 = 2,000 \text{ poor people}$$
$$2000 \div 6 = 333 \text{ poor households}$$

---

*For the only earlier comprehensive case-study of BRAC see Manzoor Ahmed, *BRAC: Building Human Infrastructures to Serve the Rural Poor,* Case Study No. 2, International Council of Educational Development, P.O. Box 217, Essex, Connecticut, 1977.

Each professional field staff is expected to organize a minimum of 333 poor (one from each household) but preferably 666 poor (one man and one woman from each poor household).

Gradually the BRAC professionals organize the poor into workable, homogeneous groups of poor. The welfare services to these groups are delivered by the unpaid helpers and paramedics. The technological services to these groups are delivered with the assistance of the para-technicians. The professional field staff, although they supervise the welfare and technical services, concentrate on the socio-political message. Their main objective is to raise the group's awareness, strengthen the groups, and foster group action.

As the groups develop the range of skills required for the job of organizing expands. The following is a rough sequence of the type of skills required:

- More *general* skills have been required of all field staff since the beginning of BRAC: communications; problem-solving dialogue: awareness-building; group dynamics; and leadership training. In addition, a general knowledge of BRAC's basic welfare programs; health, family planning, and functional education.

- More and more *technical* skills have been required over time. In those areas for which BRAC has trained paratechnicians, the professional field staff require only basic theoretical know-how: enough familiarity with chickens or silk worms, for example, to make intelligent plans for poultry and sericulture schemes. In those areas for which BRAC has not trained paratechnicians, the professional field staff must acquire enough practical skills to plan and support the schemes.

- To understand the dynamics of the village and of poverty, the professionals have been trained in *diagnostic* skills. They have been trained to develop a habit of inquiry. They have been given a framework in which to question and observe rural phenomena. They have been encouraged to record what they observe in a systematic and disciplined way. And, they have been trained to analyze their findings.

- To facilitate their many functions and programs, the professional field staff have also had to develop substantial *management* skills.

254   A QUIET REVOLUTION

The specific skills required are listed below:

Program Components	Group Development
Functional Education	Dialogue
Health/Family Planning	Consciousness-raising
Agriculture	Awareness-Building
Fish Culture	Communications
Silk Culture	Group Dynamics
Animal Husbandry	Leadership Training
Poultry	Economic Support
Horticulture	Cost Accounting
Program Management	Research and Development
BRAC Procedures	Design
Office Management	Marketing
Financial Management	Technical
Personnel Management	Diagnostic
Program Design	Habit of Inquiry
Monitoring and Reporting	Framework of Inquiry
Development Philosophy	Documentation
	Analysis

In the long run, the nature of BRAC's overall objective (to develop organized groups of poor) requires that these skills devolve from BRAC staff to the poor. This process of acquiring skills and know-how often starts with BRAC administrators who initiate, research, and develop individual programs, but must end with members of organized groups of poor. The skills devolve through the following levels of BRAC personnel:

administrators
|
professionals
|
paraprofessionals
|
unpaid helpers
|
group members

As the skills devolve theoretical know-how becomes less important and practical skills more critical.

BRAC recruits university-educated young men and women as its professional field staff. They are recruited from all over the country, not from the regions in which they are to serve. No specific disciplinary background is required as no formal discipline adequately prepares them for field work. In fact, university education is not a determining factor. BRAC insists on higher education credentials simply because, given the high rate of unemployment among the university-educated, there is an ample supply of these candidates for BRAC jobs.

In recruiting, BRAC applies several criteria and uses two screenings. During preliminary interviews, BRAC screens the applicants on their personality, and their perceptions of rural work in rural areas. BRAC recognizes that judging such qualities is a very "hit or miss" process. So BRAC has all finalists participate in a two-day series of group exercises conducted by BRAC trainers. During this "selection session," BRAC staff further observe and judge the finalists. The finalists are also able to get a taste of what might be required of them as BRAC staff and whether the job would suit their own expectations and temperament.

BRAC trains new recruits through a combination of: brief orientation sessions; apprenticeship; in-service training; and practical experience. BRAC trainers, together with senior field staff, conduct the *pre-service orientation session*. The session covers the following topics: BRAC's functional education methods and materials; BRAC's philosophy and approach to development; BRAC procedures and administrative routines; communication skills; and group dynamics. As with all of BRAC training, the recruits are engaged in group exercises and problem-solving dialogue.

Once new recruits are posted to the field, they apprentice for a few months with senior field staff. The senior staff accompany and guide the new recruits through their respective villages and responsibilities. All staff attend weekly project meetings in which the problems and progress of field plans and activities are discussed.

Throughout their field posting, field staff are provided *informal in-service training*. One field project administrator explained that the best training he offers new staff takes place during after-dinner discussions in the staff dormitory. Both the paraprofessional and the professional field staff live in office-cum-dormitories referred to, in BRAC, as camps. The communal-style of living in these camps facilitates a daily exchange of ideas and experience. When field staff report to their administrative supervisors in BRAC's Head Office, each debriefing-briefing session serves as additional informal training.

Periodically, *special trainings* are conducted to fit specific needs. When BRAC adopts a new strategy the field staff undergo a reorientation training. When BRAC's functional education materials are revised the field staff are retained in functional education. When BRAC undertakes new technical schemes, one or two field staff receive orientation training in that technical area.

The Trainers—

In 1974, BRAC promoted several senior field staff to form a small training team. They were to arrange the special training and orientation sessions for the growing number of BRAC field staff and to develop a portfolio of training material and methods. BRAC contracted a training consultant to train the trainers and to help them prepare the training materials. They prepared a set of resource materials on specific topics. The trainers draw on, adapt or combine these modules (as they are called) in preparing for different training sessions.

By 1976, BRAC had established a Training and Resource Center (TARC; in a building adjacent to the head office in Dhaka) with six full-time trainers. The establishment of TARC did not mark any basic change in training content and methods but did mark BRAC's commitment in staff and resources to training and permitted the training team to better plan and manage training activities. By that time, the trainers had developed a comprehensive set of training modules on the following topics:

—approaches to development: analysis of different approaches and target groups
—methods of communication: demonstration of different ways to disseminate ideas
—organizational and staff needs: assessment or expectations of both staff and BRAC
—role of change agents: clarifications of staff roles
—consciousness-raising: analysis of the rural situation
—leadership and social change: analysis of style, characteristics and qualities of leadership
—group dynamics and cooperation: analysis of factors in establishing group cohesion

—human development and social change: analysis of social relationships and the role of BRAC staff
—functional education methodology: training in BRAC's functional education methods and materials
—project planning: analysis of cost factors, inputs and outputs
—project management: training in principles of management (including personnel management, general management, basic monitoring and reporting)

In 1978, BRAC shifted TARC to a rural campus (16 acres 20 miles west of Dhaka) where BRAC had built dormitories, meeting rooms, a library, cafeteria and other facilities. BRAC also cultivated the land and fish ponds on the campus and developed a poultry farm. With the shift to its rural campus and given the increasing demand from the field projects for technical training, TARC augmented its basic training with certain technical trainings:

—vegetable production and management
—crop management and planning
—fruit gardening and management
—rice production and management
—poultry rearing and management
—fish culture and management
—animal husbandry and management

The production side of each technical training is designed to suit program beneficiaries. The management side of each technical training is designed to suit extension workers and field staff.

BRAC trainers are recruited from BRAC's field projects. They are experienced professional field staff who have displayed the qualities of: leadership, communication skills, and situational analysis. New trainers are given in-service training by senior trainers. Now, BRAC trainers regularly and systematically train BRAC field staff; the members of BRAC-organized and other groups of landless and poor; and the staff or other organizations.

The Administrators-

The staff of BRAC's head office in Dhaka provide the planning, administration, and logistical support required by the BRAC programs. BRAC's Executive Director carries the overall responsibility for the general policies and all individual programs of BRAC. A team of administrators help the Executive Director plan and set policy for BRAC. Each administrator has direct responsibility for one or more individual programs.

BRAC programs fall into two broad types: field and non-field. The field programs include: the three comprehensive field projects; the training, banking, and oral therapy programs; and the women's program (including the development of rural industries). The non-field programs include: the development journal, materials development; research and evaluation; and BRAC's rural craft center-cum-shop. Administrators of field programs make, at a minimum, one trip per month to each field program, regularly brief and debrief field staff when they report to head office, and daily work on planning and supporting the programs. Administrators of non-field programs supervise a team of staff at the head office. The team works together to develop and implement their given programs. Some administrators handle both types of programs.

Administrators are recruited variously. The Executive Director was the founder of BRAC. Some administrators are recruited from the field projects. Consequently, there is an emerging "career ladder" within BRAC. But some administrators are recruited from outside BRAC. Generally, the higher the level of management or substantive skills required the more likely BRAC is to recruit from outside. However, there is no hard-and-fast BRAC rule in this regard.*

A note on women staff. It should be noted that, with the exception of the Jamalpur Women's program and of the temporary Anandapur

---

*As of December 1980 BRAC engaged the following number of staff:
Administrators—11
Professional Field Staff—162
Trainers—22
Researchers—10
Paramedics—40
Paratechnicians—12
Health Helpers—152
Teacher Helpers—240

A total of 257 paid staff and 392 unpaid helpers. These numbers do not include: BRAC accountants and logistics officers; BRAC journalists; employees at BRAC's rural craft shop and traditional design center; employees at BRAC's printing press and cold storage field workers for BRAC's Oral Therapy Extension Program. Total BRAC paid staff, by the end of 1980, numbered around 580.

Women's Camp, all the social organizing and economic programming described in this book was carried out by male staff. The reasons for this are two:

1) BRAC found that experienced male staff performed as well as experienced female staff in social and economic programs for women (but not as well in health and family planning); and
2) BRAC found that if it spent the necessary will, time, and energy required in recruiting, training, and counselling women staff it did so at the cost of training and developing women group members and leaders.

In the final analysis, BRAC decided that if one sticks to an all-women model at both the staffing and beneficiary levels it leads to a certain blurring between "affirmative action" and "women in development": that is, a confusion of ends (village women participating fully in development) and means (women implementing development). This is not to say BRAC disbanded its all-women's project, the Jamalpur Women's Program, but to say that BRAC recognized that in Jamalpur its objective was to develop women staff as much as to develop village women's leadership.

In the case of health and family planning programs, BRAC recognizes that at a minimum, one needs to recruit village women as frontline workers to assist in delivery of these services to other village women. And, ideally, one would recruit women paraprofessionals and professionals as well. To do so requires political will and a flexible and supportive management. As stated earlier, in the delivery of health and family planning services particularly, such resolve and flexibility is to be recommended.

Mixing Action and Research

This appendix was written to show how BRAC encourages and trains its staff (at all levels) to learn from their experiences, to transmit what they learn, and how BRAC institutionalized a reciprocal process of implementation-learning-planning.

BRAC field staff have always been encouraged to listen, to observe, and to learn from their day-to-day work. However, over time, BRAC has had to develop its own research perspective, skills, and staff in order to train its field staff *how* to listen, observe, and learn.

Participant-Observation

BRAC field staff are posted to field situations which bring them into close and continuous contact with a set of villages and several thousand villagers. They are asked to introduce and observe the process of change. They are challenged to look into the constraints, potential and dynamics of village structure on poverty. BRAC staff are in a unique position. Few situations can match for its intensity and its continuity the opportunity BRAC field staff have to observe and to learn about rural life. Nothing can quite compare with being there.

Consider these opportunities for learning experienced daily in countless villages over many years:

—initial rounds of discussions and observations in a village
—informal surveys of village institutions, physical infrastructure, etc.
—supervision and observation of functional education classes
—supervision and observation of group meetings

—conducting and/or observation of trainings and workshops
—development and supervision of income-generating schemes
—day-to-day observations: of village relationships
                           of village power structure
                           of the process of change

Despite the daily contact with the village realities, despite continuous participation-observation by its many field staff, BRAC has not
learned as much as it might have liked or needed. BRAC has begun to
seek ways of enhancing its learning process, of teaching its staff *how* to
learn.

Action-Research

There are certain points where we don't understand people as well as we
might. Why does a cooperative succeed in one village and not in
another? Why does one person and not another respond to family planning services? There are other instances where we can't measure the
success of a program. For example, have any health lessons been learnt
by the rural clients from BRAC's health delivery system? To get at the
answer to such questions BRAC must acquire an in-depth knowledge of
the mechanisms of change.

                                          BRAC's Executive Director

How could BRAC get answers to such questions? How could BRAC
acquire more in-depth understanding? One way was to conduct formal
research. To this end, BRAC established its own research unit (in 1976)
and hired a consultant anthropologist to develop the framework and
plans for BRAC's research and to train a team of BRAC researchers.
BRAC hoped that well-designed research would help BRAC look into
the mechanisms of change and to find solutions to problems encountered in the field. At issue was not more information but more useful
and critical insights.

BRAC's research unit has conducted several studies, including:

—*Who Gets What and Why:* an analysis in one village of different
  strategies negotiated by different households to obtain and control
  resources
—*The Net:* An analysis in several villages of different strategies used
  by the rich and powerful to control and exploit the poor and
  powerless

—*Peasant Perceptions Series:* a presentation of the perspective of the poor on certain critical issues: famine and credit, to date.

However, BRAC did not feel that research in and of itself was sufficient. Rather, BRAC was looking for a mix of action and research. In the words of BRAC's Executive Director, BRAC was seeking to "mix research with commitment and involvement."

One way to bring about this mix was to ensure that BRAC researchers have a clear idea of conditions in the field. To this end, BRAC researchers have been required to spend some time in field work. Some research studies have been conducted by teams composed half of field staff and half of research staff. Another way to bring about this mix was to integrate a research perspective into BRAC's field work. In order to bring this about the field staff would have to acquire two critical research habits: the habit of inquiry and disciplined observation and the habit of analysis and disciplined recording.

BRAC field staff now receive periodic trainings in BRAC's research framework and methods. They are told the value of what they observe, the value of detail. They are regularly asked to conduct interviews, to write profiles of villagers, and to gather different types of information. They are asked to conduct simple surveys of what people affected by BRAC's projects want, how they evaluate BRAC's program, and their suggestions for improvement. They have been asked to draw up profiles of the organized groups of poor with which they work— including a history of the group and the problems, successes, and failures experienced in group action. Their findings are analyzed and discussed in sessions with senior field staff and/or research staff.

Although most field staff now recognize the importance of inquiry and observation, only a few have developed a habit of analysis and disciplined recording. BRAC is still trying to design adequate methods to capture and analyze the collective experience of its field staff. BRAC staff maintain field diaries, but these are often incomplete or lack the type of information required. BRAC has designed village and group files in which information is to be recorded regularly, but BRAC staff do not find the time and energy to maintain these files on any regular basis. BRAC has designed forms to record the minimal village statistics (vital registration, crop figures, price indices of basic commodities), but again the staff do not find the time and energy to maintain these records. BRAC staff periodically report on programs to BRAC's head office, but there is little cumulative data and no analysis of trends over time in these reports. Despite these limitations, BRAC has made significant steps in integrating a research perspective into all its activities.

As discussed in chapter one, BRAC learns so it can plan. Let me summarize the special features of BRAC that facilitate this implementing-learning-planning process and certain weaknesses of BRAC that hinder it.

First, the strengths:

1. Diagnosis of poverty in real human terms. BRAC field staff are in daily contact with the villages and with the poor. They are encouraged to learn and are required to transmit what they learn.
2. Participation of the poor. There are several mechanisms for the poor to be heard not only by the field staff but by the institution as a whole.
3. Realistic goals and objectives. At weekly and monthly project meetings, the problems and progress of the program are discussed. The staff evaluate and discuss what worked or did not work and why. Targets and objectives are reassessed in light of these discussions.
4. Flexible plans. BRAC field staff concur that both BRAC's short-term and long-term objectives are clear. Moreover, BRAC goals are dynamic. Goals are set and reset each month.
5. Phased planning. BRAC does not at any one time plan very far ahead. Rather, during one phase of field activities (with the help of surveys, research, observation and other tools) the next phase is discussed and planned.
6. Decentralized planning. Generally, BRAC planning is done by or in consultation with those who have responsibility for implementing the plans. Within the BRAC field project, the field staff have the discretion and are encouraged to act on their own. The field staff are able to respond to the dynamic of the problem and of the situation.

Next, the weaknesses:

—although field staff have always been encouraged to observe and listen, only more recently have they been taught how to observe and listen

—although the poor whom BRAC organize participate directly in the formulation of the schemes and activities of their individual groups, their voice is heard only indirectly in the larger plans of BRAC

—although for the most part BRAC plans and goals remain flexible, the administrators in BRAC's head office occasionally stick to certain generalized orthodoxies which may not necessarily fit the realities.

—although BRAC remains flexible and learns through trial-and-error, BRAC runs the risks that every error becomes a virtue and that lessons are learned prematurely (without allowing time for the process of change to work itself out)

—although there is local discretion within the field projects, there is very little decentralization on matters of personnel and overall directions for BRAC

—although this centralized authority may be required by the scale and scope of BRAC's activities, it does lead to certain problems and discontent.

These weaknesses notwithstanding, the BRAC program is noted for its flexibility, responsiveness, and learning.

APPENDIX IV

Map of Bangladesh

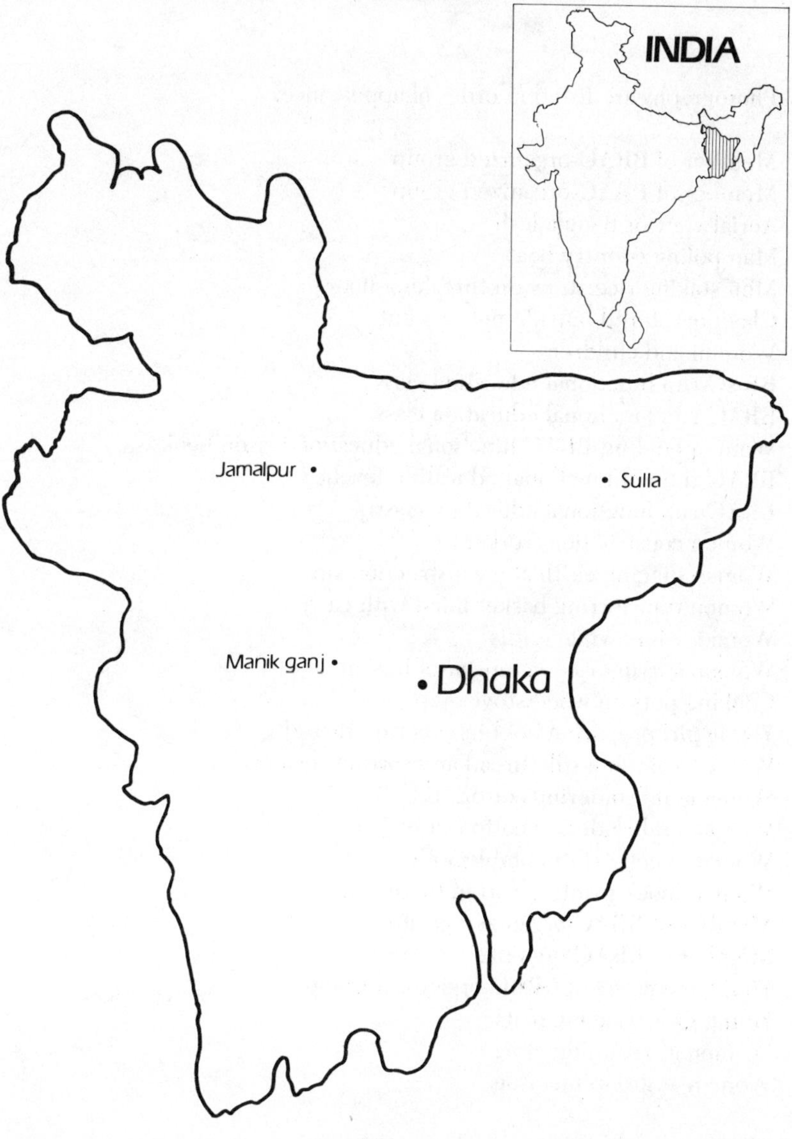
INDIA
Jamalpur
Sulla
Manik ganj
Dhaka

List of Photographs

Photographs are listed in order of appearance.

Member of BRAC-organized group
Member of BRAC-organized group
Aerial view of Bangladesh
Man poling country boat
Men staking rice straw on threshing floor
Clay pots stored outside potter's hut
Women and children
BRAC-run functional education class
BRAC-run functional education class
Women holding BRAC functional education lesson books
BRAC-trained functional education teacher
BRAC-run functional education class
Women construction workers
Woman digging earth at a construction site
Women transferring basket filled with earth
Woman winnowing lentils
Woman stirring rice in mortar of husker
Cooking pots on wood stove
Young girl preparing bobbin of cotton thread
Women spinning silk thread and sorting cocoons
Woman embroidering cotton sari
Woman embroidering cotton quilt
Woman block-printing tablecloth
Woman block-printing cotton by the yard
Member of BRAC-organized group
Member of BRAC-organized group
Young members of BRAC-organized group
Young girls weaving mats
Women at group meeting
Woman at group meeting

All photographs were taken by the author.

Bibliography

RELATED READINGS ON WOMEN AND
RURAL DEVELOPMENT IN BANGLADESH

Abdullah, Tahrunnessa Ahmed. 1974. *Village Women As I Saw Them*. Dacca: The Ford Foundation. (First published as "Palli Anganader Jemon Dekhechi," Comilla: PARD, 1966).

Abdullah, Tahrunnessa; Florence McCarthy; and Sondra Zeidenstein. 1977. "Programme Assessment and the Development of Women's Programme: The Views of Action Workers." Paper presented at the South and South East Asian Seminars on Women and Development. Dacca.

Abdullah, Tahrunnessa Ahmed and Sondra Zeidenstein. 1975. "Socio-economic Implications of HYV Rice Production on Rural Women of Bangladesh." International Seminar on Socio-economic Implications of Introducing HYVs in Bangladesh. Comilla: Bangladesh Academy for Rural Development (BARD).

——. 1976. *Finding Ways to Learn About Rural Women: Experiences From a Pilot Project in Bangladesh.*" Dacca: The Ford Foundation.

——. 1977. "Some Health Practices of Rural Bangladesh." in *Sishu Diganta*, A Child's Horizon, Dacca: UNICEF.

——. 1977. "Rural Women and Development," *Role of Women in Socio-Economic Development in Bangladesh*, Dacca: Bangladesh Economic Association.

——. 1977. "Livestock Care in the Village," ADAB News, IV, 6. Dacca: ADAB.

——. 1982. *Village Women of Bangladesh: Prospects for Change*. New York: Pergamon Press.

Adnan, Shapan, Rushidan Islam and the Village Study Group, Dacca. 1977. "Social Change and Rural Women: Possibilities of Participation," *Role of Women in Socio-Economic Development in Bangladesh*. Dacca: Bangladesh Economic Association.

Adnan, Shapan and Village Study Group. 1975. "The Preliminary Findings of a Social and Economic Study of Four Bangladesh Villages," Dacca.

——. 1975. "Social Structure and Resource Allocation in a Chittagong Village," Dacca.

——. 1976. "Land, Power and Violence in Barisal Villages," Dacca.

——. 1977. "Differentiation and Class Structure in Village Samaj," Dacca.

Ahmed, Manzoor, 1977. *BRAC: Building Human Infrastructures to Serve the Rural Poor*, Case Study No. 2 International Council for Educational Development, Essex, Connecticut.

Alamgir, Mohiuddin. 1975. "Some Aspects of Bangladesh Agriculture: Review of Performance and Evaluation of Policies," *Bangladesh Development Studies*, III, 3.

———. 1976. "Economy of Bangladesh: Which Way are We Moving," Bangladesh Economic Association, Second Annual Conference, Dacca.

Alamgir, Susan. 1977. *Profile of Bangladeshi Women: Selected Aspects of Women's Roles and Status in Bangladesh*. Dacca: USAID.

Arens, Jenneke, and Jos van Beurden. 1977. *Jhagrapur: Poor Peasants and Women in a Village in Bangladesh*. Amsterdam: Third World Publications.

Aziz, K. M. A. 1979. *Kinship in Bangladesh*. Dacca: ICDDR, B.

Bangladesh Academy of Rural Development (BARD). 1975. *The Socio-Economic Implications of Introducing HYV in Bangladesh. Proceedings of the International Seminar*. Comilla: BARD.

Bangladesh Bureau of Statistics. 1975. *Statistical Yearbook of Bangladesh—1975*, Dacca.

———. 1978. *Statistical Pocket Book—1978*, Dacca.

Bangladesh Economic Association. 1977. *Role of Women in Socio-Economic Development in Bangladesh*. Dacca.

Bangladesh Rural Advancement Committee (BRAC). 1972–82. Newsletters and Reports. Dacca.

———. 1978–82. *Peasant Perception Series*. Dacca.

———. 1979. *Who Gets What and Why: Resource Allocation in a Bangladesh Village*. Dacca.

———. 1980. *Appropriate Technologies under Pressure*. Dacca.

Barkat-e-Khuda. 1980. "Time Allocation among people in Rural Bangladesh." DERAP Publications, Chr. Michelsen Institute. No. 101.

Begum, Saleha and Martin Greeley. 1979. "Rural Women and the Rural Labour Market in Bangladesh: An Empirical Analysis." Draft Paper prepared in Dacca for I.D.S. (Brighton, U.K.) Project.

Bertocci, Peter J. 1975. "The Position of Women in Rural Bangladesh." International Seminar on Socio-Economic Implications on Introducing HYVs in Bangladesh. Comilla: BARD.

Bertocci, Peter. 1976. "Rural Development in Bangladesh," *Rural Development in Bangladesh and Pakistan*, ed. Robert D. Stevens, Hamza Alavi and Peter J. Bertocci. Honolulu: University Press of Hawaii.

Blair, H. W. 1974. *The Elusiveness of Equity: Institutional Approaches to Rural Development in Bangladesh*. Ithaca, N.Y.: Cornell University Press.

Brehmer, Margaret, Marty Chen, and Eikbal Hussain. 1976. "Anandpur Village: BRAC Comes to Town" in *World Education Reports*, No. 13, New York.

Cain, Mead. 1976. "Demographic and Socio-Economic Profile of the Study Village: Results from the Census," Bangladesh Development Studies. Dacca: BIDS.

————. 1977. "The Economic Activities of Children in a Village in Bangladesh", *Population and Development Review*, III, 3.

————. 1977. "Household Time Budgets," Village Fertility Study Methodology Report #1, Bangladesh Institute of Development Studies (Mimeo). Dacca.

————. 1978. "The Household Life Cycle and Economic Mobility in Rural Bangladesh." Centre for Policy Studies Working Paper. New York: The • Population Council.

Cain, Mead, Syeda Rokeya Khanam and Shamsun Nahar. 1979. "Class, Patriarchy and the Structure of Women's Work in Rural Bangladesh." Centre for Policy Studies Working Papers No. 43. New York: The Population Council.

Chaudhury, Rafiqul Huda. 1974. "Labor Force Status and Fertility," *Bangladesh Development Studies*, II, 4. Dacca: BIDS.

Chen, Lincoln et al. 1974. *Maternal Mortality in Rural Bangladesh*. Dacca: The Ford Foundation.

Chen, Lincoln and Rafiqul Huda Chaudhury. 1975. *Demographic Change and Trends of Food Production and Availabilities in Bangladesh* (1960–1974). Dacca: The Ford Foundation.

Chen, Lincoln, Sandra Huffman, and Penny Satterthwaite. 1976. *Recent Fertility Trends in Bangladesh: Speculation on the Role of Biological Factors and Socio-Economic Change*. Dacca: The Ford Foundation.

Chen, Marty. 1977. "Women Farmers in Bangladesh: Issues and Prospects," ADAB Newsletter, Vol. IV, No. 6, Dacca: ADAB.

————. 1981. "Organizing the Poor in Bangladesh: Evolution of an Approach to Rural Development," HIID Rural Development Seminar Series. Cambridge, Mass.: Harvard Institute for International Development (HIID).

————. 1982. "A Structural Analysis of Women's Work in Rural Bangladesh," Harvard—MIT Women in Development Seminar Series. Cambridge, Mass.: HIID.

Chen, Marty ed. 1977. *Women in Agriculture*, Bangladesh ADAB Newsletter, Vol. IV, No. 6. Dacca: ADAB.

Chen, Marty and Ruby Ghuznavi. 1977. *Women in Food-for-Work: The Bangladesh Experience*. United Nations World Food Programme, Dacca and Rome.

————. 1980. "Rural Bangladesh Women in Food-for-Work," Editor Alfred D'Souza, *Women in Contemporary India and South Asia*. New Delhi: Manohar Publications.

Chowdhury, Nuimuddin, and Afroz Gul. "Role of Women in Productive Activities in Bangladesh: A Preliminary Analysis." *Role of Women in the Socio-Economic Development of Bangladesh*. Dacca: Bangladesh Economic Association.

Clay, Edward J. 1976. "Institutional Change and Agriculture Wages in Bangladesh," *Bangladesh Development Studies*, IV, 4. Dacca: BIDS.

Clay, Edward J. and Md. Sekandar Khan. 1977. "Agricultural Employment and Under-employment in Bangladesh: The Next Decade." Unpublished UNDP/FAO Working Paper. Dacca: UNDP/FAO.

Dixon, Ruth B. 1978. *Rural Women at Work, Strategies for Development in South Asia*. Baltimore: Johns Hopkins University Press.
———. 1979. "Four Programs of Employment for Rural Women in India and Bangladesh." *Development Digest* 17(1): 75–88.
Ellickson, Jean. 1975. "Rural Women," *Women for Women*, Dacca, University Press Ltd.
———. 1975. "Observations from the Field on the Condition of Rural Women in Bangladesh." International Seminar on Socio-Economic Implications of Introducing HYVs in Bangladesh. Comilla: BARD.
Farouk, A. and M. Ali. 1975. *The Hardworking Poor—A Survey on How People Use Their Time in Bangladesh*, Dacca Bureau of Economic Research, Dacca University.
Germain, Adrienne. 1976. "Poor Rural Women: A Policy Perspective," *Journal of International Affairs*, XXX, 2.
———. 1976. *Women's Roles in Bangladesh Development: A Program Assessment*. Dacca: The Ford Foundation.
Gerard, Renee. 1977. "A Feasibility Study of Productive/Income-Generating Activities for Rural Women in Bangladesh," Women's Development Program, UNICEF, Dacca.
Harriss, Barbara. 1978. "Executive Report to the Steering Committee on Post Harvest Operations, Government of Bangladesh of the Task Force on Rice Processing & By-Products Utilization." Unpublished report.
———. 1978. "Post Harvest Rice Processing Systems in Rural Bangladesh: Technology, Economics & Employment." Paper presented for Bangladesh Agriculture Research Council, Dacca.
———. 1978. "Rice Processing Projects in Bangladesh: An Appraisal of a Decade of Proposals." Paper presented for Bangladesh Agricultural Research Council. Dacca.
Hoque, Naseem. 1976. *Non-formal Education for Women in Bangladesh*. Supplementary Paper No. 5, Program of Studies in Non-Formal Education, Michigan State University, East Lansing.
Huq, M. Ameerul ed. 1976. *Exploitation and the Rural Poor*. Comilla: BARD.
Huq, M. Nurul. 1973. *Village Development in Bangladesh*. Comilla: BARD.
Institute of Statistical Research and Training. 1977. *Statistical Profile of Children and Mothers in Bangladesh*, Dacca: University of Dacca.
IRDP Population Planning and Rural Women's Cooperative Program. 1974–1977. Reports. Dacca: IRDP.
Islam, A. K. M. Aminul. 1974. *A Bangladesh Village: Conflict and Cohesion: An Anthropological Study of Politics*. Cambridge, Mass.: Schenkman Publishing Company.
Islam, Mahmuda. 1975. "Women at Work in Bangladesh," *Women for Women*. Dacca: University Press Limited.
Islam, Meherunnessa. 1977. "Food Preservation in Bangladesh," Women's Development Programme, UNICEF, Dacca.
Islam, Shamima. 1976. "Women, Education and Development in Bangladesh: A Few Reflections," *Role of Women in Socio-Economic Development in Bangladesh*. Dacca: Bangladesh Economic Association.

Jack, J. C. 1927. *The Economic Life of a Bengal District*. London: Oxford University Press.

Jahan, Rounaq. 1974. *Women in Bangladesh*. Paper written for the IXth International Congress of Anthropological and Ethnological Sciences, Chicago, August 1973. Dacca: The Ford Foundation.

———. 1975. "Women in Bangladesh," *Women for Women*. Dacca: University Press Limited.

Jahan, Rounaq and Hanna Papanek. 1979. *Women and Development. Perspectives from South and Southeast Asia*. Dacca: Bangladesh Institute of Law and International Affairs.

Kabir, Khushi; Ayesha Abed; and Marty Chen. 1976. *Rural Women in Bangladesh: Exploding Some Myths*. Paper presented at the Seminar on the Role of Women in Socio-Economic Development in Bangladesh. Dacca: The Ford Foundation.

Khan, Akhter Hameed. 1963. *The Role of Women in a Country's Development*. Comilla: BARD.

———. 1971. *Tour of Twenty Thanas*. Comilla: BARD.

———. 1974. *Reflections on the Comilla Rural Development Projects*. Overseas Liaison Committee, American Council on Education. OLC Paper No. 3, Washington, D.C.

Khan, A. R. 1976. "Poverty and Inequality in Rural Bangladesh," Working Paper in World Employment Program Research, Geneva: International Labor Office.

Khatun, Saleha and Gita Rani. 1977. *Bari-Based Post Harvest Operations and Livestock Care: Some Observations and Case Studies*. Dacca: The Ford Foundation.

Khatun, Sharifa. 1977. "Equal Educational Opportunity for Women: A Myth," *Role of Women in Socio-Economic Development in Bangladesh*. Dacca: Bangladesh Economic Association.

Korten, David. 1980. "Community Organization and Rural Development. A Learning Process Approach," *Public Administration Review*.

———. 1981. "Rural Development Planning: The Learning Process Approach," *Rural Development Participation Review* Ithaca, N.Y. Cornell University.

Lindenbaum, Shirley. 1968. "Women and the Left Hand; Social Status and Symbolism in East Pakistan," *Mankind* VI, 11.

———. 1974 *The Social and Economic Status of Women in Bangladesh*. Dacca: The Ford Foundation.

Martius-Von Harder, Gudrun. 1975. "Women's Role in Rice Processing," *Women for Women*, Dacca, University Press Ltd.

McCarthy, Florence E. 1977. "Reports on Use of Loans by Female Cooperative Members." Dacca: IRDP.

———. 1977. "I.R.D.P. Pilot Project in Population Planning and Rural Women's Cooperatives. Third Report. June 1976–May 1977." Dacca: IRDP.

——— 1978. "The Status and Condition of Rural Women in Bangladesh." Position Paper for Women's Section, Planning and Evaluation Cell, Ministry of Agriculture and Forests. Dacca.

McCarthy, Florence E., Saleha Sabbah and Roushan Akhtar. 1978 "Rural Women Workers in Bangladesh." Working Paper for Women's Section, Planning and Development Division, Ministry of Agriculture and Forests. Dacca.

O'Kelly, Elizabeth. 1977. "Simple Technologies for Rural Women in Bangladesh." Women's Development Programs, UNICEF, Dacca.

Papanek, Hanna. 1971. "Purdah in Pakistan: Seclusion and Modern Occupations for Women," *Journal of Marriage and the Family*.

———. 1973. *"Purdah: Separate Worlds and Symbolic Shelter," Comparative Studies in Society and History*, L, 3.

Rahman, Jowshan Ara. 1976. "Role of Women in Population Planning." *Role of Women in Socio-Economic Development in Bangladesh*. Dacca: Bangladesh Economic Association.

Salahuddin, Khaleda. 1977. "Women in Productive Activities," *Role of Women in Socio-Economic Development in Bangladesh*. Dacca: Bangladesh Economic Association.

Sattar, Ellen. 1974. *Women in Bangladesh: A Village Study*. Dacca: The Ford Foundation.

———. 1977. "The Position of Women in Secondary School Education in Bangladesh," *Role of Women in Socio-Economic Development in Bangladesh*. Dacca: Bangladesh Economic Association.

Senaratne, S. P. F. 1975. "Micro Studies, Employment and the Strategies of Development," unpublished manuscript, Sri Lanka.

Sobhan, Salma. 1978. *The Legal Status of Women in Bangladesh*. Dacca: Institute of Law, Dacca University.

Women for Women Research and Study Group. 1975. *Women for Women*. Dacca: University Press Ltd.

———. 1979. *The Situation of Women in Bangladesh*. Dacca: Women's Development Programme, UNICEF.

Zeidenstein, Sondra. 1975. *Report and Commentary on IRDP Women's Program, The First Year*, Dacca: Integrated Rural Development Program (IRDP).

———. 1976. *Report on the First Two Years of the IRDP Pilot Project on Population Planning and Rural Women's Cooperative*. Dacca: IRDP.

———. 1977. "A Bangladesh Project for Rural Women." Paper presented at a Population Council Seminar. New York: N.Y.

Zeidenstein, Sondra and Laura Zeidenstein. 1974. "Observations on the Status of Women in Bangladesh." *World Education Issues*, No. 2, New York.

RELATED READINGS ON WOMEN AND
RURAL DEVELOPMENT ELSEWHERE

Ahmed, Manzoor and Philip H. Coombs. 1975. *Education for Rural Development: Case Studies for Planners*. New York: Praeger.

Antrobus, Peggy. 1980. *Hanover Street: An Experiment to Train Women in Welding and Carpentry*. SEEDS Pamphlet Series. New York: N.Y.

Agarwal, Bina. 1981. "Agricultural Modernization and Third World Women: Pointers from the Literature and an Empirical Analysis," Rural Employment Policy Research Programme. Geneva: ILO.

Beck, Lois and Nikki Keddie. 1978. *Women in the Muslim World*. Cambridge, Mass.: Harvard University Press.

Bhatt, Ela. 1977. "A Self-Help Approach for Rural Populations: Mobilizing Agricultural Workers in India." *Assignment Children* 38 (1977): 89–91.

———. 1982. "Unionizing Self-Employed Women," *The Exchange Report*. New York, N.Y.: The Exchange.

Boserup, Esther. 1970. *Women's Role in Economic Development*. London: Allen and Unwin; New York: St. Martin's Press.

Bruce, Judith. 1976. "Women's Organizations: A Resource for Family Planning and Development." *Family Planning Perspectives* 8.

———. 1971. "Setting the System to Work for Women." *Populi*, Journal of the United Nations Fund for Population Activities, Vol. 4, No. 1, New York.

———. 1980. *Market Women's Cooperatives: Giving Women Credit*. SEEDS Pamphlet Series. New York: N.Y.

Buvinic, Mayra; Nadia Youssef; and Barbara Von Elm. 1978. "Women-Headed Households: The Ignored Factor in Development Planning." Washington, D.C.: International Center for Research on Women.

Buvinic, Mayra, Jennifer Sebstad and Sondra Zeidenstein. 1979. "Credit for Rural Women: Some Facts & Lessons." Unpublished paper prepared for Office of Rural Development, DSB, USAID, Washington, D.C.

Caughman, Susan. 1983. *Markala Women's Cooperative*. SEEDS Pamphlet Series. New York: N.Y.

Chen, Marty. 1983. *Organizing for Credit and Change*. SEEDS Pamphlet Series. New York: N.Y.

Cohen, John M. and Norman T. Uphoff. 1977. "Rural Development Participation: Concepts and Measures for Project Design, Implementation and Evaluation." Rural Development Monograph No. 2. Ithaca, N.Y.: Rural Development Committee, Center for International Studies, Cornell University.

Cornelisen, Ann. 1977. *Women of the Shadows: A Study of the Wives and Mothers of Southern Italy*. New York, N.Y.: Vintage Books.

Dixon, Ruth B. 1978. *Rural Women at Work: Strategies for Development in South Asia*. Baltimore: John Hopkins University Press.

———. 1979. "Jobs for Women in Rural Industries and Services." Washington, D.C.: Office of Women in Development, USAID.

———. 1980. "Assessing the Impact of Development Projects on Women." Washington, D.C.: Office of Women in Development, USAID.

Dhamija, Jasleen. 1981. *Women and Handicrafts: Myth and Reality*. SEEDS Pamphlet Series. New York: N.Y.

Elmendorf, Mary L. 1976. *Nine Mayan Women. A Village Faces Change*. Cambridge, Mass.: Schenkman Publishing Company.

Epstein, T. Scarlett and Rosemary A. Watts. 1980. *The Endless Day: Some Case Material on Asian Rural Women*. Oxford: Pergamon Press.

Fernea, Elizabeth Warnock and Basima Qattan Bezirgan. 1978. *Middle Eastern Muslim Women Speak*. Austin and London: University of Texas Press.

Germain, Adrienne. 1974. "Some Aspects of the Roles of Women in Population and Development." Prepared for International Forum on the Role of Women in Population and Development, United Nations ESA/ SDHA/AC.5/3/Add.1.

———. 1975. "Status and Roles of Women as Factors in Fertility Behavior: A Policy Analysis." *Studies in Family Planning* 6, No. 7, New York: The Population Council.

———. 1976. "Poor Rural Women: A Policy Perspective." *Journal of International Affairs* 30.

———. 1977. Poor Rural Women: A Policy Perspective, a Ford Foundation Reprint from the *Journal of International Affairs*, Vol. 30 No. 2.

Gulati, Leela. 1978. "Profile of a Female Agricultural Labourer." *Economic & Political Weekly* 13 (12).

———. 1981. *Profiles in Female Poverty: A Study of Five Poor Working Women in Kerala*. Delhi: Hindustan Publishing Corporation (India).

Huston, Perdita. 1978. *Message from the Village*. New York: Epoch B. Foundation.

International Center for Research on Women. 1980. "The Productivity of Women in Developing Countries: Measurement Issues and Recommendations." Washington, D.C.: Office of Women in Development, USAID.

———. 1980. "Bringing Women In: Towards a New Direction in Occupational Skills Training for Women." Washington, D.C.: Office of Women in Development, USAID.

———. 1980. "Keeping Women Out: A Structural Analysis of Women's Employment in Developing Countries." Washington, D.C.: Office of Women in Development, USAID.

Jain, Devaki. 1975. *From Dissociation to Rehabilitation: Report on an Experiment to Promote Self-Employment in an Urban Area*. Report of the Indian Council of Social Science Research. New Delhi: Allied Publishers.

Jain, Devaki (ed.) 1975. *Indian Women*. New Delhi: Publishing Division, Ministry of Information & Broadcasting, Government of India.

Jain, Devaki, Nalini Singh and Malini Chand. 1980. *Women's Quest for Power*. Ghaziabad: Vikas Publishing House Pvt. Ltd.

Jahan, Rounaq and Hanna Papanek ed. 1979. *Women and Development: Perspective from South and Southeast Asia*. Dacca: Bangladesh Institute of Law and International Affairs.

Kneerim, Jill. 1980. *Village Women Organize: The Mraru Bus Service*. SEEDS Pamphlet Series. New York: N.Y.

Mernissi, Fatima. 1975. *Beyond the Veil*. Cambridge, Mass.: Schenkman Publishing Company.

Mies, Maria. 1980. "Housewives Produce for the World Market: The Lace Makers of Narsapur." World Employment Programme Research. Geneva: ILO.

Miller, Barbara. 1981. *The Endangered Sex: Neglect of Female Children in Rural North India*. Ithaca, N.Y.: Cornell University Press.

National Committee on the Status of Women in India. 1975. *Status of Women in India*. New Delhi: Indian Council of Social Science Research.

Nelson, N. 1979. *Why Has Development Neglected Women? A Review of the South Asian Literature*. Oxford: Pergamon Press.

Omvedt, Gail. 1980. *We Will Smash This Prison!* New Delhi: Orient Longman Limited.

Palmer, Ingrid. 1976. "The Basic Needs Approach to the Integration of Rural Women in Development: Conditions for Success." Paper presented at the Conference on Women in Development, Wellesley College, Wellesley, Massachusetts.

————. 1979. *The Nemow Case: Case Studies of the Impact of Large-Scale Development Projects for Women: A Series for Planners*. Washington, D.C.: Office of Women in Development, USAID.

Reiter, Rayna R., ed. 1975. *Toward an Anthropology of Women*. New York and London: Monthly Review Press.

Rosaldo, Michelle and Louise Lamphere. 1972. *Women, Culture, and Society*. Stanford: Stanford University Press.

Sebstad, Jennifer. 1982. *Struggle and Development Among Self-Employed Women*. A Report on the Self-Employed Women's Association, Ahmedabad, India. Washington, D.C.: USAID.

Schumacher, Ilsa; Jennifer Sebstad; and Mayra Buvinic. 1980. "Limits to Productivity: Improving Women's Access to Technology and Credit." Washington, D.C.: International Center for Research on Women.

Stoler, Ann. 1976. "Class Structure and Female Autonomy in Rural Java." Unpublished manuscript for Department of Anthropology, Columbia University. New York, N.Y.

————. 1976. "Some Economic Determinants of Female Autonomy in Rural Jawa." Paper presented at Agricultural Development Council RTN Workshop on Family Labor Force Use in Agricultural Production. Hyderabad: ICRISAT.

————. 1977. "Class Structure and Female Autonomy in Rural Java." *SIGNS* Special Issue on Women and National Development 3(1).

The Exchange. 1981. *The Exchange Report: Women in the Third World*. New York: N.Y.

Timmer, C. Peter. 1974. "Choice of Technique in Rice Milling on Java." *RTN Reprint*. New York: Agriculture Development Council.

Youssef, Nadia H. 1974. *Women and Work in Developing Societies*. Berkeley: University of California. Population Monograph Series, No. 15.

————. 1977. "Women and Agricultural Production in Muslim Societies." *Studies in Comparative International* Development (New Brunswick) 12, No. 1.

Youssef, Nadia; Mayra Buvinic; Aipe Kudat; et al. 1979. "Women in Migration: A Third World Focus." Washington, D.C.: International Center for Research on Women.

Zeidenstein, Sondra ed. 1979. "Learning About Rural Women." *Studies in Family Planning* (Special Issue) 10 (11/12). New York: The Population Council.